SAGE was founded in 1965 by Sara Miller McCune to support the dissemination of usable knowledge by publishing innovative and high-quality research and teaching content. Today, we publish over 900 journals, including those of more than 400 learned societies, more than 800 new books per year, and a growing range of library products including archives, data, case studies, reports, and video. SAGE remains majority-owned by our founder, and after Sara's lifetime will become owned by a charitable trust that secures our continued independence.

Los Angeles | London | New Delhi | Singapore | Washington DC | Melbourne

Introduction to Political Ideologies

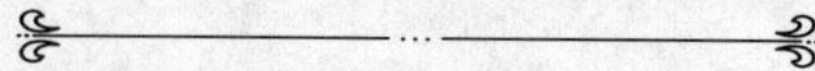

Introduction to Political Ideologies

Contexts, Ideas, and Practices

Arvind Sivaramakrishnan

Adjunct Professor, Department of Humanities and Social Sciences, Indian Institute of Technology Madras

Los Angeles | London | New Delhi
Singapore | Washington DC | Melbourne

First published in 2017 by

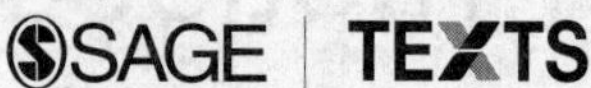

SAGE Publications India Pvt Ltd
B1/I-1 Mohan Cooperative Industrial Area
Mathura Road, New Delhi 110 044, India
www.sagepub.in

SAGE Publications Inc
2455 Teller Road
Thousand Oaks, California 91320, USA

SAGE Publications Ltd
1 Oliver's Yard, 55 City Road
London EC1Y 1SP, United Kingdom

SAGE Publications Asia-Pacific Pte Ltd
3 Church Street
#10-04 Samsung Hub
Singapore 049483

Published by Vivek Mehra for SAGE Publications India Pvt Ltd, typeset in 10.5/12.5 pt Palatino by Diligent Typesetter India Pvt Ltd, Delhi and printed at Sai Print-o-Pack, New Delhi.

Library of Congress Cataloging-in-Publication Data

Names: Sivaramakrishnan, Arvind, author.
Title: Introduction to political ideologies : contexts, ideas and practices / Arvind Sivaramakrishnan, Adjunct Professor, Department of Humanities and Social Sciences, Indian Institute of Technology, Madras.
Description: Thousand Oaks, California : SAGE Publications Inc., 2017. | Includes bibliographical references and index.
Identifiers: LCCN 2017015232 | ISBN 9789386446404 (print (pb))
Subjects: LCSH: Political science. | Ideology.
Classification: LCC JA83 .S534 2017 | DDC 320.5--dc23 LC record available at https://lccn.loc.gov/2017015232

ISBN: 978-93-864-4640-4 (PB)

SAGE Team: Amit Kumar, Indrani Dutta, Apoorva Mathur and Ritu Chopra

CONTENTS

DETAILED CONTENTS

ABOUT THE BOOK

This book is specifically intended as an introductory textbook for use at a range of levels, depending on the students' background. It arises from courses in political theory and political philosophy which I have taught at different levels for over 30 years in the United Kingdom and India, and on parts of which I have lectured in Germany. Almost every class I have met in doing so has had little or no previous experience of studying politics in any form; for example, even senior students at top-class Indian institutions have repeatedly told me that although they have heard terms like 'liberalism', 'postmodernism', and 'Marxism' used throughout their studies and in other contexts, they have never had any clear explanation of what those terms mean. I have therefore tried to render accessible to the student or the general reader the ideas which inform political action and organisation. In order to make the text accessible, I have deliberately relied on a less extensive range of sources than I would have done for a book intended to provide more detailed coverage than this one. It is possible that this book will also be of use to lecturers who are not familiar with political ideologies but have to teach them or draw upon them in related subjects.

The ideologies I have addressed here are often embodied or shown in policies, laws, and the ways public institutions work. All political actions embody *some* ideas about society, politics, and the good, as well as ideas of human nature, and therefore of what is right and fitting for human beings. This holds even if the political actors concerned have no interest in or no knowledge of political theory or political philosophy. In this book, I try to show that each of the ideologies I cover gives rise to, or in some cases specifies, a particular view of human beings and therefore issues into a particular view of how we should organise our political systems and political participation. For example, in a theocracy, the priesthood would have final authority in such matters, and in a technocracy, the experts, such as biologists or engineers, would have final authority; each group would almost certainly consider very different kinds of evidence and give very different kinds of reasons for their decisions.

LAYOUT

For each of the ideologies I have covered, I have followed a layout which is similar to that of several other teaching books, particularly at introductory levels, in similar areas. I start with a brief historical outline before covering the main ideas involved, with examples; I then show some of the problems arising, again with examples wherever possible.

The chapters follow a broad conceptual sequence, and I have given a chronological sequence between them wherever that would be helpful. In the Marx chapter, I have specifically attempted to outline the main concepts in Marx's work, because my experience has been that despite a substantial and continuing global debate on various form of Marxism, few students have the opportunity to encounter Marx's own main ideas.

Each chapter is followed by a list of extension exercises and suggested readings. Readers can reach the sources for the exercises by going through the companion website: https://study.sagepub.in/as_IPI

CONCEPTS OF THE STATE

Almost all the ideologies I have covered below give rise to, or in some cases explicitly specify, a concept of the state, or a similar form of political organisation, which is in conformity with their respective accounts of human nature, human action, knowledge, and forms of human association. Therefore, I have not attempted to provide any one concept of the state, and where appropriate I have indicated the kind of state or states which particular ideologies generate. The point is for us to see how each ideology, among other things, creates a conception of the state or other political body or bodies.

The overall aim of the book is to aid the reader to identify and evaluate the assumptions underlying a wide range of examples of public matters, including the state and institutions within it, so that they can ask more incisive and better-informed questions about major public issues and identify ways to develop an enhanced understanding of those issues.

ACKNOWLEDGEMENTS

The students taking the courses in which I have covered almost all these topics for a good many years now—in the United Kingdom, India, and Germany—have always shown me, and continue to show me, the significance of the themes involved. That dates from the time when, as a graduate student at the University of Southampton, I attended Raymond Plant's first-year politics lectures so as to enhance the support I gave to the students in my tutor group. The lectures were a model of clarity and intellectual authority, and the undergraduates' work for the tutorials amply confirmed that. Among others who made contributions to my thinking that they might recognise in these pages were David Pugmire, Ronnie Beiner, Peter Johnson, and Alan Pleydell. My former tutor Tony Manser would also have recognised his own influence.

More recently, Nalini Rajan, Dean of Studies at the Asian College of Journalism, Chennai, put the idea for this book to me while I was teaching a related course at the College. Amit Kumar, Executive Editor at Sage, was immediately receptive to my initial proposal; he and his colleague Indrani Dutta, Senior Development Editor, responded quickly and attentively to points arising as the text progressed. Four anonymous reviewers made a range of prompt and constructive comments on an earlier draft. Gail McFarlane always provided sharp and anchoring insights into the issues and into the kinds of questions the activity of writing raises. My many friends at IIT Madras, particularly Milind Brahme, Sadanand Menon, Sudhir Chella Rajan, and Gita Jayaraj, have consistently sustained a context for argument and the development of ideas in the light of events; to them too, I remain indebted.

ABOUT THE AUTHOR

Arvind Sivaramakrishnan is an Adjunct Professor and a former Visiting Professor in the Department of Humanities at the Indian Institute of Technology Madras. From 2008 to 2014, he was Senior Deputy Editor on the *Hindu*, writing editorials, specialist articles, and book reviews on international politics, public policy, and political theory; he combined his duties with teaching and research as an Associate Professor at the Asian College of Journalism, Chennai. He took his degree and doctorate, as well as a postgraduate diploma in social administration and a professional teaching qualification, at the University of Southampton, where he also taught politics. Since then, he has taught at Suffolk College, Ipswich, the Centre for Economic and Social Studies, Hyderabad, Southampton Institute of Higher Education (now Southampton Solent University), and Taunton's College, Southampton (now Richard Taunton Sixth Form College). He has published a range of academic papers in politics, political philosophy, public policy, and related fields, and has conducted research seminars and research training sessions at universities in the European Union and India. His books include *Public-Interest Journalism* (2014), *Public Policy and Citizenship* (2012), *Short on Democracy* (2007), and *Through a Glass Wall* (2007). He is currently coediting, with Dr Sudarsan Padmanabhan, a book on elections and electoral processes.

1 CHAPTER

Fascism

Historically, all societies have had, and continue to have, fascist elements and fascistic groups. Only rarely, however, do fascist groups or political parties come to hold political office; a few have even been elected in democratic systems, but they have not usually remained in office for long. Nevertheless, they often have considerable social and political influence, which is shown by specific developments, such as the spread of a climate of fear or intimidation without obvious or widespread physical violence. To create such climates, fascist movements often use particular phrases or other forms of language which express veiled, indirect, and menacing threats (Arendt 1951: 336). The use of violence to propagate a climate of fear is, nevertheless, a notable feature of fascist movements; violence and explicit or implicit threats of violence are often intensified with the help and collusion of public officials who sympathise with fascism.

In modern times, there have been only four explicitly fascist states. These are:

Italy	1921–45	Leader: Benito Mussolini, also called *Il Duce* (the Leader)
Germany	1933–45	Leader: Adolf Hitler, also called *Der Führer* (the Leader)
Spain	1939–75	Leader: Francisco Franco, also called *El Generalísimo* (the High Commander), or *El Caudillo* (the Leader)
Portugal	1939–74	Leader 1932–68: António de Oliveira Salazar

In several other countries, political and cultural life has at times taken on a fascistic character. Among these are Imperial Japan, especially during the Second World War, Argentina under Juan Perón (1945–55), and India during the rise of the Bharatiya Janata Party (BJP) in the 1990s and then during the period of BJP-led coalition government from 1998 to 2004. Indeed, in India, it was very noticeable that specific terms were consistently used so as to obliterate the differences between the terms '*Bharatiya*', 'Hindu', and 'Indian', with the declared intention of equating the meanings of all three terms. This strategy, which seems not to have been abandoned, had been explicitly adopted as early as 1950 (Noorani 2000: 10–11). I shall provide other examples as we proceed, so as to show the ways in which fascistic tendencies and climates were and are created and maintained.

FASCISM: THE MAIN IDEAS

- Symbolism
- The nation as an organic unity
- Ultranationalism
- Glorification of the past
- Permanent struggle and permanent mobilisation for war
- Antirationalism and action based solely on the will
- The leader principle

Symbolism

Symbolism is a strong feature of all fascist systems and fascistic groups. The word 'fascism' is derived from the Latin word *fasces*, which meant an image showing a bundle of rods tied together at one end, with an axe blade pointing through the rods. This was the symbol of the magistracy in ancient Rome, and by the late nineteenth century the Italian word *fascia* was being used for political groups or bands, most of which were made up of revolutionary socialists (Heywood 2007: 203). The term became more explicitly associated with what we today call fascistic ideologies when Mussolini formed paramilitary groups during and after the First World War; today this is the most common connotation of terms like 'fascist' or 'fascistic'.

All fascistic movements set great store by their particular symbols, and particularly by the dissemination of a small number of symbols. The Nazi swastika is probably the most famous fascist symbol, but others include the black shirts worn by followers of Sir Oswald Mosley, who led the British Union of Fascists in the 1930s. The use of symbolism in Indian politics is often very striking and has been hotly disputed. In July 2016, the Bombay High Court started hearing a public interest litigation case in which the claimant argued that the BJP's use of the lotus, a national cultural symbol, as a party political symbol violated the Emblems and Names (Prevention of Improper Use) Act 1950 (Press Trust of India 2016).

The Nation as an Organic Unity

Fascist doctrines rely heavily upon an assertive and exclusivist concept of the nation. According to this concept, nations are not bodies among other nations, which are at least formally equal in respect of treaties, in systems of international law, and in multilateral bodies such as the United Nations or other groupings of countries. In those kinds of contexts, nations are called states, almost all of which today are constituted bodies with highly articulated internal systems. In contrast, fascist theories take the nation not as a constituted body but as an organic unity among many nations; for fascism, those other nations are permanently hostile to it and would even overwhelm or destroy it. Fascism therefore requires an 'intense and militant' sense of national identity as a matter of survival and national regeneration through the repeated reassertion of national unity (Heywood 2007: 215). For fascism, this national regeneration is founded on the idea that national membership is racial membership, and is therefore defined by racial purity or purity of descent.

The idea of race as the unifying or defining principle of nationhood has taken different forms in different fascist countries. The basis of Italian fascism was the supremacy of the fascist state, in which the will of Mussolini ruled over the individual. At least in theory, this did not involve any theory of rank order or hierarchy among different races, and Mussolini's anti-Semitic laws—passed after 1937—were created mainly to placate Hitler (Heywood 2007: 220).

Nazi Germany, on the other hand, had as one of its key principles an explicit theory of racial hierarchies. This is a form of racialism inherited from nineteenth-century and other theories of racial categories according to which there are inherent or innate differences between the different races of the world; such theories identify racial differences by skin colour, physiognomy, and other features. Secondly, they usually see cultural differences as resulting from biological differences.

According to Nazi theory, however, all races fell into a hierarchy. For example, according to Nazism white-skinned people constituted the highest race; for them the Nazis used the term 'Aryan', which they took from the work of the French racialist thinker Joseph-Arthur de Gobineau (Heywood 2007: 222–23). The term 'Aryan' then came to have an even narrower sense, referring to white-skinned, blond-haired, blue-eyed people. All other races were considered inferior, and the hierarchy listed Slavs, Balts, Jews, and others in descending order, with Gypsies, Asians, and Africans below those.

This meant that for the Nazis, race was the essential and defining element of nationhood and national membership, and only those descended from any one race could be members of the nation concerned. This theory of purity by descent or by blood therefore meant that intermarriage between races amounted to contamination or defilement, or pollution and even degeneracy. Hitler saw Jews in particular as destroyers of the culture created by what he considered the Aryan master race. While the Nazis were particularly extreme in their thinking on this, all fascistic thought involves purity by descent, with the attendant fear of contamination through interbreeding. The theory of racial unity also involved a claim to long inheritance over many generations of life in one country or area; the Nazis in particular called this principle that of blood and soil, or in German *Blut und Boden*. Nevertheless, the concept of race as the unifying organic principle of a nation leads to what has been called ultranationalism.

Ultranationalism

This is the idea that because nations are based on racial membership, they transcend state boundaries. Hitler himself saw the Aryan nation as encompassing Germans, Nordic peoples and British peoples. The Nazi annexation (the *Anschluss*) of Austria in March 1938, and from October 1938 onwards the annexation and invasion of Czechoslovakia (where large numbers of ethnic Germans lived), were part of Hitler's attempt to unify the Aryan nation within one territory.

It also follows that for fascism, state borders are irrelevant. The Nazis considered the Aryan nation to be a nation irrespective of where Aryan people lived, and they held the same to be true of all other nations. At one time, Hitler thought he could therefore unite all Aryans; for example, in the 1930s, sections of the British ruling classes, including certain members of the Royal family, greatly admired him, and the tabloid newspaper the *Daily Mail*—still one of the country's biggest-selling papers—openly supported him. Hitler seriously believed that Great Britain, the world's greatest imperial power, would join his Aryan cause.

Glorification of the Past

The idea of reunifying the nation also means that fascist movements see the contemporary world as having been corrupted by the geographical coexistence of different races. For the Nazis, that meant the Aryan nation's identity and purity were under permanent threat from lower and lesser races. Fascist theorists, and Nazi theorists in particular, responded by asserting that at some unspecified time in the past, the Aryan nation had existed in a state of purity, before other nations had corrupted it or tried to contaminate it. For the Nazis, this past was a rural or pastoral idyll, in which Aryan peasants lived peacefully in the countryside, innocent of the threats and corruptions of modernity. Such visions of an idyllic agrarian past mark a significant difference between Nazism and Italian fascism, because Mussolini saw fascism as providing a way to unify and modernise Italy through industrialisation.

Permanent Struggle and Permanent Mobilisation for War

All forms of fascism regard national purity as being under permanent threat of contamination or pollution by contact and interbreeding with so-called lesser races; therefore, fascism requires that nations be permanently ready for war, which could also involve invading other peoples' territory and subjugating them. The Nazis in particular ran a huge rearmament programme; this substantially aided their popularity as it provided industrial employment on a national scale—which helped the country to recover from the Great Depression. It also served to revive national confidence, which had been severely damaged by the harsh terms of the Treaty of Versailles, the treaty which ended the First World War. This form of industrialisation through militarisation also suited the German private corporations very well, as they made enormous profits by manufacturing weapons and other industrial goods for the state. Moreover, as other countries developed their own armaments, Nazi Germany needed constantly to update and refine its own weapons.

This comprehensive national preparation for war also meant that all men were regarded as part of the military, and military or military-style training was compulsory for men. The whole of society had to be organised on these lines, and fascist societies almost always have sharp divisions in gender roles. The task of men is to be ready for war, and they must be willing to go to war to save the nation; women's role is to run the home and give birth to the next generation of nation-saving warriors. These separate gender roles were particularly obvious in Nazi Germany during the 1930s, when women were sent to camps for training in how to be good Nazi housewives and mothers. During the war, however, women were increasingly drafted into industrial jobs as part of the war effort, especially as more and more men were sent to the front lines. During the Red Army siege of Breslau (the Polish city of Wrocław) in January 1945, children as young as ten were forced to join the Nazi war effort (Taylor 2011: 63; 369).

Antirationalism and Action Based Solely on the Will

The ideas of a glorious past and of racial purity went beyond permanent mobilisation for war and a permanent fear of racial contamination. The Nazis, like other fascists, saw modernity as a weakening and corrupting condition, particularly because they associated democracy with modernity. They saw democracy as producing endless negotiations and compromises, which often led to a feeling of paralysis and helplessness. The situation in Germany in 1930 gave the Nazis a lot of evidence to support that. Unemployment had reached six million or 10 per cent of the population, farmers were heavily indebted, businesses were collapsing, and parliamentary government had become impossible, with several different parties each getting only a small share of the vote. Governments began to rule by decree, and the army often intervened in politics. According to the Nazis, democracy, which they considered a political system based on reasoning, had led to this state of affairs. Furthermore, the Nazis saw all intellectual life as cold and lifeless; by implication, that included science and technology, and all other forms of reasoning (Passmore 2002: 65–66). This amounts to a comprehensive form of antirationalism.

This antirationalism instead makes the will the sole wellspring of action. In contrast to the lifelessness of reason and the messy, inconclusive compromises of democracy, a life based on the expression of the will is, according to fascism, honest and direct. This applies equally to nations and individuals, and for nations the national will is expressed by the will of the leader. Therefore, clashes of will can only be resolved by struggle; as compromise means enslavement or reduction to subordinate, even subhuman, status, this struggle has to be a struggle to the death. Every dispute then has to be and can only be resolved by a fight to the death. This is also expressed in the policy of permanent mobilisation for war, and in the very militarised life that men, especially young men, are supposed to and often made to lead in fascist or fascistic societies.

The wider consequences can be and often have been truly terrible. If the very existence of another will is a threat to any individual's will, then the very existence of another nation or culture, or as the Nazis had it another race, is a threat to the very existence of the nation. In fascist theory, the only response is the extermination or enslavement of any and all other cultures. While Nazi Germany was the only country openly to attempt the extermination of entire peoples, the principle of extermination is inherent in fascist ideology.

The Nazi policy of extermination has come to be called the Holocaust, but Hitler himself, the sole author of the policy, called it the Final Solution, in German *die Endlösung*. Hitler was obsessed with the idea that Jews were the greatest threat to the Aryan master race and that there was a global Jewish conspiracy which was combining with Bolshevism to undermine the Aryan nation. In January 1939, he said that if Jewish financiers inside and outside Europe succeeded in 'plunging the nations once more into a world war, then the result will not be the Bolshevization of the earth, and thus the victory of Jewry, but the annihilation of the Jewish race in Europe!' (cited in Passmore 2002: 114).

After the Second World War had started—with Nazi Germany's invasion of Poland on 1 September 1939—Hitler issued proclamations which licensed the killing of Jews in occupied Poland, as well as their ghettoisation and extermination (Passmore 2002: 114). The Final Solution, however, was comprehensive; the plan was to identify and exterminate all the Jews in Europe, and then to repeat the process with all other races and even the physically infirm or disabled. This plan was systematically carried out, and remains the greatest act of mass murder in history; current estimates are that six million people, almost all of whom were Jewish, were murdered in a programme which covered all of occupied Europe and towards which a large part of the entire German state apparatus was directed. The Holocaust even gave rise to a new word, genocide, and a new crime, the idea of crimes against humanity as a whole.

There have been other genocides before and since, but the Holocaust by itself raises most of the relevant questions. It required the coordination of tens or perhaps hundreds of thousands of administrators, military personnel, engineers, railway staff, and even civilians who exposed their Jewish neighbours to the authorities, and it seems to have been carried out almost without question. These features have been noted in other genocides, such as the one which was carried out in Rwanda in 1994, and they may well have been true of the Australian settlers' genocide against the aboriginal Tasmanians. The use of public documents such as electoral registers to identify and round up people for killing has been repeated in other episodes of mass slaughter; this was done to Muslim residents in Gujarat in 2002 (Concerned Citizens Tribunal—Gujarat 2002, Vol. I: 249–50).

As for the Holocaust, the fact that ordinary people took part in it as a normal working matter, rounding up and transporting millions to concentration and extermination camps across a continent, amounted to a very disturbing discovery about all humanity; one of the chief administrators of the Holocaust, Adolf Eichmann, whom Israeli agents kidnapped in Argentina in 1961 for trial and later execution in Israel, turned out to be a very ordinary person. The detailed book Hannah Arendt wrote about his trial—which she attended throughout—has been read around the world (Arendt 1977).

It is also the case that millions of ordinary people in Germany and the occupied countries had no idea that mass exterminations were taking place in the camps, often on the edges of their towns and cities; one lesson for us is that genocide can be carried out even near where we live or work without our realising that it is happening. It has also been the case that many genocides have been carried out while the rest of the world did nothing; United Nations' intervention in the Rwanda genocide was blocked by the United States and France, both of which used the threat of a Security Council veto during discussions in Security Council subcommittees (Annan 2012: 46–60; Nahory 2004).

The Leader Principle

In fascism, the individual will is part of the national will, which in turn is expressed solely in the absolute and unquestionable will of the leader. Both the currently available versions of the Fascist Decalogue, a sort of manifesto of Italy's National Fascist Party, contain the sentence 'Mussolini is always right'. One of the first watchwords in the initiation ceremony for new members of the Nazi movement was 'The Führer is always right' (Arendt 1951: 339; 370, n.18). It follows that disagreement or dissent over any decision made by or on behalf of the leader amounts to betrayal or treason. Even pointing out problems in everyday matters, let alone major policies, is potentially treason, because it means either that the will of the leader is not perfect or that all is not perfect in the fascist society concerned.

This also means that even if physical conditions make it impossible to implement the leader's will, the failure to do so constitutes treason. Towards the end of the battle of Stalingrad, which took place through the winter of 1942–43 and in which soldiers and civilians suffered hideously, the German commander General Friedrich Paulus repeatedly asked for fresh supplies as the battle started to go against his troops. Hitler had no supplies to send, and instead promoted Paulus to the rank of field marshal, because until then no German field marshal had been taken alive; Hitler apparently expected Paulus to commit suicide following the impending defeat. This time, however, the newly promoted *Generalfeldmarschall* Paulus surrendered, presumably to save the lives of his troops. He later became a very public critic of Hitler and the rest of the Nazi regime, but for the Nazis his surrender at Stalingrad would have been a treasonable act. It would also have been a treasonable act to expose the failure to send supplies to Stalingrad, as a public revelation would have destroyed the myth of the Führer's infallibility.

The idea of infallibility is part of what has been called charismatic authority, a property of the leader's own personality, which in fascism is the source of supreme wisdom and expresses the general will of the people; that general will in turn is constantly reaffirmed by rallies and popular demonstrations (Heywood 2007: 212–13). That may seem a rather theoretical point about fascism, but the fascist requirement that the will of the leader is supreme and that any clash of wills must be resolved by a battle to the death was something Hitler in particular really meant. By definition, the people, even the most fanatical supporters, can never be equal to the leader. In the final days of the war, Hitler blamed the German people for not being strong enough to keep fighting until they were all dead (Passmore 2002: 71).

Problems

It is not an exaggeration to say that fascist societies and systems are riddled with contradictions, which have often caused them enormous problems and may well have contributed to the collapse of some of them. To start with, the complexity of large modern states means that problems will inevitably arise, such as coordination, unexpected technical difficulties in large-scale projects, unexpectedly severe weather, and so on. Fascism's inherent exclusion of any expression of problems then means that the system can only be sustained by an ever-expanding series of lies about its perfection. This has inevitably led to administrative chaos even in everyday practical matters, because information about essential matters like staffing, resources, materials available, and so on, becomes not only unreliable but at times nonsensical.

A second source of administrative chaos is political. The overriding principle of the leader's infallibility means that the public have to be prevented from learning which public institutions are responsible for particular areas of activity, because if they learn that, then they can even in principle start to hold such bodies responsible for things like power supply, transport, education, and the like—which could lead to their holding the leader responsible. The typical fascist response to this consists in creating several institutions with overlapping responsibilities, so that it is never clear whether a given matter is the responsibility of the municipal authorities, or the police, or the military, or the ruling party. Even those who work in and run the bodies concerned cannot be allowed to work out what they are responsible for, and so their duties are never given to them explicitly or as stable and continuing responsibilities. So the leader makes all appointments, and moves officials constantly from one post or institution to another, while also changing the definitions and duties of each post (in practice, some officials kept their posts throughout Hitler's rule). This was very much the case in Nazi Germany, but it has also been a feature of other totalitarian systems, such as the Soviet Union under Joseph Stalin (Arendt 1951: 385–86).

The Myth of the Pastoral Idyll

Fascist movements state this idea, the myth of a glorious and idyllic agricultural past, without specification or historical evidence. Serious investigation would almost certainly reveal without exception that older periods of history were as troubled as any other periods, with war, disease, famine, and social and political oppression just as common then as we think they are now. Indeed we in our time, with the almost worldwide establishment of democratic systems, even if most of these function badly, may well be much less accepting of those things than our ancestors were. The pastoral idyll is nevertheless central to the fascist idea of a pure nation which existed in the past and has been sullied or contaminated by contact with other cultures, by disruptive industrialisation, and by other processes.

The problem here is that fascist societies also have to be permanently mobilised for war, and have to have huge industries designing and manufacturing the latest weapons and armaments so that they are not overrun by other cultures, which according to fascist theory are permanent enemies and pose a permanent threat. Quite simply, pastoral and agrarian societies can neither create nor sustain such industries or the highly trained and well-equipped armed forces that fascist systems need. Modern military equipment cannot be made from wood, mud, and stone. In addition, modern industries need highly trained scientists, engineers, and mechanics, who are all inheritors and exponents of the rational–scientific intellectualism which fascism rejects.

Gender Roles and Society

Fascist thinking lays down very clear roles for women, and sees their task as that of bearing and rearing children who will constitute the next generation of fascists. The Nazis in particular held training camps and other events at which women were instructed in how to be good Nazi mothers (Passmore 2002: 123–26). Yet even in this lay a contradiction, because the training policy made reproduction, education, and even consumption into subjects for state direction; Mussolini went so far as to make birth control a crime, so that women would continue to reproduce members of the fascist nation. In effect, these moves politicised women by taking them out of the home only to return them there (Passmore 2002: 126).

Purity of Descent

This claim is almost impossible to prove, and may well mean nothing as a matter of scientific fact. Human beings seem always to have interbred with one another, and some evidence has been identified of interbreeding between our species, *Homo sapiens*, and another hominid species, the Neanderthals or *H. neanderthalensis*; other evidence has been published of interbreeding between humans and more than one other hominid species (Sankararaman et al. 2014; Callaway 2013). Yet the claim to purity of descent, or racial purity, is utterly central to fascism, and the Nazis had their own problems proving it; for example, many eminent German and Austrian families, such as the enormously wealthy Austrian family of the philosopher Ludwig Wittgenstein and his pianist brother Paul, were of Jewish descent–but Ludwig and Paul's grandparents had converted to Protestantism, and Ludwig was baptised in a Catholic church, possibly because his mother was a Catholic. The Nazis ended up classifying people by fractions of Jewishness, such as one eighth or one quarter. This taxonomy might look ridiculous, but it often had deadly consequences for those whom Nazi officials and administrators deemed sufficiently Jewish to be sent to concentration or extermination camps.

Another element of this—an element which is almost impossible to sustain—is the claim to prior occupation of territory. Humans originated in what is now part of East Africa, and have migrated all over the world, often going in very different directions, encountering other groups of humans, and they have not necessarily stayed in the areas which they first settled. The claim to prior occupation is virtually impossible to resolve, and the timescales involved are, on the existing evidence, almost impossible to establish to the degree of certainty fascism requires for its political purposes. The only thing fascist theory can allow here is therefore empty assertion.

Freedom from the State

Fascism claims to free people from the chains and shackles of the state and its bureaucracies and rules and regulations, but it also subordinates all individuals to the single will of the leader; this subordination is total, and any dissent or disagreement becomes not just treasonable but a threat to the nation, because for fascism the leader embodies the will of the nation. In practice too, fascist societies are extremely oppressive and can be arbitrarily brutal. Fascism has nevertheless attracted much admiration in areas of the world which were themselves the victims of economic and racial oppression, and during the 1920s and 1930s, there was much more contact between the Hindu Right in India and European Fascist leaders than is often recognised today.

THE HINDU RIGHT'S ATTITUDE TO FASCISM AND NAZISM

The writings of many of the major figures of the Hindu Right between the First and the Second World War show that those leaders were greatly attracted by fascism and studied it closely. Much of this has been documented in detail, for example by Marzia Casolari (Casolari 2000). Among other things, Casolari shows that some of the leaders of the Hindu Right met Mussolini in Italy; their writings often show clear approval of Nazi policies. The political strategies and methods they adopted were also similar. For example, in 1931, B. S. Moonje, a prominent figure in the Hindu Mahasabha, made a ten-day visit to Italy, where he visited military colleges as well as the Balilla and Avanguardisti organisations, both of which were specifically dedicated to the indoctrination of youth Casolari 2000: 219–20). Moonje was particularly impressed by their aim of unifying and—as he saw it—regenerating the nation by militarising it. When he met Mussolini, he told the dictator that he would praise the Balilla and other such bodies after he returned to India; he later praised fascism in various press interviews. In 1934, he founded the Central Hindu Military Education Society, which was intended to bring about military regeneration of the Hindus and to fit Hindu youths for undertaking the entire responsibility for the defence of their motherland (cited in Casolari 2000: 221). Moonje also wrote that the Balilla sought to create a situation in which there would be no distinction 'between the soldier and the man in uniform' (cited in Casolari 2000: 222).

An even stronger position was taken by Vinayak Damodar Savarkar, who rose in political life after being released from prison in 1937. Savarkar explicitly approved of the Nazi annexation of Austria and the German-speaking provinces of Czechoslovakia (the *Sudetenländer*), because he thought that the move would 'unite all Germans and consolidate them into a pan-German state' (Savarkar 1938, cited in Casolari 2000: 223). Savarkar went even further, stating in July 1939 that a nation could be formed only if people had a desire to form one and that what would unite them was 'unity of thought, religion, language and culture' (Savarkar 1939, cited in Casolari 2000: 223). Furthermore, he had earlier praised the Nazi expulsion of Jews from Germany (which had already started) and said the 'movement of the Germans' was a national one but that that of the Jews (he assumed that there was such a movement) was a communal one (Savarkar 1938, cited in Casolari 2000: 223).

As Casolari shows, Savarkar said much more in the same vein throughout that period, and admiration for Hitler was widespread at the time. Such admiration was certainly expressed openly in the Hindu Right's publications; one of the most explicit statements of this was by M. S. Golwalkar, who said in 1939 that Nazi Germany's 'purging' of Jews had shown that different races could not be 'assimilated into one united whole' and that this was 'a good lesson for us in Hindustan to learn and profit by' (cited in Casolari 2000: 224). For the Hindu Right, being a Hindu was a matter of race and blood; the Hindu Mahasabha, of which Savarkar was president, made a statement in March 1939 glorifying Nazi Germany's 'revival' of Aryan culture, and hoping that the 'crusade' against that culture's enemies would bring 'all the Aryan nations to their senses' (cited in Casolari 2000: 224). The Hindu Right seem to have thought they were part of such a nation. We cannot know whether the Nazis would have agreed had they won the war. According to their racial hierarchy, those of Asian descent were inferior beings to those of Nordic descent.

In addition, the Hindu Right's admiration for fascism also meant that they were permanently ambivalent about British rule over India. Many of their members praised the colonial government when it did things which facilitated their agenda, for example by handing over the writing and publication of school textbooks to Indians who had similar attitudes to the Hindu Right or belonged to its movements (Dwivedi 1903, cited in Orsini 2000: 99). In addition, Savarkar had a plan to encourage Indian enrolment in the army so that those who enlisted would get military training (Bose 2004: 176).

In effect, admirers of fascism embody many of the contradictions in fascism itself. Those contradictions have been widely identified and criticised; that fact makes the appeal of fascism a very important topic, because at first sight such an internally fragmented and contradictory ideology cannot get and retain support across so many sections of many different societies.

The Appeal of Fascism

Fascist leaders have always had enormous personal popularity, whether their movements have gained power or not, and the adulation Hitler and Mussolini received is almost legendary. Yet it is not clear whether or not fascist parties themselves have become genuine mass parties, and analyses vary on this point. According to Arendt, Hitler restricted the number of actual Nazi Party members so as to maintain control over the Party, but therefore he needed and actively encouraged the appointment and rapid promotion of a very large number of sympathisers in all organisations (Arendt 1951: 354). As the number of applications to join the Party rose rapidly after Hitler became chancellor in January 1933, he ordered that membership be limited. The hardcore members numbered about 1.5 million thereafter. As many as eight million people, or about one-seventh of the German population at the time, eventually joined the party, though many of them did so because membership made jobs and promotions easier to get. The number of active members was much smaller, though a substantial proportion of those members were in essential and respected professions; they included doctors, teachers, university lecturers, and researchers in the applied sciences. In all, as many as 17 million people may have joined organisations which had strong links and associations with the Nazi Party (Taylor 2011: 227–55). Irrespective of the size of the Nazi Party itself, its attitudes had very great appeal across all classes of society. This attraction across classes is a notable feature of fascism throughout. For example, in Nazi Germany, followers included small-business people from the lower middle classes, the owners of major industrial corporations, the landed aristocracy, and sections of the clergy in the institutionalised religions.

The small-business and trading classes, or the *petit bourgeoisie*, hated and feared socialism, which had enjoyed much wider popular support after the First World War than it is often recognised to have done, and they also feared large corporations, which they thought would destroy their own prospects with mass production and economies of scale. The larger businesses and corporate classes hated socialism and feared the trade unions, and welcomed the Nazis for doing so too; they were also indifferent to the fate of the *petit bourgeoisie*, and they stood to gain colossal wealth from the Nazi rearmament programme.

The landed aristocracy, for their part, were very taken with the fascist idea of pastoral or rural stability; they too hated socialism, because they feared that if it spread, they would lose their social status, their inherited privilege, and their rural or peasant workforce. As for the older established religions, sections among them feared that the spread of socialist or other egalitarian ideas would undermine the existing social order, particularly by giving women alternatives to rearing children and running the home. Even some German socialists favoured the Nazis, for expanding the industrial economy very greatly and providing mass employment to end the Great Depression; the Nazi regime also showed what looked like a socialist element, as it provided healthcare at work, and supported families with substantial numbers of social workers, nurses, health visitors, and domestic-science teachers. Most of the German communist and socialist leaders, however, were exterminated by the Nazis in the early 1930s. For their part, various German feminists thought a self-sacrificing female elite would help the cause of national regeneration, and some of them also opposed the Left.

Appeal to Artists and Writers

Fascism has often attracted artists and writers in many countries. Among the most famous were T. S. Eliot, who held a theory of racial hierarchies, the South African poet Roy Campbell, who was an Afrikaner nationalist, the writer D. B. Wyndham Lewis, and the poet Ezra Pound; the Swiss-French architect Le Corbusier was also an open and passionate fascist. A noted filmmaker, Leni Riefenstahl, made *Olympia,* two films about the Berlin Olympics, which have been very widely broadcast since they were made. The films have been widely praised for their aesthetic qualities but clearly show Riefenstahl's admiration for Hitler and Nazism as a whole, about which Riefenstahl herself was quite open. As for other areas of activity, it happened that several major industrialists also held views very similar to the Nazis, and Henry Ford was one of them; his own views were very extreme.

While various artists' admiration for fascism poses its own questions, a continuing problem is that fascist movements and parties have gained mass support from large groups which are often very hostile to one another, such as the *petit bourgeoisie* and the corporate business classes, or the landed aristocracy and various trade-union groups. Historically, what seems to have united them as followers of fascism is that fascist leaders showed or persuaded each group that the leaders hated the same things that each group hated. The landed aristocracy feared the loss of their rural dominance, the religious bodies feared the decline of the traditional family, the corporates hated and feared socialism, and so on. One lesson for us may well be that one of the easiest ways to get millions of people's support, even if groups among them hate and fear other such groups, is to hate the same things they hate—or to pretend to hate those things.

CHAPTER 1: FASCISM

Extension Exercise

1. Read the Fascism chapter again, and note down five key points about fascism.
2. For one of the political parties listed below, select a major policy commitment or a manifesto commitment; most such statements are easily accessible on the Internet.
   - The Bharatiya Janata Party
   - The National Front (France)
   - Fidesz
   - Alternative für Deutschland
   - The United Kingdom Independence Party (UKIP)
3. In the light of the points you have identified from the chapter, write a short analysis about 600 words long, on whether or not the policy commitment for the party you have selected is fascist or not.
4. Read this article (it is quite long):
   Casolari, M. 2000. 'Hindutva's Foreign Tie-up in the 1930s: Archival Evidence'. *Economic and Political Weekly* 35 (4): 220–28.
   Then compile a list of points from the article (6 or so for each side) on this question: Which movement had the greater influence on the Hindu Right—Italian Fascism or German Nazism?
   State your conclusion, which must be based on the two lists of points; from your lists give one main reason for your conclusion.

Further Reading

Arendt, Hannah. 1973. *The Origins of Totalitarianism*. New York: Harcourt.
Hood, Stuart, with Litza Jantz. 2013. *Introducing Fascism: A Graphic Guide*. London: Icon.

CHAPTER 2

Conservatism

Conservatism is not obviously an ideology in the conventional sense of the term. It is, or looks more like, an attitude of mind or an outlook on life. It also has considerable strengths, which may help account for its enduring character. It takes different forms in different cultures, and can seem to offer grounded and pragmatic ways of responding to new problems and new challenges. Conservative outlooks and attitudes have almost certainly existed in all societies throughout human history, because particular individuals may have been of a cautious temperament or because institutions or customs have been difficult to change, but as an identifiable attitude or broad grouping of attitudes, conservatism is a modern outlook and was indeed given much of its current form by events and processes which were decisive in the formation of political modernity.

Those were the French Revolution, which started on 14 July 1789, and the industrial revolutions, which had already been in progress for some decades, particularly in Britain. Among the most accessible statements of conservatism are those by various British thinkers, such as Edmund Burke in the eighteenth century and Michael Oakeshott in the twentieth century. Burke, who was both a politician and a writer, saw the French Revolution as a great threat to the established social order in Europe (which it was), but he also saw the violence and the terror which followed it as resulting from the revolutionary leaders' attempts to create radically new societies which were to be based on abstract, and implicitly universal, principles. For Burke, obvious examples of such principles were concepts such as liberty, equality, and the like; the rallying cry of the French Revolution was *'Liberté, Égalité, Fraternité!'*, or in English, 'Liberty, Equality, Fraternity!' (Heywood 2007: 66, 70).

Another eighteenth-century figure, the Scottish philosopher David Hume, is often taken to be a conservative thinker, mainly as a result of his opposition to what have been called rationalist schools of philosophy. Hume, however, differs from Burke, in that his rejection of reason as a guiding principle or a test for political systems has less to do with the effects of imposing vast rational systems on human societies than with Hume's own theory of knowledge or epistemology (Wolin 1954: 999–1001). Hume's central epistemological principle is that all knowledge is gained from sense-experience, which he calls impressions; for him, all our ideas are only fainter copies of earlier sense-impressions (Hume 1969: 55–66). That, according to Hume, means that truth or falsehood is a matter of agreement or disagreement between ideas, or a matter confined to agreement or otherwise with facts. If something cannot be settled or decided by either of those methods, it 'can never be an object of reason' (Hume 1969: 510; Wolin 1954: 1001).

Hume asserts equally strongly that reason cannot therefore serve to settle moral questions, and indeed his whole philosophic project was to replace speculative philosophy with knowledge grounded solely in experience; the subtitle of his great work, *A Treatise of Human Nature*, is 'An Attempt to Introduce the Experimental Method of Reasoning into Moral Subjects'. One of Hume's major conclusions is that reason alone can never be, as he says, a motive to any action of the will; a little later, he says, 'Reason is, and ought only to be, the slave of the passions, and can never pretend to any office other than to serve and obey them' (Hume 1969: 460 and 462; Wolin 1954: 1002).

This is certainly not a repudiation of reason, but it does put tight limits on the scope and power of reason. It also sets Hume apart from those conservatives who hold that if an institution or a practice has withstood the test of time, it is both natural and rational. Hume accepts that through habituation or long familiarity with an institution or a practice we might come to see it as natural, but for him reasoning and rationality have nothing to do with that (Wolin 1954: 1003). Hume, who does not make a sharp distinction between society and government, sees institutions and customs as having developed in response to human needs, but for him they are more than just the product of needs. They are facts of our existence, and are desirable because they meet needs, but at this point the factual and the desirable, as Wolin says, coincide in our institutions; the institutions which exist are those which are useful (Wolin 1954: 1007). Hume himself says that justice may result from the motivation to preserve and protect self-interest, but that what makes us approve of justice is 'sympathy' with public interest (Hume 1969: 551).

This is a form of conservatism which is very different from that advocated by, for example, Burke. Secondly, Hume often adopted positions which we would call liberal today; he admired the Quakers not for their religious principles (he himself was extremely unpopular with the religious authorities) but for their refusal to compromise those principles (Price 1966: 144–45). Thirdly, one of Hume's major works, *The History of England*, which was published in six volumes between 1754 and 1761, was attacked both by Tories (later the Conservatives) and by Whigs (later the Liberals). Furthermore, in the *History* Hume speaks approvingly of the Magna Carta and of those principles in the British government which protect liberty (Price 1966: 146–50). He even says, 'My own views of *things* are more conformable to Whig principles; my representations of *persons* to Tory prejudices' (Hume 1756, cited in Price 1966: 146). If Hume is a conservative, he is certainly a complex and thoughtful one.

In the twentieth century, one of the main conservative thinkers was the political philosopher Michael Oakeshott, who showed similar anxieties to Burke's. In a famous paper, Oakeshott severely criticises what he calls rationalism, the practice of imposing planned schemes on society by applying some form of universal reasoning which according to rationalism is shared by all humanity (Oakeshott 1962: 1–13).

Burke, explicitly, and Oakeshott, less explicitly, caution us against the dangers of social transformation on the basis of abstract principles, but Oakeshott's version of those is something he calls 'technical knowledge'; that may be closer to managerialism, an ideology in its own right, which I shall cover in more detail in Chapter 10. A lot of evidence could be used to support Oakeshott's arguments; for example, in the first two decades after the war, many Western European countries tried to improve millions of people's lives by building concrete estates on the outskirts of cities, so that the beneficiaries did not have to continue living in what had often been very squalid slums. Yet the new estates themselves created their own problems, as people were dislocated from familiar surroundings, moved to remote and unfamiliar areas, and had to live in tower blocks instead of houses. Several countries abandoned the relevant policies in the late 1950s, but by then a lot of social damage had been done. After that, some countries started improving people's neighbourhoods without moving or dislocating the people involved. A conservative might say that the obsession with theory had been responsible for the unexpected problems, despite the enormous material improvements in the physical conditions of ordinary people's lives; almost all of those improvements had resulted from the explicitly leading economic and political role of the social-democratic state in industrial countries for three decades after the war. It is likely that conservative opposition to the relocation schemes was partly informed by an ideological hostility to public provision of almost any kind.

Very importantly, however, neither Burke nor Oakeshott was against change. Burke was not rigidly opposed to change, and he famously said, 'A state without the means of some change is without the means of its conservation' (Burke 1790/2014); in fact, in his time Britain had already undergone enormous changes. In 1688, the English Revolution replaced an almost all-powerful monarch with a largely ceremonial monarch and an almost all-powerful parliament, even though at the start the new parliament was composed mainly of aristocrats who had inherited their status and wealth. Secondly, in 1707 the Scottish and English parliaments were both abolished and replaced with a single parliament based at Westminster in London. Thirdly, the Industrial Revolution, which started in the middle of the century, created an urban industrial workforce and generated a new class which acquired great wealth and power; this was the emerging class of industrial capitalists, a mercantile bourgeoisie whose main concerns were trade and finance.

So Burke was not opposed to change itself, but he wanted a cautious and sceptical approach to it and to all forms of the apparently new; by accepting change hastily or wholesale and without thought, we lose stability and other valuable aspects of our lives (Heywood 2007: 66). Similarly, Oakeshott sees a person he calls the 'Rationalist' as being unaware of the value of the things we inherit; such a person 'has no aptitude for that close and detailed appreciation of what actually presents itself', or of the cultivated enjoyment of a civilisational inheritance (Oakeshott 1962: 2). This kind of outlook has been called a distinctively English form of conservatism.

CONTINENTAL EUROPEAN CONSERVATISM

Conservatism in other countries has taken different forms. For a long time, French and German conservatism were more rigid and authoritarian than their British counterpart, possibly because strong monarchies remained in existence in much of continental Europe until late into the nineteenth century. Indeed, that form of authoritarian conservatism did not change substantially until after the end of the Second World War, when—with the exception of Spain and Portugal—the great majority of the now-reconstituted western European countries became, in effect, social democracies. In these new states, what had been authoritarian conservatism became instead a form of Christian democracy (Heywood 2007: 66). A German political party, the Christian Democratic Union, is a good example of that change, as is the Italian Christian Democratic Party. Broadly, these kinds of parties favour a group-orientated, if paternalistic, approach to political economy which is more associated with Catholic social theory than with Protestant thinking. This in turn implies that such conservatives accept Keynesian-type economics, in which the state acts to protect people against the worst effects of the free market (Heywood 2007: 84–85). The state is therefore also involved in coordinating the larger groupings in civil society, such as the trade unions, churches, and larger business associations (Heywood 2007: 84–85).

CONSERVATISM IN EAST ASIA

The Japanese Liberal Democratic Party, which has held office in Japan for most of the time since 1955, is one of the few political parties outside Europe which shows similar features to its European equivalents. It favours free-market economics and what it sees as traditional Japanese values such as duty, loyalty, and hierarchy.

CONSERVATISM IN THE UNITED STATES

This is very different from the other forms of conservatism. The founding principles of the state show a strong liberal inheritance, for example, in the rejection of inherited privilege and the explicit separation of powers and personnel between the main institutions of state, that is, the legislature, the executive, and the judiciary. There appears to be no foreseeable aim to introduce, for example, inherited status or privilege as an organising social principle, even though the huge and increasing inequalities in today's American society mean that the children of the rich inherit very great advantages.

American conservatism, therefore, is expressed more in the form of rigid and severe moral principles, such as bitter opposition to abortion, very strong support for the sanctity of the family, and very deep hostility to anything even remotely related to socialism, such as trade unions or other forms of workers' organisations. Some of the moral attitudes involved have their origins in the culture and faith of the white northern European Protestants who settled in North America in the seventeenth and eighteenth centuries. Other favourite targets for those with such attitudes today are unemployment benefits and of course public healthcare provision for all except the retired and for military veterans.

One possible reason for the tone and nature of American conservatism is that the United States has never had a mass labour movement or mass labour or social democratic parties of the kinds which are very common in Western Europe and Scandinavia, and also in Australia and New Zealand.

That is the case even though at one time in the nineteenth century there were no fewer than 325 radical newspapers in the US, including some published by the US Socialist Party, and despite the fact that in the early twentieth century the trade union leader Eugene Debs was a major political figure and presidential candidate (Herman and Chomsky 1988: 4). In Europe and Scandinavia, Left movements and labour parties have had a moderating effect on conservative parties' statements of their positions and on the policies the conservatives can implement if they are to retain enough support to win elections. For example, it took the British Conservative Party a long time to live down the fact that they voted against the National Health Service (NHS) in 1946; at least in public, they are still committed to retaining the NHS, even though they continue to bring private providers into specific areas of NHS work.

In the US, however, the association of conservative attitudes with various rigid or severe forms of Protestantism mean that US conservatism is not confined to Republican voters and politicians; conservative attitudes are often held by Democrat supporters too. In the Deep South, white populations irrespective of their class were so embittered when Abraham Lincoln abolished slavery in 1865 that they started voting Democrat almost *en masse*. The Republicans did not get the southern Democrats' support again until the early 1980s, when—under Ronald Reagan's leadership—they resumed the very strident expression of positions which they had earlier moderated during the New Deal period, which the Democrat president Franklin Delano Roosevelt had started in 1933; the southern states have voted Republican since the 1980s. The moral positions the Republicans have asserted in this period are motivated by far more than just their opposition to the so-called permissiveness of the 1960s, which would allow people to adopt, or at least to be much more explicit about, a range of attitudes and practices a conservative would consider immoral. US Republicans see this as the spread of moral diversity, which they consider a threat to the cohesion and stability or order of society (Heywood 2007: 93). A general term for the many groups which hold such attitudes is the New Christian Right, and I have covered it in more detail, with examples, in Chapter 9, which is on theocracy and fundamentalism.

US Neoconservatism

This is a specific form of conservatism that developed in the United States in the late 1960s and the 1970s, as several political thinkers and politicians had grown uncomfortable with what they considered social excesses on the Left and with the Left's criticism of military spending by the state, which they feared would weaken the US both domestically and—especially—internationally (Thompson 2011). Crucially, neoconservatives reject neoliberal and libertarian demands for a minimal state. For them, the political community is the primary unit, and most neoconservatives call for the United States to be militarily strong, with a 'muscular' foreign policy—which will include a willingness to use force in other parts of the world, especially to impose democracy if needed. US neoconservative foreign policy also includes a readiness to act independently when multilateral institutions such as the United Nations adopt policies that might harm US interests (Thompson 2011).

This willingness to maintain a large and powerful military requires substantial state funding, and neoconservatives consider that in order to be powerful and robust internationally, the US also needs what has been called remoralising internally or domestically. This moral vision requires a society in which

> ordinary people work hard, read the Bible, go to church, recite the Pledge of Allegiance, practice homespun virtues, sacrifice themselves to the 'common good,' obey the commands of the government, fight wars, and die for the state (Thompson 2011).

This is a comprehensive or systematic political philosophy and is far more prescriptive than, say, British conservatism. It is also very hostile to liberalism, which asserts individual freedom, including freedom in moral matters, as a central principle, and to libertarianism, which often goes far further than liberalism and can look like an extreme form of anarchism; we shall cover liberalism and anarchism respectively in Chapters 3 and 5.

Neoconservatism has been described as a consequence of the work of the political philosopher Leo Strauss (Thompson 2011). Critics have pointed to its many and very serious policy failures, such as the invasion of Afghanistan in 2001 and the catastrophic consequences of the invasion of Iraq in 2003, which was based on the entirely fictitious claim that Iraq possessed weapons of mass destruction and was an immediate and present threat to the world, particularly certain Western countries. Yet the conceptual commitments of neoconservatism remain significant and are potentially very influential. They include a focus on great leaders rather than constitutional procedures, and rule by a class who possess superior knowledge and discernment in comparison to ordinary people, who, under this theory, are therefore considered incapable of knowing their own best interests. These kinds of principles, combined with a form of great-nation political collectivism, have led to the description of neoconservatism as a form of 'soft, American-style' fascism, even though Thompson, for example, stresses that neoconservatives are not fascists (Thompson 2011).

Indian conservatism, for its part, shows some similarities to US conservatism, including neoconservatism, but in order to identify its often complex features we need to know the main ideas in conservatism, particularly in its British forms, as these show similarities with Indian conservatism.

CONSERVATISM: THE MAIN THEMES

- Tradition
- An organic view of society; respect for hierarchy and authority
- The conservative view of human nature

Tradition

Conservative thinkers, almost without exception, set great store by tradition. Traditional institutions, customs, and practices have withstood the test of time, and have survived or adapted to the challenges which they have faced. This means that according to conservative thought the strengths and good qualities of such institutions and practices have endured, while those aspects which were not so good have been abandoned or have withered away.

As the conservative sees it, tradition also helps us to know who we are; it gives us a sense of continuity and stability, it was taught to us by our forebears, who learnt it from their own forebears, and we then teach it to our descendants without needing grand theories or formulas to justify it. That also means we need to respect traditions by observing them, by carrying out the practices they require, and by altering them only in response to sufficiently serious questions or problems which arise in the everyday course of events.

It follows, further, that traditions cannot be invented and that institutions cannot be designed or planned in great detail, because we cannot know in advance which of their features will or will not stand the test of time. The conservative attitude to tradition has been called a Darwinian outlook, because according to it whatever is fit to survive will survive and is therefore worth maintaining and preserving. Conservatives therefore generally resist very substantial changes in the law, such as the introduction of the universal franchise or significant widening of the grounds for divorce.

An Organic View of Society; Respect for Hierarchy and Authority

The conservative view of tradition is accompanied by a view of society as an organic whole. Those institutions and customs which withstand the test of time are worth preserving and thereby show that they serve a necessary purpose in society. Examples of such institutions would be the longer-lasting religions, the judicial system, marriage and the family, educational systems, and so on. According to conservative thought, such institutions have turned out to be necessary because they have endured for a long time, and therefore they serve functions rather as the organs of a living body serve the body.

That in turn means some institutions and practices are more important than others; historically, hierarchy and authority seem to have survived in all societies, and for conservatism they are both necessary and inevitable. For conservatives, society is naturally divided into classes, with some people born to rule; in such classes, each generation teaches the next generation how to accept and use authority, power, and privilege. Many conservative political parties show this clearly; for example, the British Conservative and Unionist Party had no leadership elections until 1965, because the conservative philosophy was that leaders would emerge naturally. Indeed, the Party did not even register itself as a political party until 1997, when it did so partly in response to changes in funding law, which were introduced by the newly elected Labour government. Despite some changes in its internal structure, the Conservative Party still does not involve local branches significantly in policymaking; most if not all policy is decided by the leader and other senior figures and then declared at the Party's main annual conference. Yet the Party famously relies on grassroots members for its election campaigns, particularly to get supporters out to vote during elections; that kind of local loyalty is a conservative strength.

The Conservative View of Human Nature

Conservatism rejects grand theories, especially grand theories for social or economic organisation. According to conservatism, humans are flawed and imperfect beings, and are basically self-seeking as well. So we cannot be made into perfect beings, and there is no point in trying to plan or create perfect institutions or to create perfect people by creating such institutions; if we tried to do that, we would be acting on a misconception about human nature. According to a conservative outlook, our tendency to selfishness, or envy, or malice—or worse—means that our institutions and societies will always be affected by our flaws and cannot be perfected, because we cannot be perfected. Conservatism also sees us as needing a sense of order and continuity, a sense of the familiar and the known, and therefore attempts to create radically new societies or political systems are doomed before they start, because those destroy our sense of continuity and therefore also remove any sense of constraints on our conduct. Conservatives often cite as examples the terror which followed the French Revolution, as well as the history of the Soviet Union and Nazi Germany.

This pessimistic view of human nature as inherently flawed has several consequences for a conservative view of society. We fear the unfamiliar and should therefore keep things as they are, including existing hierarchies. Secondly, we are inherently selfish, even greedy, and therefore, crime is an expression of the worst features of human nature; for conservative thinkers, it is not a product of inequality or social disadvantage (Heywood 2007: 71–72). Therefore, conservatives hold that the only response to crime is tough law with strict enforcement, because as individuals who seek our own advancement we are also responsible for our own actions. Conservative politicians and parties around the world are consistently associated with 'law and order' policies, often irrespective of the success or failure of such policies. For example, creating new criminal law creates new offences, and by definition increases crime rates; in addition, tough prison conditions may be electorally popular and consistent with a conservative outlook, but they do little to prevent those who have served sentences from reoffending.

The view of humans as inherently self-seeking also means that for conservatives, society is best organised by being left to itself. This is consistent with the organic view of society, and for a conservative the family is the basic unit of society. In conservative thinking, individuals naturally seek to advance their own and their family's interests, and according to this view any attempt to prevent them from doing so, or any attempt to redirect their efforts towards wider or more public-spirited concerns, will always fail because it is based on a misconception about human nature. For conservatives, the best and only feasible organisation of society is that which arises naturally from people's own advancement of their own and their family's interests. Some conservatives have even greatly embarrassed their own parties by saying this. For example, the British Conservative prime minister Margaret Thatcher, in an interview with the weekly magazine *Woman's Own*, once said this about society:

> There is no such thing! There are individual men and women and there are families and no government can do anything except through people and people look to themselves first (Thatcher 1987).

This was a great shock to very large numbers of Conservative voters, who overwhelmingly favour strict social norms and strict enforcement of those. The Party's propagandists and publicity managers, not to mention Tory MPs, had to work very hard to moderate the political damage their leader's comment had caused—but Thatcher had in fact expressed a core principle of conservatism.

That principle also has enormous consequences for political economy. It rules out large-scale economic planning and regulation, and it requires that we give people the maximum possible amount of economic freedom to advance their own interests. So conservatism is committed to the free market, and to the kind of society that results from the free market. It is also committed to letting failed businesses fail and at least in theory rules out government refinancing or bailouts for businesses which fail. The idea is that good ideas and good businesses will succeed, and that those which fail deserve to fail because they are not good enough to withstand the test of the market.

In sum, conservatism involves avoiding grand theories of society, especially large-scale attempts to plan societies or economies, or to create perfect societies. It also involves a general caution about change, particularly hasty or substantial change; it requires respect for tradition, hierarchy, and authority, and its view of political economy rests on a pessimistic sense of human nature. This is not at all an implausible outlook on life, and some of its most powerful arguments use substantial evidence of the terrible brutality and catastrophic failures of visionary or ill-considered attempts to redesign society in the light of a grand theory, or attempts to plan and regulate whole societies. All the same, conservatism has its problems, and we need to identify the main ones.

PROBLEMS IN CONSERVATISM

Tradition

Conservatism's respect for tradition can be a powerful asset in election campaigns, but traditions are often much more complex matters than conservatism allows. To start with, many traditions are no more than practices which happened to be repeated often enough to start being regarded as traditions. Secondly, the origins of many traditions are much more modest than they seem to be. For example, the time allocated to Prime Minister's Questions in the British House of Commons has repeatedly changed, from having no special timetabled place until the early 1880s to the current 30 minutes starting at noon every Wednesday when Parliament is in session. Yet in May 1997, when the then-split session of 15 minutes on Tuesdays and Thursdays was replaced by the current system, a Conservative MP, speaking on one of BBC Radio's main news broadcasts, lamented the change in terms so florid that a listener may have thought all of civilisation had collapsed. The Tory MP was totally deflated when the news anchor told him that the split sessions had themselves been introduced only in 1953 because the then prime minister Winston Churchill—himself a Conservative—had been too frail to stand at the dispatch box for half an hour at a time.

Conservatism, however, does not encourage the detailed questioning or scrutiny of traditions, and that reluctance is part of the general conservative caution over theorising about society. The problem here is that this approach offers us no way of deciding when to change or abandon a traditional practice or institution, because that would involve asking wider questions about the origins, worth, and purpose of the traditions concerned, with the further risk that those traditions may turn out to be a great deal less exalted than conservatism requires them to be.

This can have very serious consequences; the conservative belief that if an institution or practice has endured then it is worth maintaining could well imply that, for example, the institution of caste—which has endured for two millennia, if not longer, and has endured and resisted countless challenges—is worth preserving simply because it has endured for such a long time.

Conservatism and the Free Market

For conservatism, as we have seen, people are self-seeking beings; therefore, attempts to restrict or control the free market would go against the grain of human nature and would be bound to fail. If, however, the operation of the market requires that we change or abolish established traditions or institutions, we face a problem in conservative thought.

Conservatism requires an unrestricted market, but any reasoning about whether or not to alter or abandon a tradition because the market requires it would mean reasoning about restrictions on the market and about traditions in a way conservatism rejects. Conservatism has no conceptual resources with which to resolve this problem. This supposedly pragmatic or practical outlook on life gives us no guidance on how to decide when to alter or abandon a tradition, and none on deciding how to respond to market-driven challenges. We also need to note that conservatism faces other conceptual problems. For example, conservatives are suspicious of grand theories of society or human nature, but their own thinking is based on a very substantial theory of human nature, namely the idea that humans are naturally self-seeking beings and that they are inherently flawed beings. Secondly, the conservative reliance on piecemeal change in response to particular situations carries the implication that human knowledge is inherently limited, provisional, and temporary; this is itself a theory of knowledge, an epistemology. It may sound like a persuasive one, but it cannot accommodate the possibility that new discoveries, say, about very harmful foods (refined sugar might be one example) or very destructive global practices, such as our dependence on fossil fuels, could well require wholesale changes to entire ways of life and whole societies. Conservatism, despite its rejection of substantial theories, is founded on at least two very substantial theories.

INDIAN CONSERVATISM

Indian conservatism is rarely, if ever, adopted as a single position or set of positions, and instead it is more often shown or expressed in a complex range of ways. For example, no political party in India has called itself conservative or put forward an explicitly conservative policy programme, but several groups and some political parties have taken positions and stated policies which are in effect conservative and are best understood as conservative in the Indian context.

There is, however, no doubt that conservatism and conservative forces are very deep and powerful in India; this is only to be expected in a society noted for its age and continuity, and for the endurance and strength of its social structure and social institutions. Secondly, although the major faiths in India, such as Hinduism, have often been both doctrinally and structurally adaptable, the pervasiveness of the caste system means that challenges to the caste system, or even demands for the elevation of particular castes in the caste hierarchy, have often been met with bitter resistance, including intimidation and murder, sometimes even mass murder. Many of the challenges have amounted to threats to an existing economic order or even to symbols of changes in the economic order (Anandhi and Vijayabaskar 2013).

It is also the case that despite strongly stated commitments to structural reform, to at least a social-democratic economy, and to much else that would have transformed Indian society, the political party which has held office for the longest time, often with huge majorities, the Indian National Congress, has never seriously challenged established vested interests or much of the existing social order (Erdman 1978: 793; Prashad 2015: 43). Many of its attempts to introduce significant reforms have been fiercely resisted, even during the period of the party's greatest dominance; it took even Jawaharlal Nehru 10 years to persuade Parliament to pass four major acts on Hindu family law, and the one ending polygamy in Hinduism was passed only in 1955. The debates around these new laws, however, were largely confined to urban areas, and there was little or no will to implement them (Erdman 1978: 794).

Conservatism in its Indian forms has tended to be resistive, and possibly even passive, for long periods; furthermore, groups which might have been expected to state their conservatism explicitly have not done so. For example, at the time India attained Independence there were no fewer than 561 princely states, very few of the rulers of which wanted to merge with the Indian Union. Many leading politicians strongly pressed those rulers to join the Union, and ultimately the central government wielded great power over the princely states in the form of privy purses. It could also offer inducements in the form of ambassadorships and various ceremonial appointments (Erdman 1978: 797–98). The Indian princes were also divided, with one cause of their divisions being status differences among themselves (Erdman 1978: 797–98).

The rulers of the princely states were hardly the only ones aware of what an independent, democratic—and then republican—India would mean. For example, some of the Congress leaders led a powerful resistance to the very idea of the universal franchise; indeed many of the Constituent Assembly debates before Independence showed that the Indian elites wanted to 'share the benefits of modernisation, without surrendering the social advantages they enjoyed' (Muralidharan 2007: 39–40).

Conservative politicians in India, however, differ from their counterparts in Europe in that they have had little apparent contact with the hereditary aristocracy, who seem to have regarded them, at least before and for some time after Independence, as 'tradesmen who were not fit to rule' (Erdman 1978: 794). Some parties which have had conservative policies have tried to attract the aristocracy; the Swatantra Party, which C. Rajagopalachari founded in 1959 partly in response to the potential disturbance which nationwide social and economic change would cause, was one such, but the party never did well in elections, and in 1977, it was incorporated into a larger assemblage, the Janata Party. That in turn has been supplanted by the Bharatiya Janata Party (BJP).

In India, therefore, conservatism is an obvious feature of society in all its forms, and conservative attitudes in all classes and communities are so deep and so powerful that almost no political party or policy seems to have much effect on them. That makes Indian conservatism less of a political movement than an attitude, outlook, or cast of mind, such that social change is almost automatically treated with caution or suspicion. If there is change, it seems to proceed locally and by very small steps, with little or no change tolerated to the established economic structure and system.

Conservatism, in its many forms, remains a difficult ideology to evaluate in simple terms. The conservative reluctance to articulate specific theories or detailed political or economic plans means that its central themes, as we have seen, often conflict with one another to the point where conservatism looks completely incoherent. Yet, as an outlook, conservatism endures in several forms, and it continues to be a powerful political force, not least when societies face great uncertainty or very rapid change.

CHAPTER 2: CONSERVATISM

Extension Exercise

1. Read this article:
   Kasturirangan, Rajesh. 2009. 'In Praise of Conservatism'. *India Together*, 29 August. http://indiatogether.org/conserv-op-ed
2. In the article, identify or highlight those points which match the key points of conservatism from the chapter.
3. Using these points, write two paragraphs (each about 150 words long) on whether or not Indian conservatism is a distinct form of that ideology.

Further Reading

Robin, Corey. 2011. *The Reactionary Mind: Conservatism from Edmund Burke to Sarah Palin*. New York: Oxford University Press.

O'Sullivan, Noel. 1976. *Conservatism*. London: Everyman.

3
CHAPTER

Liberalism

Liberalism is more obviously an ideology than, say, conservatism, in that it embodies a range of specific ideas, which often result in specific approaches to political life, including the organisation of the state and society; very often liberal ideas result in a range of particular policies. Unlike conservatism, however, liberalism has often had a transformative and even revolutionary effect on societies where it has been propounded. It is also a distinctively modern ideology, though in a different way from conservatism. It is associated with production on a mass scale, that is, with the industrial revolution in the eighteenth and nineteenth centuries, and with industrial capitalism; both of those, in northern Europe at least, constituted decisive challenges to established feudal societies and their inherited hierarchies.

In English life, the term 'liberal' used to refer to attitudes and activities among the aristocracy, but in the early nineteenth century, it came to have a much more specifically political meaning (Bell 2014: 692–94). For political usage at that time, the word seems to have been derived from the Spanish word *Liberales*, which seems to have had connotations of narrowness; in Britain, the Tories used it to attack their main opponents, the Whigs. The Whigs themselves started to use the word to describe groups or individuals who sought reform without revolution, and from about the second half of the nineteenth century, the term came to mean the policies and attitudes of the newly formed Liberal Party, which was the new name for the Whigs (Heywood 2007: 23). It also came to be associated with the emerging middle or upper-middle classes, that is, the new business and financial classes, who were starting to demand greater economic freedoms and commensurate political changes (Bell 2014: 692–93). It is worth noting that the term itself says little about the specific arguments involved; for example, the English philosopher John Locke (1632–1704) is now described as one of the founding figures of liberalism, but in his time he was not called a liberal, and seems not to have been widely regarded as one until his political work came under fresh scrutiny from the middle of the twentieth century onwards (Bell 2014: 694–98).

Politically, liberalism has been adopted extremely widely around the world, though not always as an explicit commitment. Most democracies today have procedures and institutions which embody or show liberal values. Examples would be free and fair elections with a universal franchise and secret ballots, laws protecting rights, and anti-discrimination legislation. Other examples would be contributory systems of unemployment benefit, state pensions, and governmental attempts at broad forms of economic management rather than economic control. Despite the global or near-global spread of liberalism, it is far from clear how successful its application or adoption has been, and many of its main ideas continue to be strongly disputed. In addition, as I shall show below, the history of liberalism is closely associated with the spread of imperialism and the imperialist exploitation of hundreds of millions around the world; imperialism has also been associated with open statements of racial superiority by its proponents, and such statements, including assumptions or statements that some cultures are superior to others, are occasionally still made by liberal ideologues.

Liberalism arose in a specific historical and economic context and its earliest statements involved a set of ideas which challenged established ideas of society and authority. More specifically, as a body of ideas, liberalism rejects the imposition of power and authority from above, and that includes resisting the imposition of ideologies, faiths, moral principles, or ways of life including occupations and social or other activities, down to sexual preferences and orientations. I shall list the main ideas in liberalism, and then outline the implications for the organisation of government and other institutions of state. I shall go on to examine the two main forms of liberalism, and will conclude by identifying some of the problems in liberal thought.

Historically, liberalism has gone through two main phases, namely classical liberalism and modern liberalism. The modern form is a modified version of the classical form, and has faced severe criticism from supporters of the older version; such supporters, often called neoliberals, did not have much impact until the late 1970s, when politicians such as Ronald Reagan and Margaret Thatcher claimed, at least in public, to support policies which would be consistent with classical liberalism. This allegedly revived form came to be called neoliberalism, and it too has faced renewed challenges since the global financial crash of 2007–9. Various forms of modern liberalism have been put forward as alternatives, as have other ideologies.

LIBERALISM: KEY CONCEPTS

The main ideas of liberalism, however, are shared across the different forms of the doctrine. They are:

- The individual and the concept of rights
- Freedom
- Reason
- Justice
- Toleration

The Individual and the Concept of Rights

For liberalism, the individual is the basic unit of society, and the individual must be protected by a range of rights, which constitute absolute limits to actions and to the powers of official bodies. Rights also involve processes, such as the right to participate in fair and free elections, the right to freedom from the arbitrary use of official power, and the right to personal privacy. A range of roughly simultaneous processes seem to have given rise to the idea of the individual as a being protected by rights; in the late eighteenth century, feudal societies in northern Europe began to break down as the newly emerging industries needed large numbers of labourers to do the new types of work which were emerging. These were mainly routine jobs operating machines in factories, or manual jobs in extractive industries like mining. Conditions in both those types of industry were truly terrible for something like a century and a half, until mass trade unions and other labour movements had some effect, but the millions and even tens of millions who moved from rural areas to the new cities got year-round work, which gave them some relief from the seasonal rural cycle of glut and famine or near-famine. Millions were also thrown off the land by laws like the British Enclosure Acts; the country's parliament, which at that time was made up mainly of rich aristocratic landowners, passed these between 1750 and 1860, and by 1860 virtually no common land was left. The rest had, in effect, been stolen (Rosenman n.d.).

In addition, new financial and business classes were emerging; these new classes devised credit-based ways of funding manufacturing industries which made use of the many inventions that were also emerging at the time. As their wealth increased rapidly, the emerging classes began to seek more political power and thereby challenged the existing hierarchies of inherited wealth, privilege, and power. Their claim to increased power involved the idea that individuals have their own unique talents and capacities, and therefore that traditional hierarchies prevent individuals from developing those capacities. They also held that the tradition of inherited occupations allowed individuals to develop only certain capacities, or prevented them from finding out what they were best at. According to the new class then, individuals must be free to develop their own capacities, and to advance themselves in life; in Latin, the word *liber* means 'free'.

Liberal theorists also argued that everyone has a right to develop their own talents irrespective of the social class or status which they inherit, and that such a right must be protected against interference or restrictions. For liberalism, human individuals have these rights because they are human and nothing else; such theories have been called natural rights theories, and in everyday discourse the rights involved are often called human rights (Heywood 2007: 45–46).

One consequence of natural rights theories is that if we accept them then we must not interfere with human beings' freely made decisions, and furthermore, we must not exploit people or use them as instruments for our own purposes. This idea, that people are ends in themselves and not means to others' ends, was most famously stated by the philosopher Immanuel Kant in the 1780s (Kant 1948: 90–91).

Very importantly, within liberal theory, rights are not meant to protect us so that we all attain equal status in life or achieve the same things or even the same kinds of things. Instead, liberalism requires that we are protected against interference or restriction in the choice of our activities and our pursuit of those activities. This has often been called negative freedom, a phrase created by the philosopher Isaiah Berlin (Berlin 1969). Many of the rights created in modern democracies, such as those found in anti-discrimination law, express or embody the idea of negative freedom. That idea is also shown in other procedural rights, such as the right to a fair trial, to free and fair elections, and so on. These involve protections against interference, but no claim is made here that we have a right to autonomy, that is, a right to be in control of our lives. Berlin called that kind of right positive freedom (Berlin 1969).

The primacy of the individual and of individual rights in liberalism also means that we must not impose a moral or political system, or an ideology, on individuals; it also means that we must not state any substantive theory of human nature. Many liberal theorists have put forward strong critiques of the terrible consequences that have followed when ideologies or substantive theories of human nature have been imposed and then often defended at all costs. Historically, they can adduce a lot of evidence to support the liberal position; Nazi Germany would be one example, and other examples could easily be found in those colonial conquests which were inspired by religious motives, such as the Iberian colonisation of Central and Latin America. Among other examples of the imposition of ideologically driven systems would be the history of the Soviet Union and China under hardline communism, and the neoliberal financial doctrines which have dominated economic policy almost worldwide since 1980.

Freedom

The idea of the individual is of course conceptually related to the idea of freedom in liberalism. According to liberalism, we are all unique individuals, and our individuality is, so to speak, sacrosanct; we therefore have an inherent right to choose our activities, our directions in life, and almost anything else, freely and without restriction.

This can only be achieved in a certain kind of society. Liberalism requires that we organise society so that individual rights and freedoms are protected; then we can develop our capacities freely (Heywood 2007: 29–30). This can create problems, especially when our free action restricts others' freedom or freedoms; this can occur frequently in everyday matters as well as larger issues. For example, if we throw our rubbish anywhere we like, we are despoiling somebody else's surroundings, and if we play very loud music late at night or drive vehicles in any manner we like, we are limiting others' freedoms and potentially also harming them. Most liberal thinkers therefore reject the idea of unlimited freedom and instead favour keeping restrictions to a minimum. John Stuart Mill argues for limitations only to prevent harm to others, and some contemporary libertarians—who go further than liberals—advocate the freedom to harm oneself, for example by taking addictive or harmful substances. John Rawls tried to reach a sort of compromise position which would give us liberties which would be consistent with similar liberties for all (Heywood 2007: 29–31).

Reason

For liberalism, reason is an essential element in our capacity to make free decisions for ourselves. Historically, forms of liberalism have derived some of their weight from the enormous social and political changes which are broadly known as the Enlightenment. This involves the progressively widening recognition that we can reason about things that once seemed unchangeable features of life, such as established political or religious authority, natural disasters, outbreaks of disease, and so on. Politically, the Enlightenment may have started in the city states of mediaeval Italy; these wrote their own constitutions, and were involved in often confrontational relations with the Church in Rome. In other respects, the Enlightenment has derived very great energy and momentum from advances in the natural sciences, which have enabled us to explain, predict, and control many apparently uncontrollable natural phenomena, such as floods, diseases, and the like.

The liberal view of individuals' capacity to reason therefore makes individuals the best judges of what is best for themselves; therefore, too, education is essential if individuals are to be liberated from superstition, ignorance, and submission to unquestioned authority. The capacity to reason, crucially, is spread by the process of education, and enables us to reach agreement without resorting to violence; for liberalism, violence is at most the last resort.

Justice

In liberal thought, justice has to do with the distribution of rewards and punishments; in what is called modern liberalism, justice can include material benefits as a form of social justice. The liberal idea of justice is derived from the principle of foundational equality, according to which we are all of equal moral worth. Therefore, we must have formal equality in respect of opportunities and procedures, and the law must be applied equally to all of us; we must also have a fair distribution of rewards and entitlements (Heywood 2007: 33).

That, in turn, means liberal theorists oppose arbitrary discrimination, for example discrimination on the grounds of gender, ethnicity, religious affiliation, and so on. Rights therefore include the right to fair procedure, and laws against arbitrary discrimination are typically liberal in form or express liberal values. This does not have to mean equality of outcome or of social status; liberalism can accept inequality if it results from a fair process, and the idea of a meritocratic society is a typically liberal one, because it implies reward in proportion to our talents allied to our efforts (Heywood 2007: 34).

Toleration

Liberal theorists require that we do not impose ideologies, or ways of life, or beliefs, on people; that means we have to tolerate wide or even very wide diversity in society, even if we do not like people's decisions, choices, or preferences. We may even find those unsettling, disturbing, or offensive, but liberalism places a duty of tolerance upon us as a complement to the right to choose our way or ways of life. In liberalism, we have a duty to tolerate others' ways just as we have a right to their tolerance of our ways.

In practice, most liberals accept some limits to toleration, especially where harm is caused by anyone's conduct, but the controversies which result are often very fierce. One very important point here is that toleration can require us to recognise mutual dependence; for example, workers and employers may have conflicting interests, and organised bodies such as trade unions may act very forcefully in any disputes, but liberal theory recognises that each side needs the other. Most contemporary democracies have laws on the conduct of such disputes, and procedures regulating the relevant dealings. These laws do not specify the outcomes, and are characteristically liberal in form.

THE LIBERAL STATE

In view of liberalism's emphasis on freedom, justice, and the individual, only particular forms of state are compatible with liberalism. In this, liberalism differs greatly from conservatism, which accepts society and its institutions as the outcome of an organic process or as having developed in the natural course of events. Liberalism, instead, requires a certain form of state, that is, one in which institutions have specified roles and functions, such as making laws or implementing justice, with specified relationships between the main institutions of state so that none of them can dominate the others. Liberal theory has to be very explicit about these aspects of political organisation, and some of the most intense and detailed arguments about the organisation of the state have taken place in liberal theory or in response to liberal theory.

The Form of the Liberal State and Its Institutions

Historically, liberal thinkers and politicians demanded, fought for, and established constitutional government before they focused on representative government. This was mainly because they were trying to put an end to the excesses and corruptions of late mediaeval monarchies, and because they therefore regarded constitutional government as the first requirement. That involves a set of basic laws which specify the powers of public institutions and office bearers as well as the procedures they have to follow. It also specifies the limits to those powers, or creates judicial processes whereby such limits can be decided in particular cases. Constitutions therefore restrict, or at best abolish, arbitrary conduct in matters of government and politics, and liberal thinkers in general consider arbitrariness to be part of the tyranny which for them is an inevitable danger in all forms of political power (Heywood 2007: 38).

Constitutions, therefore, specify the ground rules and procedures for the conduct of political life, and also limit the powers of government. For liberals, such basic laws are essential for the protection of individual rights and freedoms; many of them would apply to private bodies and individuals as well as public bodies and personnel. In general, written constitutions are a feature of liberal political systems, and almost all contemporary democracies have written constitutions. The United Kingdom and New Zealand are two exceptions, but both of those states have laws, conventions, and institutions which would be found in most written constitutions informed by liberal thought. For example, the United Kingdom has a Human Rights Act, and New Zealand has a Bill of Rights; both these laws set some limits to governmental powers; for example, the British Human Rights Act 1998 requires that all laws passed thereafter be consistent with the Act.

As for written constitutions, India provides an excellent example, with powers and responsibilities specified for the central government and the states; the Supreme Court, the guardian and interpreter of the Constitution, can order official bodies to act in accordance with the Constitution, and can strike down legislation which contravenes the Constitution.

Representative Government: Unresolved Tensions Between Liberalism and Democracy

It may seem surprising that liberalism has an at best uncomfortable relationship with democracy, especially as most democratic constitutions in today's world express recognisably liberal commitments to things like limitations on governmental power, to rights of many kinds, to free and fair elections, and so on. Nevertheless, both conceptually and historically, liberalism has a much less comfortable relationship with representative government than it does with constitutional government. John Locke, who lived from 1732 to 1804, saw the task of government as protecting what he called natural rights (for him these were life, liberty, and property) so that individuals could pursue their private activities and advance their private interests freely. Locke also held that mixing our labour with something, say, by working on land or on raw materials, made it our own property and therefore gave us a right over it; he did, however, state cautions about the possession of excessive amounts of land or other resources (Locke 1960: 303–18). In respect of politics, all liberal theorists are nervous that any public institutions we create can start to expand beyond the limits we set for them or that they can abuse the powers we give them. In liberal thought, therefore, it is the public who give power to public institutions and officials, and it is the public who must be able to take that power away from those who hold it.

One problem for liberalism, however, is that of who the relevant public are. Partly because education is very important in liberalism, early liberals like John Stuart Mill thought that educated people were better fitted to make political decisions than, say, the uneducated or illiterate. Mill later came to accept the idea of a universal franchise, but he also held that educated people's votes should count for up to four votes by illiterates. John Locke, for his part, thought that only those who own property should be allowed to vote, because in his time only the propertied classes paid taxes.

This kind of nervousness, or even fear, of popular or mass democracy is shown very strikingly in the United States constitution, where Article 2 says the president shall be elected by an electoral college. The college vote for any given state is equal to the number of Representatives that state sends to the House of Representatives plus two for the Senators who represent the state in the Senate. For example, California, with 53 Representatives and two Senators, has 55 college votes. If a presidential candidate wins the popular vote in a state, then he or she takes all the college votes for the state. The number of Representatives is decided according to each state's population, so a presidential candidate needs to win only the seven most populous states in order to win a majority of the current total of 538 college votes. Four times, the winner of the college majority has won less of the total popular vote than the loser; for example, Grover Cleveland lost in 1888 because he won the count of total votes but was unable to persuade the college to give him a majority. More recently, in 2000 George W. Bush lost the popular vote to the Democrat Al Gore but—in a disputed count—won the state of Florida, which gave him a total of 271 college votes and therefore the presidency. Perhaps most strikingly, Donald Trump won the 2016 presidential election by 306 college votes to 232, but his nearest rival Hillary Clinton won 2.86 million more popular votes, or about 2.1 per cent more of the turnout, than Trump. Those who drafted the US Constitution were very frightened that a simple popular vote would lead to what the French philosopher Alexis de Tocqueville called the tyranny of the majority; so they could not allow a popular vote to decide the presidency. Indeed, Alexander Hamilton, one of the framers of the US Constitution, wrote a letter in which he said of the United States that democracy was 'our disease' (Hamilton 1804). The framers of the constitution therefore devised the requirement for the college vote as a safeguard against what they feared might be bad judgement by the masses.

Liberalism also gives rise to this kind of problem in imperial and international contexts. John Stuart Mill, who like his father James Mill worked for the East India Company for a time, concluded that liberal democracy would have to be imposed on the Indian civilisation by force, because its cultural values were too far removed from those of liberalism for a reasoned introduction to take place (Bhabha 2004: 132–44). At the end of the twentieth century, the idea of liberal interventionism became something of a media fashion for a short time, particularly as a way of trying to justify the Western invasion of Afghanistan (which was valid in international law) and the illegal invasion of Iraq, which was led by the United States and the United Kingdom. Yet liberal intervention seems never to have been proposed in respect of Saudi Arabia, a very powerful Western ally, or in respect of Nigeria and India, both of which have free and fair elections, even though both are tainted by severe corruption and inequality, which cause enormous problems for hundreds of millions in respect of access to education, healthcare, and the justice system, whether civil or criminal (Transparency International 2011: 11–13, 2013).

This kind of problem is hardly new in the history of liberalism. Domenico Losurdo's unrelenting critique of the doctrine's record shows that the American Revolution, which was started in the name of liberty, involved what was in effect official consecration of the institution of slavery (Losurdo 2011: 14). This was not the kind of slavery recorded in antiquity but permanent, hereditary slavery determined by the colour of people's skin—that is, slavery or permanent subordination by descent. According to Losurdo, a central factor here was that the emerging merchant and financial classes saw anything and everything as a tradable commodity, including human beings, or more specifically human labour power, the capacity to perform work; it was these classes who defined themselves as liberals (Losurdo 2011: 29–36, 241–44).

In the conceptual home of liberalism, Great Britain, this meant the forced expulsion of peasants from the land and the enclosure by law of common land; the measures taken were of 'unprecedented harshness'. Even absolute monarchy might have provided a possible protection against the enclosures, but Britain's executive monarchy had been abolished in 1688, when the nobles who then composed Parliament created the doctrine of parliamentary supremacy and made the monarch a figurehead. One consequence was that the whole sphere of politics and legislation was defined so narrowly as to exclude material living conditions and the system of structural economic relations; this also made it almost impossible to raise seriously the fact of slavery as a public matter (Losurdo 2011: 188–92). As Western colonialism spread, a further result was the imposition of colonial control based on repression and genocide or near-genocide, whether in Australasia, the United States, or the expanding French empire. Indeed, slavery was in many places replaced by what Losurdo calls servile—meaning indentured—labour; the United States, for example, imported 10,000 Chinese labourers to build railroads in inaccessible parts of what was then the Far West (Losurdo 2011: 222–24).

It should therefore be surprising that liberalism, with its record, has been so apparently successful in our time, with rights and anti-discrimination legislation now a routine feature of almost any democratically constituted polity, irrespective of whether or not such rights are observed in practice. One possible reason is that liberalism continues to be as much the ideology of ruling classes and putative or aspirant ruling classes as it was during the period of its early successes. As this form of class ideology, it would therefore rely on passive conceptions of citizenship, tight control of official information, and a variety of ways in which access to the public sphere is restricted or controlled.

That, however, is not a complete explanation, because the flaws in the practice of liberalism have been and continue to be exposed globally. A philosophic difficulty—one which applies to any ideology—is that the historical record does not exhaust or end the possibilities in any system of political ideas. Indeed, it is not clear what our world would even look like if the historical record were all there is to any ideology. What would such a state of affairs mean? The rejection, for example, of Marxism on historical grounds is common enough, but the same point is just as true of liberalism; in sum, we need, whether we like it or not, to continue taking liberal ideas seriously.

Political Pluralism

Liberal states, by definition, allow a wide range of political opinions and parties, and this is consistent with the liberal principle that people are free to support policies they like, in freedom from coercion by the state or private bodies or individuals. This also means people are free to choose political representatives, and that the representatives themselves can offer a range of policies and attitudes to the electorate. Therefore, liberal states are characterised by a range of ideas, viewpoints, and political parties.

Civil Society

This is a very important feature of liberal political systems. Liberal theorists distrust and fear what they see as the state's tendency to encroach upon more and more of the individual's life, and they require limits to the state's reach so that individuals can freely follow their own interests, including business and commercial interests, and continue their own activities without state interference. These would be things like voluntary societies, sporting and artistic activities, recreational pursuits, and the like. For most liberal theorists, and in practice in most liberal systems, people spend most of their time in civil society, which includes the right to freedom of association. Civil society is therefore the space of all activities not connected with the state. The German philosopher Hegel calls it the aggregate sphere of interests (Hegel 1967: §182–239).

Liberal Economics

A broadly free-market or capitalist economy is essential to liberalism, because economic freedom is part of liberal thinking. Liberal theory has a substantial economic element, and broadly shows two main tendencies. One is formed by classical liberalism and neoliberalism, and the other is often called modern liberalism.

CLASSICAL LIBERALISM AND NEOLIBERALISM

These forms of liberalism involve a strong form of egoistical individualism, according to which we are rationally self-interested beings and have a strong capacity for self-reliance. On this view, we are like individual atoms which make up society; individuals are the basic units of society, and we have natural rights because we are individuals. We have already noted the principle of a negative right to freedom from coercion, and the right to life, liberty, and property. Not all liberals have seen this in quite the same way; the US Declaration of Independence famously states the right to life, liberty, and happiness, though in many of the earlier debates people like Thomas Jefferson had used phrases like 'public happiness'. Jefferson himself had written of a right to be a 'participator in the government of affairs' (cited in Arendt 1963: 126–29).

Economic freedom was and remains an essential element in liberal theory. Adam Smith, for example, saw the economy as a set of interrelated markets; this overall system, he thought, would work best when left to itself. The theory is that the aggregate or overall results of self-interested individual actions (Smith's 'invisible hand') would automatically produce the best outcomes in the most efficient way.

In liberal theory, however, economic freedom of this kind also involves a strong commitment to the state, and liberals do not call for the abolition of the state. They see it instead as a necessary evil, but they need it to enforce contracts, to provide protection against attack by other countries, and to maintain internal order; this can require a strong, comprehensive, and highly militarised state. That would be very different from the kind of thing John Locke, one of the major figures in classical liberalism, envisaged, namely a 'nightwatchman' (cited in Heywood 2007: 45).

There are some differences between classical liberalism and neoliberalism, which is often said to be the dominant contemporary form of liberalism, having had wide currency from the late 1970s until the financial crash of 2007–9. These differences, however, are not fundamental, and some neoliberals see themselves as the true inheritors of classical liberalism. The classical form of liberalism was founded on philosophical theories of human nature and of economics, and not all liberals were completely confident about the benefits of the free market. Adam Smith himself was deeply worried about the effects of the division of labour and about other consequences for the unrestricted market; he says the division of labour results in our doing a small number of repetitive tasks to the point where anyone in that position would become 'as stupid and ignorant as it is possible for a human creature to become', and he adds here that this is inevitable 'unless the government takes some pains to prevent it' (Smith 2007: 203).

Neoliberal theorists, on the other hand, have both a rigid commitment to the free market and a strongly conservative social philosophy. Like classical liberals, they require a strong but very limited state to enforce the law, including contract law, and to protect the state against disorder or attack. Milton Friedman considered that taxation for government spending would fuel inflation without reducing what he thought was a 'natural' or inevitable rate of unemployment (Friedman 1968: 8–10). Another famous neoliberal, Friedrich von Hayek, sees the operation of the free market as a natural law, like the laws of physics; this means that any intervention in the economy is based on a misconception. Hayek also says that while we act to advance our immediate self-interest, the overall workings of markets are so complex that no individual can predict the aggregate outcomes of their own actions in the market (Hayek 1976: 32–33, 69–74).

I shall cover the main conceptual problems of liberalism in a later passage in this chapter, but here we must note that the empirical record of neoliberalism has been severely criticised, both before and after the global financial crash of 2007–9. One major criticism is identified as dating from the 1970s, when it seems to have been agreed by the US government (in particular) and the US financial sector that in any kind of economic crisis the financial institutions must be protected by the state irrespective of all other consequences. The financial institutions, in particular the commercial banks, almost certainly knew how insecure they were, and how financially dangerous even their everyday business activities were, despite the fact that under a liberal ideology organisations which are not efficient in the market must fail. In the 2007–9 crash, the major commercial banks simply demanded and got $700 billion in public funds; hundreds of millions of ordinary people paid the price for that as large-scale unemployment spread throughout the world (Harvey 2013).

Secondly, the scarcely credible amounts of paper money generated by unrestricted financial speculation meant that the only place such monies could be invested was in more paper money, that is, in stocks and shares or financial instruments completely unconnected to productive activity. This amounts to a colossal inflation of notional asset values, which is combined with the near-elimination of credit for all but the best-paid workers (that is, the highly qualified professionals), and means that apart from the very rich, fewer and fewer people can even consume such goods as they still produce (Harvey 2013).

MODERN LIBERALISM

Both classical liberalism and modern liberalism involve a moral element. According to them, market competition makes for efficiency; we rise or fall according to our own efforts, and the unequal outcomes of markets only reflect natural inequalities between human beings in respect of their ability and effort. So the state must not try to equalise natural inequalities, and we deserve to end up wherever we end up. This runs through all forms of liberalism, and has been called social Darwinism, by analogy with Darwin's theory that hierarchies are entirely natural and that the fittest and strongest survive and come to dominate (Heywood 2007: 51–52).

One version of liberalism, nevertheless, requires that we attempt to equalise several aspects of society so that we all get the best possible chance to achieve the best we can achieve. This version is called modern liberalism. Historically, it is most closely associated with the New Deal implemented by the US president Franklin Delano Roosevelt between 1933 and 1945, and with the mixed economies of the post-war period in north-western Europe and Scandinavia. Conceptually, it originates with John Maynard Keynes' book *The General Theory of Employment, Interest, and Money*, which was published in 1936. Roosevelt was attempting to get the US economy moving again during the Great Depression which followed the financial crash of 1929, and tried to introduce substantial spending by the US federal government by way of deficit funding in the expectation of future revenues from an improved economy. Keynes provided a theoretical explanation of why the standard assumptions of mainstream economics could not explain the persistence of economic depression despite the consequent fall in prices, labour costs, and so on.

Part of Keynes' argument was that in times of economic uncertainty, ordinary people spent less rather than using any savings (if they had any), which meant slumps in consumption; that in turn made capitalists reluctant to invest, as they could not be confident of future sales and therefore future profits. Secondly, giving ordinary people money, say, as tax breaks, meant they were far more likely to spend the added money immediately than, say, very rich people or large businesses, for whom such monies were simply not necessary for their survival or for everyday necessities (DiLeo 2009).

Both Roosevelt and Keynes had highly political motivations too. Roosevelt promised to save capitalism by reforming it, and he was deeply troubled by the extent of poverty and suffering the Great Depression had caused; in 1933, US unemployment reached 25 per cent. Roosevelt also had to overcome strong resistance from opponents who contended that the increased cooperation the New Deal needed between the federal government and the states amounted to a violation of states' rights under the 10th Amendment to the US Constitution; they also thought federal funding for the states would give Washington increased power over policy at state level. Keynes, for his part, saw two main problems. One was that in any slump people simply spend less, and the circulation of money is reduced, with a much greater impact—the multiplier effect—on all economic activity. Secondly, Keynes could have left the matter at that, as a contribution to economic theory, but he was much more worried that the effects of a slump would make socialist or communist ideas much more attractive to ordinary people. Keynes hated and feared both socialism and communism, so he proposed something similar to Roosevelt's New Deal; the state would spend money, and if needed would embark on large-scale public projects, in order to get people back into work, to get money circulating again as a direct result, and to minimise or eliminate the attraction of socialism or communism.

At that time, this form of political economy was revolutionary and highly controversial, but both Keynes and Roosevelt saw their policies as temporary. In Roosevelt's second term of office, which lasted from 1936 to 1940, the US suffered a second slump, which meant that even the limited Keynesian measures Roosevelt tried were not working. For his part, Keynes seems to have thought that government spending to revive the economy would be needed only until the economy was running again under its own steam.

What seemed to rescue the US economy was government-funded war production for US allies as the Second World War intensified. That continued and accelerated after the US entered the war in December 1941; for the rest of the war the government ran what was in effect a command economy. The war effort required what has even been called 'war socialism'; it included enforced savings, controls on money, credit prices, and labour, government borrowing—such as war bonds or war-loan stock—and the rationing of food, petrol, and much else. These had already been applied during the First World War (Mattick 1969, cited in DiLeo 2009).

Such interventionism, nevertheless, has sources in liberal theory. Modern liberalism is associated with what can be extensive state intervention and regulation to moderate the worst effects of the unrestricted market. The intervention usually takes the form of unemployment benefit, retirement pensions, state-funded education, and state-supported healthcare systems. Another common feature is that of potentially far-reaching legislation, with courts or tribunals to enforce laws against arbitrary discrimination on the grounds of gender, race or ethnicity, caste, or faith. These kinds of laws, sometimes expressed as constitutional provisions, are found in virtually all democracies, and are intended to end or at least reduce the effects of long-standing attitudes and social structures which systematically disadvantage very large groups of people—in the case of women, one half of humanity. Such laws are meant to aid progress towards equality of opportunity, not equality of outcome. Among political philosophers, John Rawls has put forward a noted argument in support of such measures, holding that if people did not know their own social position, they would support greater equality as being fairer than greater inequality; Rawls also holds that inequality should be accepted only if it works to benefit the poorest. Secondly, Rawls considers that—once again, behind a 'veil of ignorance'—people would support freedom or liberty for each person provided that was compatible with similar freedom for all (cited in Heywood 2007: 57–58).

In practice, most state-benefits systems are based on liberal and not socialist theory, because they require individuals to contribute through systems such as national insurance, which is usually deducted from employees' pay and also requires employers and the state to contribute. This also applies to many healthcare systems, such as most of those in western Europe and Scandinavia. Two notable exceptions are the British National Health Service and the Cuban healthcare service, both of which are founded on explicitly socialist conceptions of universal entitlement and free treatment at the point of need. The value of such systems to tens of millions of people is incalculable; the British NHS, founded by the socialist Aneurin Bevan in 1946, is the most trusted and valued institution in the United Kingdom, with a standing higher even than that of the monarchy (Leys 2011; Leys 2001: 165–210).

Modern liberalism, therefore, involves protections against the worst effects of the free market, but it also requires individuals to accept responsibilities such as pension contributions or other such payments, and it also includes provision for procedural rights such as rights to free and fair elections, to fair trials, and to anti-discrimination legislation. So for modern liberalism, procedural rights are far more acceptable than the idea of material rights, which under this theory are not rights at all. This corresponds to the distinction between negative rights, such as freedom from interference, and positive rights.

MULTICULTURALISM

The status of multiculturalism as an ideology is not necessarily clear, and the term 'multiculturalism' itself has had widespread use only since the early 1990s or thereabouts. It has been described as an ideological space rather than an ideology, meaning that it is an area in which the nature of diversity and civic unity or civic commonality are discussed (Heywood 2007: 313). Multiculturalism, nevertheless, shares a number of features with liberalism, even though there are tensions between it and several major ideologies, and therefore I shall outline it here rather than in a separate chapter; a substantial literature on multiculturalism does exist, and I shall draw upon it as we proceed.

Of course, almost all societies today are made up of different cultural inheritances in their own ways, but that is hardly a new state of affairs, and the expanding body of research on languages, music, art, and archaeology, not to mention other fields, shows long histories of cultural complexity and diversity. For example, most of the grammatical structure of the English language today is a composite of Anglo-Saxon, Norman French, and other forms of French, and it was only towards the end of the sixteenth century that English showed a form we can recognise today; needless to say, those earlier forms of the language are unrecognisable as the English of our time, whether in vocabulary or grammar (Sanders 2004: 1–134). This holds in different ways for almost all areas of culture around the world, and we shall see that many of the central issues in multiculturalism involve the question of what constitutes a culture in the first place.

Multiculturalism as a contemporary political position seems to have started with the deepening realisation among African-Americans that the end of the US civil war might have put an official end to slavery but that it had certainly not put an end to severe racism and racial discrimination against African-Americans. Indeed, in the early twentieth century several US states, particularly the southern states, had laws enforcing racial discrimination until the federal government passed several laws against that in the early 1960s. The campaigner Marcus Garvey (1887–1940), who was born in Jamaica, had earlier started a 'Back to Africa' movement, but the strongest expressions of what was then called black consciousness came from figures in the US such as Martin Luther King, who led a non-violent civil rights movement, Elijah Mohammad, who led the Black Muslims (now the Black Nation) for over 40 years, and his fellow leader Malcolm X. Like the Black Power movement and its associated Black Panther Party in the 1960s, the Black Muslims rejected non-violence and supported more confrontational methods, including a readiness to use arms. It is worth noting that, like several other such movements around the world, the US movements asserted forms of cultural or ethnocultural identity as a means of resisting what were often ancient and brutal forms of systematic oppression and racial or cultural subjugation. Not only in the US but also in former imperial powers such as the United Kingdom and France, assumptions of racial and cultural superiority were widely shown in the tone and forms of language and in the range and scope of, for example, media coverage. Resistance to this came from movements like the language-based Québécois separatist movement in Canada and the Basque movements in Spain, and ethnonationalist movements such as those of the Maoris in New Zealand and aboriginal peoples in Australia (Heywood 2007: 311).

In the second half of the twentieth century, other forms of multiculturalism arose as the United States and other Western countries imported relatively large amounts of cheap labour from very poor parts of the world, either for post-war reconstruction or (in the case of the United States) for agricultural work as the economy expanded very rapidly. Today, it is hard to believe that some of the governments concerned even thought that those they imported—who largely came from the poorest classes in their countries of origin—would go back after a few years. The percentages involved are not great, despite what is often inflammatory media coverage of the topic; in 2011, about 10 per cent of the current British population were of South Asian or Afro-Caribbean descent (Institute of Race Relations 2017).

In the last quarter of a century or so, industrial countries in particular have experienced significant influxes of refugees as a result of war, ethnic conflict, and other forms of political upheaval, some of which are well documented as having been exacerbated by foreign intervention. Examples of the latter would be the invasion of Iraq in 2003, the legality of which in international law is severely disputed, and the use of a United Nations Security Council resolution in 2011 to cause regime change in Libya on the pretext of a no-fly zone for the protection of civilians. It is very likely that the related movement of refugees has gained the attention it has because Western countries are affected; in the early 1970s, India took about eight million refugees from what became Bangladesh, and in the 1990s, several countries in the Great Lakes region of Africa took a total amounting to over a million people fleeing from genocidal wars.

Multiculturalism as Policy

This dates from the mid-1960s and early 1970s, when Canada and Australia officially called themselves multicultural societies. At about that time, public-service staff in many industrial countries also started modifying policies and everyday practice—for example, in healthcare and education—as they came to see that earlier assumptions about uniformity of culture and language were actively harming substantial sections of their societies or preventing the relevant groups from making the best use of the institutions and services concerned. In the early 1990s, public debates on multiculturalism expanded greatly, with intense arguments for and against the idea (Heywood 2007: 310). Multiculturalist policies are based on the recognition that particular cultural groups may have distinctive needs and that the adaptation of policy and practice to such needs both reduces unjustifiable discrimination and amounts to a celebration of diversity and complexity in modern societies. This kind of approach has even been extended to the design of countries' constitutions, as in Bosnia–Herzegovina, and to major political institutions, as in Belgium and the devolved British province of Northern Ireland (Heywood 2007: 312).

In sum, multiculturalism requires the detailed articulation of issues arising from the experience of colonial subjecthood, the attitudes of former imperial cultures, and questions of identity and culture, minority rights, and diversity. The issue of postcoloniality is a vast one, and I shall not cover it here; major writers such as Frantz Fanon and Edward Said have written famous works on it, among other things showing the impact of colonial subjecthood on colonised peoples, and contemporary novelists like Salman Rushdie have included acerbic passages on colonial and postcolonial encounters and relationships.

What we need to note here, rather, is that although claims to the public recognition of diversity and demands for the redress of past collective harm have been strongly justified and have often resulted in substantial changes to law, policy, and public institutions, the issues raised by the idea of multiculturalism can be almost intractable or insoluble. For example, liberalism requires that we tolerate diversity, but that we cannot accept cultures or subcultures in which individual rights are violated. For example, the United Kingdom accepts the jurisdiction of Jewish civil tribunals (called Beth Din) and Islamic Sharia councils in respect of family disputes, because in English law (in particular) the parties in a civil dispute can refer the matter to an agreed third party; as long as the process is agreed and the outcome is reasonable, the decision does not have to be based on English law. The Beth Din jurisdiction was approved by an Act of Parliament in the nineteenth century. As it happens, Sharia domestic councils in the United Kingdom seem to adjudicate more on divorce than anything else, and 90 per cent of the divorce cases they hear are initiated by women (Sivaramakrishnan 2008).

Problems over cultural identity, however, arise when particular practices violate existing rights under liberal or liberal-democratic systems of law. The British foreign ministry, the Foreign and Commonwealth Office, has a unit dedicated to assisting British residents or citizens who are victims of forced marriages (not arranged marriages freely entered into by both partners), and in the United Kingdom the practice of female genital mutilation (FGM) has been a criminal offence since 1985. It is also a criminal offence for British nationals or residents to participate or assist in FGM outside the United Kingdom, and British public-service staff in healthcare or teaching have a legal duty to report the offence if young people under 18 are the victims. We need to note, nevertheless, that the current Conservative government is yet to implement that section of the Equality Act 2010 which would enable a minister to declare caste discrimination an offence under the Act (Bhatnagar 2016; United Kingdom 2010).

A further problem over cultural identity has to do with what it is to belong to a particular group and whether or not members have significant authority to declare themselves not bound by the given group's ways in respect of particular issues. This in turn raises wider questions of who in a group has the authority or power to decide who does and does not belong and why. The point is that there is no avoiding questions of the substance and content of the rights claimed or of the cultural practices at issue. An uncritical separation of faith and the state is of no help here, because in practice that closes down discussion rather than creating a space in which the relation between faith (or traditional cultural practices) and the state can be articulated and addressed. The results can be very serious; too much of, for example, the current debate in many European countries about possible bans on the hijab have excluded European women who happen to be Muslims from any serious exploration and expression of what equality, citizenship, and faith might mean to them; that can hardly be what liberal advocates of cultural rights intend, but it is nevertheless the case (Kennedy 2011: 65).

Other major ideologies also have their problems over multiculturalism. Conservatism is, unsurprisingly, one of the ideologies most incompatible with it, because according to conservatism shared values and shared practices and traditions are part of a shared history and form a national identity; for most conservative thinkers, therefore, nationalism overrides or takes priority over multiculturalism (Heywood 2007: 328).

One of the main problems for any account of multiculturalism is the matter of inequalities of power and status, that is, structural inequalities. Indeed, the relative neglect of this in a lot of work on multiculturalism means that advocates of multiculturalism have often sought recognition, advancement, or redress through the assertion of cultural or ethnic identity. That in turn opens the possibility that practices such as child marriage could, at least in theory, be justified as being central to any given culture. That shows another significant area that multiculturalism seems to have neglected, namely the question of what constitutes a culture in the first place. Any serious examination of that will very quickly show the complexity and variety of almost every culture on the planet, and the mutability of any and all cultures.

In what may well be a response to that matter, Nasar Meer and Tariq Modood, for example, have shown the need to think in these terms by pointing out that what they call interculturalism has to be a political discourse if it is to enable us to express and address the wide range of concerns which inevitably arise from the fact that our identities are complex, as are the areas in respect of which we are significantly equal and significantly different (Meer and Modood 2011). As Bhikhu Parekh says, all cultures are continuing conversations (Parekh 1999). They are permanently involved in, so to speak, exchanges with their own inheritances and those of other cultures, however different those others might seem to be. That in turn means engaging with the substance of cultural practices and ideas no matter what their background or origins, but it is not clear if liberalism can accommodate that engagement without abandoning its purported neutrality on such matters.

LIBERALISM: THE MAIN PROBLEMS

Liberalism, at least on first acquaintance, offers a very great deal. For example, it requires that we do not impose moral, social, or political systems or ideologies on people, and that we accept and tolerate individuals' right to choose their ways of life freely; it also requires that we protect the relevant rights and freedoms so that people can make their own decisions and choices. We need to see, however, if liberalism can fulfil its promises.

Abandoning Any Substantive Ideology

The reasons for this are understandable, in view of the horrors which many proponents of any number of ideologies, religions, and other moral and political systems have inflicted on humanity. The problem, however, is that the liberal position itself amounts to a substantive ideological commitment, that is, a commitment not to impose moral or political systems or positions on people—but it also implies not intervening, say, when a system or an individual causes serious harm in the service of an ideology. Liberal theorists are not always aware of the problems they face here, and we have already noted Mill's call for liberal values to be imposed on India by force; we have also noted the contradictions in liberal interventionism.

The Right to Choose

In liberal doctrine, the individual, as we have seen, is the basic unit of society and is the holder of a right to make free choices and decisions, whether in occupation or way of life, or in moral and political attitudes, or in sexual preferences, and so on. This idea is highly attractive, particularly in contrast to the kinds of coercion which social and political systems often impose on people, and it has had an enormous impact on entire societies around the world. It has also given rise to very extensive protections in law and in institutional systems.

The problem here is that seeing the individual as a chooser and nothing else makes it impossible to evaluate the choices and decisions individuals make, because any such evaluation infringes their right to choose. In addition, if we accept individuals' right to choose as inviolable, then we are also unable to examine whether or not they—or we—are manipulated or coerced into decisions, or brainwashed, or simply deceived, or whether our decisions are made from prejudice, misinformation, or self-deception. We could even choose to stuff ourselves with junk food, or consume other harmful substances, or choose to watch unending violence on television or on the Internet, or anything else; but raising any questions about such conduct would mean investigating the substance of people's actions, as well as the relevant backgrounds and reasons, and the wider social and political contexts in which people make their choices. The only thing that liberalism, however, can accept or protect is the right to choose (Beiner 1992: 26–27).

The Concept of Rights

Further difficulties arise over the way liberalism protects the individual; it does so by means of rights, such as the right to choose, the right to freedom of expression, to freedom of association, and so on. Yet the idea of rights is riddled with problems. For example, the right to freedom of expression has even resulted in a US Supreme Court decision which, albeit indirectly, confirmed that students at George Mason University had the right to hold an ugly-woman contest on campus (*Chronicle of Higher Education* 1993). Such a contest exposes the organisers' misogyny and hate, but under liberal principles the only thing that counts is the right to hold the contest.

Similarly, there is no point in having a right to something which is not worth having. For example, in certain states of India the practice of appointing unqualified teachers on very low salaries in place of qualified teachers has been researched and documented as undermining the aims of the Right to Education Act, which was passed in 2009 (Rao 2009).

The example of the ugly-woman contest reveals even more problems with the idea of rights. The right to freedom of expression often clashes with the right to freedom from expressions of prejudice and bigotry, but if rights are absolutes, that is, if they are inviolable, then clashes of rights cannot be resolved within liberalism. An endless series of examples can be found; the right to a traditional way of life is often claimed, but the tradition or traditions in question might and often do require, say, the subjugation of women, or compel compliance in other ways which violate liberal principles (Kymlicka 1995: 94; Green 1995: 264–65).

In practice, attempts are often made to evaluate rights claims under another formula, for example, under utilitarian calculations of relative good or harm, or in terms of costs and benefits. This, however, leaves unaddressed the question of how particular things came to be seen as goods in the first place, and it accepts that rights to those goods are not absolute. As for the neoliberal or libertarian principle of leaving it to the market to decide which rights are to take priority, that in effect abolishes the idea of rights, and in addition ignores the fact that the market itself depends on non-market values. One of these non-market values is the idea that a contract is morally binding and legally enforceable, and another is the dependence of market exchanges depend on the parties' trust and confidence in one another (Smith 2007: 86–87).

Another way of preserving the idea of rights against challenges involves giving a special status to procedural rights, such as the right to a fair trial or to free and fair elections. These have been regarded by some liberal theorists as absolutes, in contrast to say rights to employment, or to other material goods such as public housing, which are ruled out on the grounds that they require money and will be the subject of endless dispute over how much is to be spent on them; those rights have been called material rights or economic rights. The distinction can seem very attractive, but the problem is that fair trials and free and fair elections themselves require considerable expenditure in the form of institutions and staff, and so on. There is therefore no difference in kind between supposedly procedural and supposedly material rights, and the only dispute is therefore over how much we are prepared to spend on them (Plant, Lesser and Taylor-Gooby 1980: 73–97).

A further issue here is that of whether or not we are in any position to choose. If we are seriously sick or starving, we are not choosing beings in the sense liberalism takes us to be. Most contemporary liberals seem to have accepted this point, and even an extreme proponent of liberalism like Friedrich von Hayek advocates a social safety net, with the implication that as an economy expands so too will the safety net (cited in Plant 2010: 141–42, 256). Hayek, however, regards the expansion or contraction of an economy as the operation of a natural law, because according to him the aggregate or overall outcomes of individual market decisions cannot be predicted. This is a philosophical claim about the nature of knowledge itself, an epistemological claim, but Hayek is well aware of its dangers, and in effect says we must not tell people that where they end up in life is a matter of unpredictable overall outcomes and not their own efforts. He is afraid that if we do tell them that, then they will lose the incentive to work (Hayek 1976: 69–74; Plant 1982: 348). The consequence is that we have to lie on a global scale in order to protect Hayek's god, the market (Sivaramakrishnan 2012a: 78).

In sum, liberalism promises a lot, and in practice has been at least in part responsible for the global recognition that in democracies, political power needs to be justified, legitimised, and controlled by public processes and institutions. It has, however, probably never been implemented fully, in any of its forms. Neoliberalism has been severely criticised since its revival in the early 1980s, and in the wake of the 2007–9 global financial crash even international financial institutions have admitted that many of its precepts do not work. As for the implementation of neoliberalism, detailed arguments have been put that far from replacing the state with the market, neoliberalism has amounted to a takeover of the state by commercial financial bodies and very large manufacturing corporations, with so-called light-touch regulation or no regulation at all, or sweetheart tax deals and the location of profits in tax havens which effectively enable corporations not to pay taxes in the countries where they make their greatest profits, or even to pay no tax on colossal corporate sell-offs. In 2013, the Vodafone corporation, for example, held that it was not liable for UK tax after selling its holding in the US corporation Verizon for £84 billion, as the relevant share was owned by a holding company based in the Netherlands and was therefore not liable for UK tax. Objectors to the deal, including the chair of the relevant parliamentary oversight committee, maintained that Vodafone itself is based in the southern English town of Newbury, and should therefore have paid tax on the deal (Grice 2013).

As for other forms of liberalism, they share with neoliberalism the promise of all manner of freedoms, but they also share the fact that liberalism as a whole is full of problems, for example over clashes of rights and over the unstated dependence of the theory on a very substantial theory of human nature, namely the idea that humans are choosing beings above all else. In effect, liberalism delivers us into its own forms of captivity, forms created by the very terms on which it is founded. Many of the conceptions of rationality involved—for example, the idea that we are rational choosers—have been very severely criticised for what are no less than gross assumptions about what it is to be rational at all; for example, one utility theorist has even said that our own brains are an obstacle to rationality (Glimcher, Dorris, and Bayer 2005; Fine 2010; Sivaramakrishnan 2011). The rational conclusion from that would seem to require a global programme for the removal of all human beings' brains. Even the Nazis, as far as we know, did not think of that. As for liberalism, at best it is a genuine ideology, a way of thinking which unintentionally but systematically misleads us; at worst, as in the case of Hayek, it can be sustained only by a gigantic lie. It has promised an enormous amount, and—despite its undoubted impact and its successes—its failures to deliver are not only empirical but conceptual.

CHAPTER 3: LIBERALISM

Extension Exercise

Use this article

> 'India has second-highest number of child marriages:
> Unicef'. http://www.thehindu.com/news/international/south-asia/India-has-second-highest-number-of-child-marriages-Unicef/article11131187.ece

and this report

https://www.unicef.org/publications/files/Improving_Children_s_Lives_-_Transforming_the_Future_9_Sep_2014.pdf

to write a liberal-multiculturalist justification of child marriage AND a liberal-multiculturalist criticism of the practice.
From the set sources, use information on a range of countries. The total length should be about 1500 words, divided equally between the two arguments.

Further Reading

Beiner, Ronald. 1992. *What's the Matter with Liberalism?* Berkeley: University of California Press.
Smits, Katherine. 2003. 'Liberalism's Identity Problem'. *Polity* 35 (3): 347–67.

4
CHAPTER

Marx

This chapter is specifically about the main concepts in the work of Marx, because there are many varieties of Marxism in many areas of public discourse, but although there are fierce arguments around all of them, the main ideas Marx himself developed often disappear in some of the controversy. Marx himself started as a student of philosophy, and although he never studied under the philosopher Georg Hegel his own work has led to his being called the greatest student ever of the work of Hegel (Jacoby 1981: 22).

Marx's early works, such as *The German Ideology* and the *Economic and Philosophic Manuscripts of 1844*, are philosophically very rich, but Marx came to think that many of his German contemporaries—called the Young Hegelians—who claimed to follow Hegel had underestimated the importance of economic forces in shaping our lives and our institutions. Marx also concluded that those forces caused deep suffering for the great mass of humanity, and that the task was to change that state of affairs. In *The German Ideology* he famously says: 'The philosophers have only *interpreted* the world, in various ways; the point is to *change* it' (Marx 2000: 173).

Marx seems not to mean that the task of philosophy is to change the world, but that we are faced with the urgent and pressing task of altering our economic and social systems so that they do not cause the kind of mass suffering with which we are only too familiar. In any case, even in his most politically committed work, Marx shows sharp philosophic insight and considerable philosophic ability, not least in his precise analysis of concepts and in his meticulously structured arguments; despite his criticism of Hegel's great work on the state, the *Philosophy of Right*, Marx's own approach and his methods show strong inheritances from Hegel (Collier 2004: 117–29). Collier also notes here that Marx's reputation today is probably higher in philosophy than it is in any other academic discipline, even though most of his writing after 1845 lies in social science and political commentary (Collier 2004: 117–29).

Marx wrote *The German Ideology* from late 1845 to the middle of 1846, and thereafter spent much of his life campaigning for change and writing about the problems inherent in the then-emerging system of industrial capitalism. Although his work is often assumed to be difficult, if not impenetrable, he worked as a journalist for much of his life, and he often writes with great flair and wit; almost two thirds of Volume I of *Capital* read like first-class investigative or campaigning journalism on the appalling conditions in English factories in Marx's time.

BIOGRAPHY

Marx was born in the German town of Trier in 1818. His parents, Heinrich and Henrietta, had Jewish origins but had adopted the Protestant faith so as to make it easier for Marx's father to advance his law practice. The family were financially comfortable, and when the young Marx was seventeen he was sent to the University of Bonn to read law. He got into trouble for drunkenness and was wounded, though not seriously, in a duel; so his parents transferred him to the University of Berlin (Singer 1980: 2). The young Marx disappointed his family again, by abandoning law for philosophy, in which he was already showing his talent. That he became one of the greatest thinkers in the Western tradition and indeed the history of the world hardly needs saying, but he never became a professional academic, even though he received a doctorate in 1841, for his thesis on the Greek philosophers Democritus and Epicurus (Singer 1980: 2).

Marx became a journalist instead, and remained one for most of his life, writing for several journals and papers which the authorities in many countries disliked and even closed down. At the time, it was not unusual for journalists to campaign openly on major problems of the day, and Charles Dickens was another famous journalist who criticised social and political conditions; so was Charles Mayhew, who is less well known than Marx or Dickens. In our own time, Glenn Greenwald has gained an international reputation for campaigning journalism on global surveillance and for protecting the whistle-blower Edward Snowden over illegal US government surveillance.

For his part, Marx joined, and later became the editor of, the *Rheinische Zeitung* or *Rhenish Gazette*, but the public authorities closed the paper down after he exposed poverty among winegrowers in the Mosel region; Marx then became co-editor of the *Deutsch–Französische Jahrbücher*, or *German–French Yearbooks* (Singer 2000: 2–3). The new job enabled Marx and his childhood friend Jenny von Westphalen to get married; they moved to Paris in 1843, but the paper was closed down by its backers when the Prussian government confiscated copies of a particular issue and ordered that the editors be arrested (Singer 1980: 2–3).

Unable to return to Germany, Marx went back to writing philosophy, and the family lived on their savings; Marx's *Economic and Philosophic Manuscripts* date from this period. Marx moved among the many German communists then in Paris, and he also got to know Friedrich Engels, whose father was a German cotton-mill owner in Manchester and who had become a revolutionary socialist. The French government, however, gave in to pressure from the German government and expelled Marx, so the family moved to Brussels. The Belgian authorities banned Marx from political activity, but he soon breached their order, and also started work on what later became the book *Capital*, which is equally widely known as *Das Kapital*.

Intellectually, this was a highly productive time for Marx. He wrote *The German Ideology*, and he was very active in various communist movements. Moreover, in February 1848 he and Engels published the now legendary *Communist Manifesto*. Marx was also inspired by the French revolution of that year, as were many other European movements. The Belgian government ordered him to leave the country at 24 hours' notice, but in France the new government almost simultaneously revoked the previous government's order banning Marx from France; the family moved to Paris and then to Germany. Marx started another paper, the *Neue Rheinische Zeitung* or *New Rhenish Gazette*, but the Prussian government crushed an attempted revolution in Germany, and would not grant Marx renaturalisation. Marx, who had moved back to France, was then expelled from Paris again. In August 1849 he and his family moved to England.

Marx spent most of the rest of his life in London; in their first few years there, the family struggled both financially and with the deaths of three of their young children (Singer 2000: 5–7). Thereafter, however, things got easier for them. Horace Greeley, editor of the *New-York Tribune*, published an article by Marx almost every week for the next 10 years, and in a very short period in 1857–8 Marx wrote much of what later became *Capital*. It was meant to be one in a series of six works on economics, including of course political economy (Marx 2000: 37). Marx continued to be very active in politics; he was elected to the General Council of the International Workingmen's Association, later known as the First International, which was founded in 1864, and his lectures to them on the Paris Commune were so successful when published in 1871 as *The Civil War in France* that Marx even welcomed the notoriety it earned him as a noted communist and activist (Singer 1980: 7–9).

The Paris Commune was put down with terrible brutality, which has not been sufficiently widely noted (Collier 2004: 14–15). The end of the Commune was a bitter blow for its supporters, not least because a number of socialist and socialistic movements had sprung up in Great Britain and Germany in 1848, but Marx continued writing. His *Critique of the Gotha Programme*, which appeared in 1875, contains reflections on a postcapitalist society; he seems to have planned to do much more work on that and on the state, but he died in 1883 and was buried in Highgate Cemetery in north London.

MARX: THE MAIN CONCEPTS

The main concepts in Marx's works are:

- Species being and the social nature of labour
- Modes of production: subsistence production and commodity production
- The division of labour
- Alienation
- Profit in capitalist society: the labour theory of value and the theory of surplus value
- The falling rate of profit
- Ideology and commodity fetishism

Species Being and the Social Nature of Labour

For Marx, we are of course a form of animate life, but what differentiates humans from animals is the character of human productive activity. Many animals produce things, such as nests, tunnels, hives, and so on, and some of these are very complex indeed. Many also cooperate to obtain food; wolves hunt in packs, lions in a pride cooperate to single out particular animals from herds before they attack them, killer whales and dolphins hunt cooperatively, and so on. Animals, however, produce or cooperate to produce what according to Marx is only what they need for themselves or their young; they produce only under the compulsion of physical needs. Humans, in contrast, produce even when they are free from pressing physical needs, that is, when they do not need to produce solely for survival.

It is true that in practice, enormous areas of human activity take place under terribly oppressive compulsions, but Marx covers that matter in great detail in other areas of his work, as we shall see. What Marx means by saying human productive activity is something we engage in freely is that we are the only species that produces over and above what we need for survival, and that we produce reasoningly, by thinking about what we make, by collaborating in production, and by evaluating what we do and how we do it. Marx calls us species beings, because we can only be understood as this species.

This also means we transform the world by our reasoning activity upon it, that is, by acting reasoningly on it. The evidence for that is all around us, in the form of agriculture, buildings, cities, extractive industries, and indeed in the form of whole landscapes which we have transformed, say by clearing forests for farming or construction, or by damming rivers for reservoirs or power generation. The results have not always been entirely benign, and we have also caused colossal environmental damage and destruction, but at least in principle we can act reasoningly and collaboratively to redeem some of the damage and prevent or minimise future damage.

Marx, furthermore, recognises that in the process of transforming the world we transform ourselves and our sense of human capacities and possibilities. Today, almost all classes of people in almost all countries live substantially longer than they did even a century ago, and terrible diseases which used to kill tens of millions—or more—are now easily diagnosed and cured or kept under control so that we can continue to live almost as though they did not exist. We have also devised techniques and instruments which make routine activities out of what would have been almost unimaginable achievements in times past. To take just one example, we are now thoroughly familiar with the practice of transporting a quarter of a million tonnes of cargo halfway around the world in a few weeks, aboard ships over 300 metres long and over 50 metres in beam. A key insight, perhaps the central one, Marx has here is that we cannot do any of this as individuals acting entirely on our own (even our physical survival on our own is something for which we are very poorly equipped in comparison to any number of other species).

Marx's point here is that production, the labour involved in production, and our very sense of who and what we are as humans—that is, of what it is to be human—are themselves social creations. In addition, our sense of human needs and capacities is also social, in that it is shaped by the historical epochs or periods in which we find ourselves (Avineri 1968: 73). This does not mean there is no continuity or development, as we accumulate knowledge and draw upon it as we live our lives (Avineri 1968: 79–84).

At no point does Marx hold that we are solely the products of the historical and material conditions of our lives. If we were, we would be robots, unable to change or transcend our particular times and situations; as Marx might have put it, we would be locked into our time and place with no prospect of transforming the world and in the process educating and transforming ourselves (Marx 2000: 58, 172, 403–4; Avineri 1968: 68–72). We are material beings of course, but we are material beings who are shaped by nature and who for our part reshape nature and ourselves by acting intentionally, collaboratively, and reasoningly upon it (Avineri 1968: 73–75). In effect, our consciousness is a social creation, and production is a social activity.

Modes of Production: Subsistence Production and Commodity Production

For Marx, the form our humanity takes, namely the way it is expressed in our ways of life, is particular to our historical period; therefore our needs, or more precisely the ways we conceive our needs, are particular to our historical period. Marx is very clear that our needs are not totally bound by our time, but the ways we meet our needs and the ways we produce what we need are shaped by the period in which we live. That may seem obvious, but it means that our systems or modes of production, and the instruments we use for production, are particular to our time. Therefore, the instruments, tools, and machines we use have to be understood in their historical context, not simply as new objects or inventions to be seen in abstraction. Instead they show and represent the organisation of human consciousness and human activity (Avineri 1968: 76). The things we create in and through our activity express and embody our humanity. Our productive instruments, the means of production, and our productive systems, the relations of production, are therefore always changing and developing as we evaluate them in the light of our purposes. We improve some, discard others, and so on. Marx holds that when seen in overall terms, the productive systems—which he calls the modes of production—fall into two major and very different historical forms. The first was subsistence production and the second, which continues today, is commodity production.

Subsistence Production

Marx sees subsistence production as a feature of preindustrial or feudal societies and the societies which came before them. In subsistence production, we produce primarily to meet our needs, and sell any surplus produce only if we have any. For example, we might sell certain fruits or vegetables when they are in season and we have more than we can use. We must remember that Marx says very little about barter, and that unlike most conventional economists he does not seem to assume that barter preceded currency-based systems of exchange. In any case, the idea that barter preceded currency exchange has been severely criticised by David Graeber, who shows with extensive evidence that for thousands of years, human societies have used forms of currency-based exchange, including accounting records, debts and various forms of currency (Graeber 2012). So in subsistence production, our needs come first, and sale comes second; we sell only any surplus, that is, anything which is over and above our needs.

Commodity Production, or Production for Exchange: The Class Structure of Society

This is a radically different system from subsistence production. In this mode of production, we produce goods to sell them, that is, we produce them in order to participate in systems of exchange. According to Marx, the transition from subsistence production to commodity production took place in late-mediaeval Europe. At that time, demand for goods grew rapidly as international trade expanded, and the existing productive forces could not meet this rising demand. Furthermore, according to Marx this was also the first time technical innovation could serve to meet rising demand (Avineri 1968: 154).

Technological or technical innovation itself now came to depend on the accumulation of capital. This was a key development. Wealth was ceasing to be seen as residing or inhering in natural objects, or land, gold, or the like; instead, it was being reconceived in terms of produced goods, in effect as the accumulated result of labour. The new sense of wealth saw itself as embodied in the goods produced by labour applied to natural resources or to machinery, or both (Avineri 1968: 178, 154, 162).

Yet technological innovation itself did not cause the change from subsistence production to commodity production. According to Marx, the main cause of the change was social and political; at that time, sections of urban society in Europe were starting to engage in economic activity of a kind which was increasingly independent of the existing feudal and religious authorities. For example, the emerging corporations and communes developed a concept of property and the inheritance of property which, in effect, enabled members to trade in property and to accumulate wealth through their economic activity. This amounted to the emergence or creation of a sphere of economic activity which was relatively free of political and religious restrictions and regulations. Hegel had called this sphere civil society, the aggregate sphere of interests, and Marx uses the same phrase too; it is still used to mean much the same thing (Hegel 1967: §182–239; Avineri 1968: 154–56; Marx 2000: 159–61).

This new social development, as Marx recognised, was truly revolutionary. It enabled natural resources and land to be turned into commercial goods, and also enabled the commercialisation of agriculture. Therefore, by about 1700, social conditions and powerful financial incentives had arisen which drove the development of the forms of technology required for the exploitation of the new commercial assets, namely land and natural resources (Avineri 1968: 155–56).

In addition, those whose main activity was participation in civil society—that is, neither in politics nor religion nor in politico-religious activities—very quickly became a new class in society, which Marx calls the bourgeoisie. They posed such powerful challenges to the existing order that both feudal and religious institutions swiftly gave way to them.

The transformations that resulted were enormous, and amounted to the creation of a whole new mode of production, as commodity production replaced subsistence production. In this system, we produce goods not for subsistence or to meet our own needs, but for exchange, that is, for sale. This, as Marx notes, drives technological innovation, which enables us to produce far more than we can consume; the point of production is to sell what we produce.

The emergence of commodity production as an entire system had another immensely important consequence; as commodity production emerged, the old feudal and religious social hierarchies disappeared, and were replaced by only two classes. So in a commodity-producing society, one class is the bourgeoisie, that is, those who own land and other resources as well as the factories and other instruments of production. The other class is very much larger, and is made up of the former peasants and artisans; they have no property and can sell only their labour power, that is, their capacity to work. Marx calls this class the proletariat (in ancient Rome the word *proletarius* meant a citizen of the lowest rank).

Marx sees the advent of the new mode of production—capitalism—as revolutionary, because it transforms entire societies. He also sees it as progressive, because it eliminates the restrictions of feudal and religious hierarchies, and it exposes the nature of those hierarchies, which concealed exploitation behind claims of divine right, inherited superiority, and religious authority (Marx 2000: 159). The new system has done this:

> In one word, for exploitation, veiled by religious and political illusions, it has substituted naked, shameless, brutal exploitation. (Marx and Engels 1848)

According to Marx, when the last restrictions on capitalism have been removed, the system starts changing under its own internal forces and imperatives. For example, the Corn Laws in Britain were repealed in 1846, and in 1847 the first of a series of laws curbing unregulated economic activity was passed. This was the Factory Act of 1847, also called the Ten Hours Act, because it made ten hours the legal maximum for the working day. In the next 30 years or so several other regulatory laws were passed; these included the Artisans' Dwellings Act 1878, which laid down minimum house-building standards, the Education Act 1870, which required all children aged between five and eleven to attend school, and many others. The Sanitary Act 1866, which made local municipal authorities responsible for water, sewerage, and street cleaning, may well have been a significant factor in the relatively quick elimination of cholera in the United Kingdom. Furthermore, the ban on trade unions was lifted when the Combination Acts were repealed in 1824.

Many of these laws were passed precisely because the processes of unrestrained capitalism had exposed the effects and the problems of the system itself. It is also the case that sick workers and uneducated children—who will become workers as they grow up—are a hindrance to the further development of capitalism. Marx sees such laws as resulting from the processes of capitalism itself, and that insight is part of his conclusion that every mode of production contains the logic of its own transformation. He never, however, says capitalism will collapse (Avineri 1968: 174; Marx 2000: 188–95).

The Division of Labour

Commodity production, as we have seen, is the system in which goods are produced for sale, or in economic terminology, for exchange. The most efficient form of this system requires that all productive tasks be divided into their component elements, with tasks allocated to single workers or single groups of workers; those workers will perform only the set tasks. This can involve specialisation, but that depends on the particular jobs concerned. In practice, the division of labour could have one worker fetching, say, sand,

and another fetching cement; a third would add water and mix the two, a fourth would deliver the mixture to a fifth, and the fifth would apply the wet cement. This division of the work increased the speed and volume of production enormously; the concept of it was identified before Marx's time, and Adam Smith's treatment of the topic is famous. Smith greatly approves of the increased productivity which the division of labour enables, and recognises that tasks can be separately apportioned in industrial work to a far greater extent than they can in agriculture (Smith 2007: 9–11). He is, however, also deeply troubled about what the process does to the worker:

> The man whose whole life is spent in performing a few simple operations, of which the effects are perhaps always the same, or very nearly the same, has no occasion to exert his understanding or to exercise his inventions in finding out expedients for difficulties which never occur. He naturally loses, therefore, the habit of such exertion, and generally becomes as stupid and ignorant as it is possible for a human creature to become. (Smith 2007: 603)

In the same passage, Smith adds:

> But in every improved and civilized society this is the state into which the labouring poor, that is, the great body of the people, must necessarily fall, unless government takes some pains to prevent it. (Smith 2007: 603)

Marx, however, is much more incisive about the division of labour. To be human is to act reasoningly upon the world, to transform it and ourselves in the process. Yet the division of labour freezes our main activity. It restricts us to a single, very often repetitive, task, or to a very small range of repeated operations, and subordinates all our other activity, even most of the rest of our life, to our main task or tasks. The rest of what we do has the purpose of making us fit for our specified task and nothing else. This in turn means that we have to depend on other people who are themselves participants in a system of commodity production and who are also confined to single tasks. We need one group of them to produce the food we eat (and even specific groups to produce specific kinds of food), another group to produce our clothes, yet another to produce our shoes, and so on. We even need specific groups of people to deliver such produce to markets near our homes so that we do not spend too much time restoring ourselves for the next day's work. In effect, the division of labour, which is a necessary feature of commodity production, makes us more and not less dependent on others. In addition, commodity production—that is, capitalist production—can survive only if all production is turned into commodity production. It is indeed a form of totalitarianism.

The point here is that in commodity production, we are not directly dependent on the people who produce the goods we need in order to do our own work in the productive system. We are instead dependent on the objects they produce; if on our way home after work, or on our day off, we cannot do our household shopping or rely on, say, the ready availability of everyday necessities when we need them, then we cannot perform our designated work. Everyone else in the system is also dependent on us to turn up at work on time and to produce the particular goods we produce in the time specified, so that they can buy the goods in order to keep working themselves. This universalises our dependence on others and depersonalises our relations with others, because it does not matter who has produced these everyday necessities as long as the relevant goods are available in the market when we need them, and preferably also where we need them. Furthermore, we are now dependent on the objects and not those who produce them (Avineri 1968: 163–66).

Alienation

This universalised and depersonalised dependence separates us and sets us apart from our fellow workers, but it has another and very serious set of consequences. As workers in a system of commodity production, we do not own the means of production, but we still have to participate in the system or starve to death. The only commodity we have to sell is our labour power, that is, our capacity to work (Marx 2000: 554–56 and 488–92; Collier 2004: 76). We sell our labour power to the owners or controllers of the means of production, and then we work for them, producing goods for them to sell; in return we receive a wage for the sale and exercise of our labour power.

That may seem to be no more than a statement of the obvious, but Marx reveals the main consequences of the process. For him, the essence of human nature is that we reasoningly and collaboratively produce things, and the evidence of our humanity is the things we create, including systems and institutions. In capitalist production, however, we have no option but to sell our capacity to create to the controller of capital. They then decide what we create, the conditions in which we create it, and the disposal of it.

Therefore, the controller of capital, the capitalist, controls the expression of our humanity. Our humanity itself is alienated from us, and is now embodied in the object we create for the capitalist. It is embodied in, say, the billions of matchsticks or paperclips or anything else that we produce over the course of our working life, and therefore the capitalist controls the disposal of our humanity. We lose our humanity to the system of commodity production, to capitalism, and to the capitalist; we are alienated from ourselves, from nature, and from the rest of humanity (Marx 2000: 84–95, 547–50, 554–61; Avineri 1968: 105).

It follows that as workers, we come to regard free time and free activity solely as time and activity not connected with work. In the *Economic and Philosophic Manuscripts*, Marx says the worker is

> …at home when he [*sic*] is not working and when he works he is not at home. His labour is therefore not voluntary but compulsory, *forced labour*. It is therefore not the satisfaction of a need but only a means to satisfy needs outside itself. How alien it really is is very evident from the fact that as soon as there is no physical or other compulsion it is avoided like the plague. (Marx 2000: 88)

Marx concludes that as workers, we feel freely active only in what he calls our animal function—eating, drinking, and procreating, or 'at most' in our dwellings and personal adornment; in our human functions we are reduced to animals (Marx 2000: 88; Avineri 1968: 106). In sum, commodity production, the system in which we produce for sale first and foremost, dispossesses us of our humanity; alienation is a truly terrifying condition. In a system of commodity production, we have to sell our humanity if we are to survive at all; our labour power is itself a commodity in this system. The question then arises of how this particular commodity serves to make a profit for the capitalist, and how it does so systematically, not randomly.

Profit in Capitalist Society: The Labour Theory of Value and the Theory of Surplus Value

Here Marx uses the labour theory of value, which originates in the work of the economist David Ricardo (1772–1823); Adam Smith also based his thinking on this theory, but Ricardo was a much stronger supporter of capitalism than Smith (Collier 2004: 76). Ricardo's main distinction here is between use value and exchange value. The use value of a thing is simply its usefulness to us, that is, how useful we find it. Exchange value, on the other hand, is the ratio at which commodities exchange for one another, or the relative price of commodities. For Marx, the standard of measurement here is the amount of labour time necessary to produce any one item. Therefore, under the labour theory of value the value of an item is the amount of labour time it takes to produce the item. This does of course change over time, as we devise new methods and instruments to help us produce the item. So the value of the worker's labour power, which is essential to the production of goods, is the length of time it takes to produce the food, clothes, and shelter which the worker needs in order to be fit and ready for the next day's work; this is also shaped by its particular social and historical period, that is, by the state and condition of society at any given time.

The use of labour power in production adds value to commodities; eight hours of labour adds eight hours' worth of value, but the value of the labour power actually used is the amount of time needed to get the worker ready for the eight hours' work. Furthermore, in any economy that has advanced beyond primitive subsistence levels, this length of time—that is, the value of the worker's labour power—is invariably less than the length of time the worker can work. So, if it takes four hours to produce the food and so on that the worker needs, the worker covers the cost of their labour in four hours, and the remaining four hours of their working day adds another four hours to the value of the commodity they produce. A very rough analogy might help here: it might take us half an hour (or a good deal less if we are in a hurry) to prepare and eat our breakfast in the morning, but once we have eaten it we are fit to work for a much longer period, say until lunchtime. The length of time we can work is much greater than the time it takes us to get fit for work, and therefore what the capitalist buys is not the worker's labour but their labour power, or as Marx puts it in *Value, Price and Profit*, labouring power (cited in Collier 2004: 79–82).

For Marx, the difference between the length of time it takes to get us fit for work and the length of time we can then work is the explanation of how profit is generated in capitalist production; these profits are not randomly but systematically generated (Marx 2000: 492–508; Collier 2004: 81–84). The worker is paid the value of their labour power, but that is always less than the value they generate for the capitalist. Secondly, the worker physically produces the next generation of workers by having children who will follow them into the workforce (Collier 2004: 84).

One very important point about the theory of surplus value is that it holds irrespective of the length of time for which the worker works. If they work for eight hours, the value of their labour power is always less than eight hours, and the difference between the two is the surplus value the worker creates for the capitalist. Similarly, if the worker works for an hour, the production of the goods to get them fit to work for one hour takes less than one hour, and again the surplus value is the difference between the two lengths of time. The worker's labour time is not only a commodity in the capitalist system. It is the only systematic source of profit in the capitalist system; it is inherent in the process of commodity production, and therefore the use of the worker's labour power is the central generator of capitalist profit.

One contemporary question that has been raised about the generation of surplus value is that of how it is created by the use of labour power in processes which do not produce, so to speak, physical objects for sale as commodities. How value is generated by services has nevertheless been of interest for some time now. Marx was starting to take note of this issue at the time he died, but that means his notes on it are sketchy and incomplete, though we have some of them in Volumes II and III respectively of *Capital* (Marginson 1998: 576–81). Marginson proceeds to develop the analysis in more detail so as to show how services generate surplus value (Marginson 1998: 582–85); we need also to note the great importance of this type of analysis in view of the almost total financialisation of the world's economy.

Ideology and Commodity Fetishism

In everyday talk, ideology usually means a set of ideas or beliefs about political or social life, that is, about how we should organise whole societies, or about the kinds of policies we should have on, say, healthcare, education, and so on. For example, the chapters of this book have titles like 'Fascism', Conservatism', and so on. We also say that an education policy is informed by a social-democratic ideology, or a neoliberal one, or whatever.

Marx, however, is very precise about what an ideology is. In commodity production, we devote most or all of our working lives to a specific task which our employer assigns to us or employs us to perform, and out of our wages we buy the everyday necessities which enable us to perform each day's work. We have made a contract with the capitalist, we work as individuals doing a job, and out of hours we refresh and restore ourselves as individuals. Yet, as Marx shows, in such a system we are in fact more and not less dependent on one another; because we are at work all day, we need others to produce our daily necessities, to construct and maintain or repair the machines and instruments we use at work. We also need the capitalist to pay us, and they need us—or rather, they need us to exercise our labour power—in order to produce the goods they sell and from which they make their profits.

So the individual nature of our contract and our work is only a superficial appearance. We are in fact located in a wide range of social relations which are necessary features of the capitalist production process. The process, however, appears to us as an individualist one, that is, as one in which we as individuals and our employer as an individual entity make a contract with one another. The superficial features of the process look like the reality of it, and if we mistake the appearance for the reality then we are in the grip of an ideology.

Another example of an ideologised concept is the very widespread idea that a contract of employment is an equal agreement which both sides freely reach. Yet when we examine the contract more closely, we see that the parties who agree the contract are not on an equal footing. The employer can find someone else, but the worker has to accept the job or go without an income until they find another one—or starve. Furthermore, even the worker's wage is not freely set by either the worker or the capitalist. The wage is the value of the worker's labour power, that is, the time it takes in that particular society at that time to reproduce the worker's labour power for the next day's work. The contract appears to have been reached freely by free individuals, but the economic relations, or material relations as Marx calls them, which underlie the contract show it to be inherently unequal. If we think the contract is equal, we are misled by its apparent equality and therefore have an ideologised conception of it.

The point here is that an ideologised conception is not a lie, and it is certainly not the result of a conspiracy. It is instead the systematically misleading appearance of a system of production relations. Just as importantly, it misleads all who participate in this type of productive system. The employer and the worker share the same idea about the nature of the contract, because the surface or superficial appearance of the contract misleads both of them. Thirdly, an entire system of production can by its very nature mislead an entire society. That is what Marx means by an ideological misconception, and that is what it is for us to be in the grip of an ideology. For Marx, the way to free ourselves of it is to examine the underlying production relations—that is, to examine who or which class of people own the means of production and which class have only their labour power to sell in order to survive.

Marx's arguments here are very far-reaching. For example, he never says the system of production relations determines or causes the various ideas we hold, or that the productive system totally shapes our culture and our society; he never subsides into a totally materialist or mechanistic conception of society (Avineri 1968: 42). His exposure of the nature of ideology, nevertheless, shows that if we want to understand how our institutions work, and why our society has the form it has, we have to include the material relations of production in our explanation.

For example, colossal financial crimes have been committed throughout recent history, in the form of corporate tax fraud, the comprehensive rigging of interest rates, and much else, but virtually no prosecutions ever take place, and even when they do and the perpetrators—almost invariably minor figures in the crimes concerned—are convicted, the punishments are so feeble as to be worse than a joke. Neither the major corporations nor those who head them seem to be prosecuted, despite their fear of exposure. It is not an excuse that financial crimes or other corporate crimes can be so intricate as to make successful prosecution difficult. The brute fact is that such crimes are committed by enormously rich bodies and individuals, and that such perpetrators are intimately bound up in networks of social and political power to such an extent that major political institutions and individuals are complicit in the crimes, often because they cave in to pressure not to prosecute or because they create a working culture in which regulatory bodies are expected not to implement laws which already exist. The history of the Merck prescription painkiller Vioxx, which has been called the worst drug disaster in history, shows what seems to have been obstruction and concealment by the Merck corporation, together with what may well have been the US Food and Drug Administration's weakness or collusion in licensing the drug in 1999.

Vioxx was recalled in 2004, but the ban was lifted with conditions in 2005; at the time of writing, 11 years later, the drug has apparently not yet been reintroduced. It was associated with about 38,000 deaths in the United States (Drugwatch 2014). Other scandals around very harmful drugs include the birth deformities caused by Thalidomide in the 1950s and 1960s; the drug was intended to reduce morning sickness during pregnancy. It was many decades before the eventual conglomerate owner, Distillers Company, paid compensation. At the time of writing, new information is emerging daily about what look very much like highly systematic actions by globally famous car manufacturers to cheat pollution tests by installing a purpose-built device in car engines. Once again, one question will be that of whether or not states take any action against the manufacturers as corporations or if only individuals will be charged—that is, if any action at all is taken.

Marx's arguments over this kind of issue are part of his comprehensive analysis of commodity production; the apparent nature of the production relations involved conceals their true nature, and even the items we produce and consume take on a misleading appearance. That may seem surprising, but the argument starts with the recognition that an object produced as a commodity, that is, as a thing produced for sale, is objectified labour, or more specifically, objectified labour turned into capital; it has been called crystallised labour (Marx 2000: 472–78; Avineri 1968: 117–19).

A commodity is, however, a commodity only if there is a market for it, that is, if it has been produced specifically for sale in the market and if there are people willing to buy it. The fact that people want to buy an item creates a relation between the worker and the buyer, and the item is literally an objectified expression of this relation (Avineri 1968: 118). The relation of course changes according to the demand for the item, or in response to other factors such as technological improvements or modifications; and as the theory of surplus value shows, the sale of the commodity also makes a profit for the capitalist.

Therefore, the worker, the buyer, and the capitalist are all involved in a set of relations, but these relations can now be expressed in terms of the commodity, the state of the market for it, and the surplus value the capitalist makes from its production. The social relation between the people involved is replaced by relations between commodities, including the worker's labour power; we end up seeing not the social relations but the relations between objects and systems, such as the production line and the market where we buy the commodity in question. Marx calls this replacement of social relations by relations between things and systems commodity fetishism.

Major Contradictions and Incoherences in Capitalism

Marx, as we have already noted, is never completely materialistic or mechanistic, and he is always aware of the power of social ideas and long-established social systems even in economies which are otherwise completely or almost completely capitalist. For example, he notes that in Great Britain, the new class of the bourgeoisie effectively controlled the whole of civil society or the sphere of interests, while the old landed aristocracy still ruled officially through the institutions of state (Avineri 1968: 42).

Secondly, Marx exposes the powerful element of moral coercion which is inherent in capitalism, despite the widespread claims and beliefs that the system is founded on freedom. First of all, money reduces all human values to a single, interchangeable or apparently universalisable measure. Moreover, any accumulation of money—capital—amounts to deferred consumption; if we save money, we postpone both our consumption of goods and our participation in activities. In respect of capital, Marx says:

> The less you are, the less you express your life, the more you have. (Marx 1844: 51)

What we have more of is money—the very thing which can purchase the things which meet our needs and express our lives. Yet, to accumulate it at all, we have to live a certain kind of life—that is, give our working hours to the capitalist, scrimp and save for anything beyond the necessities, and so on. That then shapes the whole or almost the whole of our lives, and amounts to a comprehensive vision of how we should live; it is therefore a blanket moral requirement, and its acceptance is an essential part of the emergence and survival of capitalism (Avineri 1968: 110).

A further problem here is inherent in the logic of commodity production. The capitalist has to keep the value of the workers' labour power as low as possible, and even force it consistently downwards, so as to maximise the surplus the worker generates. Yet if workers are paid so little that they cannot buy the goods they themselves produce, then the system is at risk of collapsing because the market for goods shrinks rapidly, in what may be a negative form of Keynes' multiplier. Such shrinkages can have an enormous impact, and the global crash of 2007–9—whence we are yet to recover—has been described as a crisis of aggregate demand (Sen 2009). This also serves to show how whole economies may well depend less on gigantic corporations than on ordinary people's buying and selling ordinary everyday things.

What has also emerged in this process is the role of finance capital; particularly in the Anglophone world, political and other pressures on governments have led to very great relaxations on finance, with the result that enormous notional or paper profits can be made very quickly without any apparent need for the use of labour power in production. Quite simply, the worker's labour power—the worker, the human being—is all but eliminated from the process of making profits. One result has been that astounding amounts of money are claimed as profits and held solely in notional form; even in 2007, the notional total of derivatives was $595.3 trillion, or 11 times the world's annual output (Birch and Mykhnenko 2010: 11–13). It is difficult to know what this kind of money even means, especially as it seems only to be invested not in production but in yet more financial instruments and other such holdings.

Marx never claims that the absolute position of the workers will deteriorate endlessly under capitalism, but his analysis shows that there is no limit to the extent of the inequalities between the working class and the bourgeoisie. In industrial capitalism the bourgeoisie, furthermore, can and do reuse the surplus value the workers create for them by turning more and more areas of life into commodities. That process brings yet more workers under their control, and is also necessary to capitalist society; as we have seen, in order to be a worker at all in commodity production, a worker has to have their daily necessities available in the right quantities, in the right place, and at the right time, because their whole life is subordinated to being at work on time for a specified period of time. Unless capital is used thus, it remains 'dead labour' (Avineri 1968: 124).

The Falling Rate of Profit

One result of 'dead labour' is the falling rate of profit, which is also inherent in this system of production. Capitalists may form a class in the system, but they are also in continual conflict with one another and with their workers, because in this system they are under constant commercial pressure to reduce the costs of production. The only way to do that is to reduce the time it takes to produce an item, because that reduces the labour time used. An obvious way to do that is to install machinery, which is a form of crystallised or 'dead labour', because it is not itself a source of labour power or labour time.

Marx calls machinery constant capital and labour power variable capital. The ratio of the two is for him the rate of profit (in Volume III of *Capital*, Marx calculates this as the percentage of surplus value in the total investment by the capitalist, namely constant and variable capital). As more and more machinery increases productivity and reduces the amount of labour power needed, so the ratio of variable capital to constant capital falls, because less and less labour power is used; therefore the ratio of surplus value, or profit, to investment also falls. Marx calls this the falling rate of profit. In addition, the value of each item produced falls, because progressively less labour time goes into producing it. It makes no difference that higher volumes of production mean that what Marx calls the 'absolute mass of surplus value', that is, the total profit, rises (Marx *Capital* 1999 Vol. III: chapter 13). For the capitalist, the only response is to produce more and more, which means the market could collapse through overproduction. It could also, as we have seen, mean that the state has to colonise other regions of the world and turn the colonised peoples into captive consumers for the surplus goods produced by capitalism.

SOME PROBLEMS IN MARX

Here I shall not go into questions about how socialist movements or political parties might bring about socialism, as those questions have been covered very extensively both within such groups and in the literature on Marx and Marxism. Instead I shall look briefly at some philosophic difficulties or potential difficulties in the work of Marx.

The first is Marx's distinction between use-value and exchange-value. Marx says use-value is limited by the properties of the thing in question, and that exchange-value is the ratio or proportion at which it is exchanged for another commodity in the market. The idea of use-value, however, is more problematic than it seems to be at first sight; the relevant properties of a thing are themselves not independent of particular societies or ways of life, and an item can serve many uses, as a tool or a memento, or an ornament, and therefore use-value is itself a social creation (Sivaramakrishnan 1998). Marx shows some recognition of this, but does not make it very clear (Marx 1887: chapters 1 and 2).

The second problem emerges in Marx's account of alienation. His critique of capitalist production for expropriating our humanity itself is extremely powerful, but he regards our humanity is expressed in the things we do and embodied in the things we create, and therefore in a completely capitalist system it is not clear what other form of humanity we know. That is, we may be unable to say what is being alienated from what, unless we posit or assume some human essence which underlies any particular historical expression of our humanity. That raises other problems in turn; one possible way for us to proceed might be to say that as we are reasoning and collaborative actors in and on the world, then capitalism reduces us to robotic subjects of its own imperatives, that is, to something no longer recognisable or intelligible as human. That condition is one in which both the capitalist class and the proletariat find themselves, and Iring Fetscher, for example, has identified a strong conception of human nature in Marx's work; according to this, we are collaborative and creative beings whose sociality and creativity are controlled and redirected by capitalism to its own ends (Fetscher 1973; Sivaramakrishnan 1998).

Some Further Questions Arising

Marx is very clear that there is no question of going back to preindustrial societies; there is no way of knowing how, for example, preindustrial feudalism or other hierarchies could be revived or reinstated. That, however, leaves open the question of how societies which are still primarily feudal, or agrarian and feudal, are to be transformed into socialist societies without going through an industrial revolution and its attendant horrors. This is an issue that faces all socialist movements in the developing world, and Marx's own work is not necessarily an automatic source of help here, partly because he seems to consider it necessary for preindustrial societies to become industrial capitalist ones before they can become socialist ones.

Secondly, Marx's account of history is never mechanistic, but he is pessimistic about the prospects for the emergence of capitalism in societies which have never been feudal in the first place. He saw feudalism as a precondition for the commercialisation of land and agriculture, and he held Portuguese society was not feudal, so the mercantile civil society which transformed the rest of Europe did not develop there (Avineri 1968: 156).

One implication is that those who try to bring about socialism in very traditional non-feudal societies cannot use Marx's work as a formula for their own action but instead need to engage with it and draw upon it with a very clear sense of their own historical and social location. There are no easy options in the form of one model or another. That may seem like cold comfort, but Marx himself calls on us to investigate whether any society has sources of social or societal behaviour which might contribute to the development of socialism—even though that requires a clear understanding of capitalism (Avineri 1968: 152–53).

Many socialist leaders around the world have been well aware of the need to know the workings of capitalism very well and to develop socialism for their own societies. Fidel Castro and Che Guevara both rejected the Soviet model when they overthrew the dictator Fulgencio Batista in Cuba in 1959; so did the Chilean president Salvador Allende, who was elected in 1970. Guevara also saw how the then-communist countries were failing to improve civilian production systems while putting vast amounts of money into military research and production under the pressures of the Cold War (Guardiola-Rivera 2013: 96–98). Guevara was very alert to the implications of technological developments, and he saw how capitalist corporations were using new technologies solely to increase their profits. In 1962, he said, 'Electronics has become a fundamental political problem', and tried to reorientate Cuban society and the economy so that technological innovation and production would foster a common ethics in which willing commitment would be central (Guardiola-Rivera 2013: 96). In India, although political parties on the Left have often been severely criticised, with substantial evidence, for a wide range of failures, communist leaders have always known that their task is the enormously difficult one of devising a compelling socialist position for India (Prashad 2015: 140–232).

Those are the kinds of things all who engage in socialist political activity have to face, but what must not be forgotten in any study of Marx, and no doubt in any attempt to draw upon him, is his fierce passion for the productive life of human beings (Singer 1980: 43). Marx's lifelong analysis of capitalism, and his rage against it, both show how capitalism, despite the immense productive energies it liberates, systematically chains human creativity and productivity to its own ends, and crushes all other forms and expressions thereof. It even shapes our very nature as human beings (Singer 1980: 34). Yet Marx shows us how the forces of capitalism, the system of commodity production, are not forces of nature, or supernatural forces. They are human creations, and if we see them as anything else we enslave ourselves to them and to the controllers of capital.

SOCIALISM, COMMUNISM, AND MARXISM

These terms cannot be easily understood in isolation from a knowledge of Marx's own writings, and one reason for that is that Marx himself says, '[W]e do not anticipate the world dogmatically, but rather wish to find the new world through the criticism of the old one' (Marx 1843). Marx was also well aware that when we change our views and ways of life we usually do so more in response to intolerable conditions and less because we are attracted by some vision of a better life in the future (Ollman n.d.). One difficulty we face, however, is that Marx died before he could carry out his stated intention of writing about future society, though the notes he left on that have been published as Volumes II and III of *Capital* and have received attention from some very distinguished Marx scholars (Ollman n.d.).

The terms 'socialism', communism', and 'Marxism', however, are very widely used, often without specification and often in complete ignorance of what they mean (particularly when they are used as general terms of abuse). Here I shall provide only a brief outline of them, in the hope that readers can draw upon this material and on the material above to inform their sense of political positions they might hear or read about.

A socialist system is one in which the state owns the means of production, that is, plant and equipment, as well as natural resources and property such as land. This is sometimes called state socialism, and the most obvious historical examples of it have been the Soviet Union, the People's Republic of China, and Cuba, plus the Democratic People's Republic of Korea; the former German Democratic Republic may also have been an example of state socialism. This system can work extremely well; for example, the British National Health Service, as I have noted in Chapter 3, is the most loved and trusted institution in the United Kingdom, and some visitors to Cuba who have received treatment under the country's healthcare system have also spoken very highly of it. In mixed economies, such as the largely social-democratic systems of western Europe and Scandinavia, state-owned institutions are usually described as being in public rather than state ownership; that includes almost all educational institutions in the countries concerned. The terms 'public ownership' and 'government ownership' are used in India, where for example three quarters of the banks are in the public sector, as are the railways.

Comprehensive state socialism, however, has been severely criticised, only partly for a mixed record of success and failure (for example, the Soviet and the Chinese education systems have received much less criticism than many of those countries' other systems). Some of the sharpest criticisms have been directed at state socialism for its centralisation of power and political authority among a very small elite at the top of the respective countries' communist parties; it has even been called state capitalism (Wolff 2012).

In contrast to socialist systems, a communist system involves staged progress towards full communism. The first stage would be what Marx, in a famous phrase, calls the revolutionary dictatorship of the proletariat (Marx 1875). This would be, as Marx says, 'still stamped with the birthmarks of the old society from whose womb it emerges' (Marx 1875). Marx does not seem to say exactly what these transitional 'birthmarks' would be, or how long they would last, but in the *Manifesto of the Communist Party* he and Engels set out a number of specific measures that such a system would implement, including a 'heavy' progressive income tax as well as state control of transport and the means of communication. The system would also abolish landed property and direct all rents or profits from land to public purposes (Marx and Engels 1848; Ollman n.d.). There is nothing particularly utopian about any of this, and some of it has been very successfully implemented around the world for many decades.

Marx's use here of the term 'dictatorship of the proletariat' has caused problems, and it is quite likely that he did not mean dictatorship in the usual sense; he used the term in opposition to the French socialist Louis Blanqui's proposal that a future workers' state would have be organised on elitist lines, and—writing more than half a century before the terrible dictatorships of the twentieth century came into being—he probably had the severely limited dictatorships of Roman times in mind (Ollman n.d.). Ollman also points out here that the democratic rule of the whole working class—which would bring former capitalists and landowners under its ambit—would be more democratic than anything we have today, even under our current bourgeois conceptions of democracy (Ollman n.d.).

This would nevertheless be a transitional and transformative stage on the way to full communism, in which the means of production and natural resources would be genuinely communally owned. Marx's work on this, like his work on the state, is incomplete, but his writings on the Paris Commune and its distribution of political and administrative power give us a key to his thinking. Crucially too, Marx was very insistent that in the new system work would have to be 'human, agreeable, or at least bearable', and in a draft text on surplus value he also argues in detail that eliminating the unnecessary work we do in the existing productive systems would give us a great deal more free time for the use of our creative capacities; the unnecessary work may amount to as much as nine tenths of the use of all labour power (Marx 1999: 54; Ollman n.d.). While Marx did not live to start specifying what a communist society would look like, he did say enough to show that it would involve a profoundly different sense of productive value in almost every sense from the ones we have today: each of us would produce according to our ability, and would receive according to our need (Marx 1875).

Marxism

A flourishing debate has always existed over what Marxism means and—even if particular groups or political parties reach agreement on what it means—on how it would best be implemented. This was as true in Marx's own time as it is in ours, and we have seen above that Marx himself was involved in various disputes about the policies and directions the various groups he founded or joined should take. The crucial point is that all these disputes, discussions, and disagreements are grounded in or derived from analyses of our situation or condition, and that these analyses draw upon the major themes in Marx. That means there is no one defined or definable Marxist position or perspective, and it also means that we have to know something about Marx's own work in order to understand the issues that arise in and around the enormous field of Marxist debate and literature.

Clearly, there is no question of my encompassing the immense variety and range of Marxist arguments, policies, and parties, or the colossal amount of work on those themes. Socialist and communist movements and parties in non-communist countries, however, have had to devise approaches which they consider constitute the best ways to achieve socialism and then, possibly, communism. These have been outlined clearly in much of the literature, and I shall only summarise them briefly here, with the reminder that almost all the debates and arguments involve the question of the relations of production—that is, of ownership and control—in the political economy of any society where socialist or communist movements exist; this of course includes the analysis of major institutions and practices such as religion (Molyneux 2008). We must also remember that Marx's thinking, like that of Sigmund Freud, has had an enormous impact far outside perhaps even the widest field such thinkers could have intended to cover. Famous artists in many areas of work have been deeply influenced by Marx, and we shall encounter some of these in Chapter 8, on poststructuralism and postmodernism. Marx's language and terminology also inform our language in many and often unexpected ways, and significant works of literary analysis have been explicitly informed by Marx's work; one such is Raymond Williams' *Marxism and Literature*, which was first published in 1977. For the present, then, I shall offer only very brief summaries of possible paths towards socialism.

Evolutionary Socialism

This might be the most widespread form of socialist approach, and dates from as early as the early or mid-nineteenth century; in 1824, for example, the British government repealed the Combination Acts, which had been passed in 1799 and 1800 respectively and prohibited trade unions as well as other forms of combination or combined action by workers. Within 30 years or so, several successful trade unions existed, and in due course they formed the British Labour Party. Similar developments took place in most industrial countries over the next 75 years or so, with vast policy developments after the Second World War; the United States, however, is something of an exception in that the proportion of the US workforce which is unionised is much smaller than it is in other industrial countries. Today, the European Convention on Human Rights (a creation of the Council of Europe, an older and larger body than the European Union and one distinct from the EU), protects the right to trade union membership under Article 5, which states a right to freedom of association.

In addition, most industrial countries, and several in the non-industrial world or the global South, have long had social-democratic or socialist parties, which have often held office and continue to be major bodies in their countries' political systems. Socialist Members of the European Parliament also form a single bloc within that assembly, and in both France and Italy the Communist Party has at times been a substantial political presence.

Very generally, the thinking within and behind socialist or social-democratic parties in contemporary democracies is that socialism can be achieved by gradual or in some cases by parliamentary means. It hardly needs saying that this approach has been fiercely criticised, for example by Ralph Miliband (1924–94), a Polish refugee who served aboard British warships during the Second World War and then became one of the great English-speaking Marxist academics. Miliband considered that the demands of electoral politics would override and then put an end to any possibility that capitalist production relations would be replaced by one based on workers' control of the means of production, or any other genuinely socialist system of production relations. He also openly denounced many of the positions taken by social-democratic parties, such as the support for the Vietnam War stated by the then-ruling British Labour Party in the 1960s.

Revolutionary Socialism

This seems to have had its greatest appeal at the height of unregulated capitalism in the middle of the nineteenth century, and then again during a series of almost worldwide rebellions against colonialism or gross oppression by domestic oligarchies or plutocracies.

Indeed, its greatest successes probably occurred in the latter contexts, and examples could well include the Bolshevik Revolution of 1917, the Chinese Revolution of 1949, the Vietnamese defeat of French rule in Indochina in 1954, and the Cuban overthrow of the Batista regime in 1959.

In conditions of great mass oppression—which have never fully disappeared and may well be reappearing in former industrial countries with the financialisation of the world's economy—the motivation to revolution may be entirely understandable, but revolutionary movements seem rarely to establish stable and tenable systems which retain public assent. This can of course be due to a range of causes, but in respect of Marx's work we need to bear in mind one continuing issue—if not a persistent problem—for communist or other socialistic parties. This is the matter of the ways in which people understand themselves and their position in relation not only to one another but to whole groups of people, whether in their own society or in any other or others. Mobilising people—especially those who live solely or primarily by selling their labour power, namely the overwhelming majority of human beings—as a single class has always been immensely difficult anywhere in the world. In India, soon after Independence, the Left divided sharply along caste lines (Prashad 2015: 98–125). In the former colonial power, the United Kingdom, about a third of the working class have consistently voted Tory.

CHAPTER 4: MARX

Extension Exercise

Do these exercises in whichever order you like:

1. Summarise this article in about 1000 words:
   Hudson, Michael. 2010. 'From Marx to Goldman Sachs: The Fictions of Fictitious Capital'. *Michael Hudson on Finance, Real Estate and the Powers of Neoliberalism*, 30 July. http://michael-hudson.com/2010/07/from-marx-to-goldman-sachs-the-fictions-of-fictitious-capital1/
2. Using the Marx chapter and the article cited here, explain in 600–800 words the theory of surplus value and the way surplus value is generated in the delivery of services: Tregenna, Fiona. 2009. '"Services" in Marxian Economic Thought'. https://www.repository.cam.ac.uk/bitstream/id/534127/0935.pdf

Further Reading

Mandel, Ernest. 2002. *An Introduction to Marxist Economic Theory*. Chippendale, NSW: Resistance Books.

Collier, Andrew. 2004. *Marx*. Oxford: Oneworld.

Both are outstanding short works.

5

CHAPTER

Anarchism

Where Marx shows how powerful and constricting capitalist or commodity-producing systems are, he leaves open the possibility that we can create better systems, and his intended work on the state may have addressed some of the relevant issues. He died before he could complete that work, but he clearly intended to write about the postcapitalist state. Liberal theorists, for their part, have never hesitated to expound their accounts of the state, even if they often disagree with one another over the state.

In sharp contrast to both Marx and liberals, anarchists express far greater suspicion about all forms of the state and about other forms of authority, both political and religious, even if many of them criticise capitalism in terms very similar to Marx's own. Indeed anarchists were significant participants in nineteenth-century socialist movements; the International Workingmen's Association, or First International, was created when Pierre-Joseph Proudhon's followers joined forces with Marx's followers in 1864, even though their disagreements caused the organisation to collapse in 1871 (Heywood 2007: 176). Since then, anarchists have at times gained quite substantial political support, for example among landless peasants in Russia shortly before the 1917 revolution, and have left a strong influence on the thinking and organisation of trade unions in France, Italy, and Spain, as well as in Argentina, Uruguay, and Mexico (Heywood 2007: 176). That influence has persisted despite decades of fascism in Spain and brutal military regimes in Latin America and Central America.

More recently, anarchist ideas have found fresh expression in the Occupy movements in the United States and, less obviously, in the United Kingdom, in the wake of the 2007–9 financial crash. Among other things, such movements have focused on the failure of social-democratic parties like the Democrats in the United States or Labour in the United Kingdom to oppose the policies which caused the crash. They have also pointed out the way the state bailouts for the failed banks involved helped the banks to consolidate their hold on landed property and their influence on policy and legislation. For example, the crash put millions out of work, and those with mortgages often had their homes repossessed by the banks who had lent them the money in the first place.

Anarchism's central concern over episodes like this is that they are not episodic but systematic; according to anarchist thinkers, established power invariably expands far beyond the limits apparently placed upon it, and far beyond what the public would tolerate if they knew about it. Anarchist critics often cite a very impressive body of evidence for this. In earlier times, the French Revolution soon collapsed in a reign of terror, and the Russian Revolution resulted in a state which, by the time it collapsed in 1991, had almost no public assent whatever. More recently, global scandals have emerged over the extent of electronic surveillance by the US government, including illegal surveillance of its own citizens and hacking the phones used by heads of government even in friendly states; the process relied upon willing cooperation by major IT corporations. In India, highly repressive colonial legislation has never been repealed or has been repealed, reintroduced, and vigorously used despite severe criticism and damage to the possibility of peaceful dispute resolution; the Armed Forces (Special Powers) Act 1958, which has even been used with retrospective effect, is an obvious example (Das 2012). Noam Chomsky, perhaps the most famous anarchist thinker today, has spent many decades detailing abuses of power by the US government and its allies (Chomsky 2003).

The anarchist suspicion of established power also extends to religious authority. Here again, the evidence is very substantial; the Roman Catholic church has publicly admitted to covering up several scandals of child abuse by priests, and sharp criticisms have been made of concubinage in Hindu caste society as a religiously sanctioned abuse of economic power and social status (H. Singh 2014: 72–73). It is perhaps not surprising that anarchism has had considerable influence in certain countries and regions which have historically had strong religious traditions; these include France, Spain, and almost all of Latin America (Heywood 2007: 183). The anarchist critique of religion, however, applies to all religions because of their claim to spiritual authority, which in many cases is unquestionable; a great strength of the anarchist analysis of religion is that religion works hand in hand with political and financial power (Heywood 2007: 183–84).

The anarchist critique of the religious claim to authority is further strengthened by the fact that religions impose standards of good and evil, or acceptable and unacceptable conduct. Those standards are enforced and policed by priests, imams, rabbis, and any number of other religious authorities, and according to anarchists amount to an enormous number of controls on humanity, even to the extent that thinking certain kinds of thoughts becomes a sin.

ANARCHISM'S GLOBAL APPEAL

In view of the extent of oppression, suffering, and abuse of power all over the world, we should not be surprised that anarchist tendencies are found all over the world; anarchist thinkers have influenced political movements in India, China, Japan, Korea, and parts of Africa, not least during the struggles for liberation from colonial domination. In the period immediately after the Russian Revolution, anarchists were so popular that the Bolshevik party almost regarded them as rivals (Ward 2004: 10–13). Indeed, where the state has collapsed, which it has done in terrible civil wars (many of which result from global drives for natural resources), a return to self-generated, local community-based organisation and dispute resolution may well offer fresh hope (Ward 2004: 12).

Anarchist thinking is also found in records from earlier times; ideas which we would today call anarchist occurred in ancient slave rebellions, and figured in the thinking of Diggers in the English revolutions in the 1640s; they also appeared in the French revolutions of 1789 and 1848, and the Paris Commune of 1871 had an anarchist element. One of the most successful anarchist movements was the one led by Emiliano Zapata in Mexico in 1911; although Zapata himself was ambushed and killed in 1919 and his mentor Ricardo

Flores Magón was imprisoned in the United States and murdered in prison, the Zapatista legacy survives in the form of Ejército Zapatista de Liberación Nacional (EZLN), the Zapatista Army of National Liberation. In Brazil, a contemporary anarchist movement is the Movimento dos Trabalhadores Rurais Sem Terra (MST), the movement for rural workers. Both aim to regain control of land from large cattle-ranching oligarchies which have dispossessed peasants of communal lands (Ward 2004: 16).

Anarchism has had this kind of global appeal despite frequent allegations that it has an optimistic and even utopian view of human nature, according to which, societies must be founded on and informed by mutual respect, compassion, and cooperation. This has even been called a mystical streak in anarchism, a belief in 'almost unlimited possibilities' of self-development, with the implication that all human beings can create harmonious societies and lead harmonious lives (Heywood 2007: 184).

Yet leading an anarchist life can take enormous moral and physical courage. Gandhi may well be the outstanding modern example of that; he was partly influenced by the writings of Leo Tolstoy, which have an anarchist element, and he inspired millions of Indians to withstand enormous physical and political violence by the imperial British state without retaliating violently or hating the colonisers themselves. Gandhi in turn inspired leaders elsewhere, such as Martin Luther King in the United States (Heywood 2007: 199, 315). Contemporary anarchists have also been influenced by philosophic insights in Taoism and Zen Buddhism, particularly on the nature of self-reflection, respect, and natural harmony (Heywood 2007: 199).

Such ideas may be very attractive, but anarchist movements have never held significant political office, and anarchist arguments for the reform of the state and the economy seem to figure only rarely in general political life. Anarchist thinking, however, has and continues to have much greater influence than it is often recognised as having. The reason for this neglect, which amounts to censorship by silence, are very serious; they also tell us something about the nature of established political and economic power, irrespective of the ideological positions taken by those who have such power.

Historically, anarchism's greatest successes came during the Spanish Civil War, a bitter conflict which ended in 1939 with victory for the fascist general Francisco Franco and led to 36 years of dictatorship. During the Civil War, the largely anarchist Republican movement held substantial areas, most notably the province of Catalonia, for long enough to establish a functioning system based on and embodying anarchist thought. In the 1930s, Spain already had a mass anarcho-syndicalist trade union, the Confederación Nacional del Trabajo (CNT), and the Federación Anarquista Ibérica (FAI), which spent some of its time in the political underground. In July 1936, the CNT in particular decided to fight the Morocco-based Spanish generals who revolted against the government of the day, the Popular Front government in Madrid. On 18 July, the government was formed and re-formed thrice in one day, and the ministers involved then concluded that resistance to the generals would be futile, but the CNT moved swiftly, seizing the weapons held by military garrisons and by the civil guards, the Guardia Civil. Crucially, the CNT also took control of factories, transport systems, and land; at that time, only two per cent of landowners owned 67 per cent of the land, and many of the smallholdings were too small even to feed a family (Ward 2004: 21–23).

Especially in Catalonia, the locally based and anarchist-inspired economy was highly successful, and the province's political life took on an anarchistic character which still endures. The workers of the CNT–FAI took over the transport system in the provincial capital Barcelona, and improved it substantially (Ward 2004: 21–23). The Republican side faced enormous military and political odds, and was eventually betrayed on several fronts. The Western democracies blockaded Spain under a purported non-intervention agreement which United Kingdom and France favoured, but the United States and the United Kingdom covertly helped Franco's forces (Chomsky 2008). Secondly, the Soviet Union under Joseph Stalin decided to help the Republicans, but it did so on terms which effectively destroyed the Republican movement. It insisted on extortionate payments for weapons, thereby bleeding Spain's gold reserves, and further required that the anarchists subordinate themselves to the existing Popular Front, the government which had already decided not to resist Franco. Stalin's motives were utterly instrumental. He could not face the prospect that an anarchist or anarcho-socialist movement in Spain could undermine the Spanish Communist Party, and he also feared that the anarchists would take control of British investments in Spain; Britain was a presumed Soviet ally in a 'democratic alliance' against Nazi Germany (Ward 2004: 21–23; Guérin 2010: 128–30).

In addition, the Spanish government itself may have been alarmed by the success of the CNT's rapid moves to reorganise not only agriculture but all work, with the free participation of peasants and other workers. The CNT had over a million members at the time, and one of its regional congresses in Catalonia decided to collectivise land—but the peasants were given a choice in this; the slightly better-off opted for individual property while the poorer farmers chose collectivisation. Among the workers, 90 per cent chose to join collectives, creating a rare joint movement of both agricultural and industrial workers (Guérin 2010: 130–31). Under the broad umbrella of the trade unions, the collectives were run as groups of small units, and in accordance with anarchist principles, membership was not compulsory; even those who had opted out could trade through shops run by the collective or by communal bodies, and could receive some of the benefits of membership. In Catalonia, where there was a tradition of small and medium-sized farms, only a few pilot collectives were created, but in the neighbouring province of Aragon, more than three quarters of the land was socialised.

Anarchist thinking seems to have been followed as closely as possible; for example, regional planning was federal in nature. Agricultural yields improved immediately, with the collectives turning out to be more successful than the communes, and when graduates of agricultural colleges contributed their knowledge, yields rose by 30–50 per cent; in the Levant, the citrus farmers outperformed big private farmers even in business dealings, accounting for 70 per cent of the trade. The local bodies, furthermore, organised lectures, films, and plays, which the largely illiterate peasants relished; they also showed a degree of solidarity which greatly impressed the visiting British Independent Labour Party member Fenner Brockway. The number of people involved in such agricultural self-management soon reached half a million, in a total of some 900 collectives (Guérin 2010: 134–35).

The Catalonian achievements in industrial self-management were even more impressive. Catalonia was the most industrialised area in Spain, and for four months in 1936 almost all the factories and public services in the provincial capital Barcelona were under workers' self-management; in fact many of the private owners, who were terrified of the workers, had fled (Guérin 2010: 136–38). In October 1936, 600,000 attended a trade-union congress in Barcelona, and it was highly significant that qualified engineers from the professional classes participated in this, unlike their counterparts in Spain and Italy. On 24 October, the Catalonian government issued a decree confirming or ratifying the new state of affairs; all establishments with over 100 workers were to be socialised, and in fact farms of all sizes were socialised because many of the farmers were heavily in debt. The new system was highly successful, especially in running urban services, and foreign observers were full of praise for the workers' enthusiasm and commitment.

The successes were, however, undermined even by the pre-Franco government; some of its pro-Soviet ministers feared the prospect of genuine workers' control, and they also decided against the takeover of private factories and lands. Vincente Uribe, the strongly Stalinist minister of agriculture, even told private landowners that the Communist Party's weapons were at their disposal, and he ensured that they got imported fertilisers which were denied to the socialised farms. Uribe and his fellow Stalinist Juan Comorera, who was put in charge of the Catalan economy, even mobilised small and medium-sized farmers against the socialised farmers; they disguised large landowners as smallholders, and then privatised the organisation of food supplies in Barcelona. As if that were not enough, the 11th Division, under Enrique Lister, invaded Aragon with tanks (Guérin 2010: 139–40).

Even then the peasants resisted, and as soon as the Líster division had gone, they rebuilt their collectives. The Communist Party seemed to realise how much damage it had done, though whether its leaders realised how much they had reinforced the position of the landowning classes is less clear (Ward 2004: 24). Perhaps the question arises of whether the Republican government was even on Franco's side. The Spanish Civil War ended in April 1939, and Franco's regime, which endured for nearly 40 years, was so brutal that after his death the Guardia Civil themselves had to be protected against violent revenge by the public.

The historical record is that anarchist movements have been hated, feared, and crushed by all forms of established power, whether by broadly capitalist states or communist (or state-capitalist) ones, or by established religious authorities. Anarchist ideas, including ideas on political economy, are therefore essential to an understanding of the challenge anarchism poses to all forms of authority.

THE MAIN ANARCHIST IDEAS

Anarchist thought falls into two broad types, namely collectivist anarchism and individualist anarchism. Although the greatest difference between the two lies in their respective approaches to economics or political economy, they have a strong common element in their implacable opposition to the moderated or managed capitalism favoured by social democrats or Keynesians, and to the now-defunct state-socialist or state-capitalist systems, of which the most obvious examples were the Soviet Union, China until relatively recently (though China remains a one-party state), and North Korea, or more precisely the Democratic People's Republic of Korea.

Collectivist anarchists reject social democracy for doing nothing more than softening capitalist exploitation without ending it or replacing it with a better system; they reject state socialism for creating exploitation by the state as well as a monopoly over political power. Individualist anarchists reject social democracy for, in effect, enabling the emergence of both public and private monopolies, and for limiting property rights and individual freedoms (Heywood 2007: 185–86).

Collectivist Anarchism

This takes a range of forms, and is closer to the generally socialistic origins of anarchism than individualist anarchism, which is a somewhat later development. Like socialism, collectivist anarchism relies on a view of human beings as social beings who are better suited to cooperation and collaboration than they are to the pursuit of individual self-interest (Heywood 2007: 166). This is not a naïve idea that humans are inherently good; the anarchist view is that when we recognise our common humanity, we do not need government, which according to anarchists always replaces freedom with oppression and makes it impossible to achieve any significant social solidarity, which Kropotkin called mutual aid (Kropotkin 1902). The eighteenth-century English philosopher William Godwin, who has influenced much anarchist thinking, held that free individuals could reach reasoned agreement about how to live and work together, and did not need a higher authority. According to collectivist anarchists, free and voluntary organisation is the best defence against, and the best alternative to, the self-aggrandising tendencies of the state and the corresponding imperatives in capitalism.

This has two related sources. One lies in the work of Peter Kropotkin, a nineteenth-century Russian geographer. During his extensive travels in Russia, and then while in exile, Kropotkin observed many different forms of cooperation, and was particularly impressed by the watchmakers in the Jura region of Switzerland. They were self-employed craftsmen and organised themselves without any authority or direction from above (Ward 2004: 85–86). In the eastern regions of what was then the Russian Empire, Kropotkin also saw how central administration and funding, together with ignorance, incompetence, and corruption, destroyed ancient local institutions and practices. The rich got richer, the poor got poorer, and the administrative system was suffocated by boredom and embezzlement. As Ward says here, similar literature can be found on almost any other empire or nation-state (Ward 2004: 87).

Kropotkin, however, never made the mistake of thinking people were naturally good, but he saw a potential for good in all human beings, and concluded that human beings are social beings; they are better suited to working together, possibly even for a common good, than to advancing their own self-interest. Furthermore, Kropotkin concluded that when people recognise that, they cooperate better than they compete, and then do not need regulation or control by government. Government, according to anarchists, replaces freedom with oppression and makes social solidarity, which Kropotkin calls mutual aid, impossible (Heywood 2007: 186).

This does not have to be confined to small or localised activities, and indeed the scale of the work or the system concerned may well be irrelevant. The railway networks of

Europe and Asia, and the postal systems of virtually the whole world, coordinate their work so well that it is possible to travel by rail across two continents, or send a letter from anywhere to almost anywhere, with minimal involvement by any government (Ward 2004: 88–89).

The Spanish example also shows that organisation does not have to mean bureaucracy. Even the British welfare state, which is actually a nationwide range of services and organisations, arose not from the great expansion of state services after the Second World War, but from the vast network of local mutual societies and friendly societies that the working classes had created in the nineteenth century (Ward 2004: 27–28). In fact, the British National Health Service (NHS), the most loved and trusted institution in the country—which ranks higher in public regard than the monarchy—has its origins in the Tredegar area of South Wales. The Tredegar Workmen's Medical Aid and Sick Relief Fund (later the Tredegar Workmen's Medical Aid Society), which ran from 1890 until 1995, took a voluntary contribution from every worker in the district and provided medical care to everyone who lived within the district. Indeed, the principle of the NHS is still precisely that; it is funded from general taxation, and all who are resident in the United Kingdom are entitled to free treatment, sometimes including long-term care. At that time Tredegar was in the constituency of Ebbw Vale (which is now part of the Blaenau Gwent constituency), and the MP for Ebbw Vale, Aneurin Bevan was the Labour minister for health who created the NHS and saw it inaugurated in July 1948.

The internal organisation of the NHS, however, has often been anything but local, and both staff and patients—virtually all the United Kingdom's 64 million people—have often been reduced to helpless bewilderment, and sometimes worse, by a permanent ferment of top-down reform and bullying managerialism, which for the last two decades or more seems to have had the sole purpose of ensuring that numerical targets and little else are met (Sivaramakrishnan 2012a: 18–21). This top-down control has been a consistent process irrespective of the party in power in London, even though some of those involved in it have admitted mistakes; various hospital architects have acknowledged that some of their hospital designs had been badly misconceived, and even some of the many management consultants brought in have later recognised at least some of the damage they have done (Ward 2004: 28–29).

It may be impossible to tell how many millions of ordinary people have paid the price for that, or indeed what kind of price they have paid. In addition, many of those on the British political centre-left were badly shocked to discover in the early 1980s and thereafter that substantial proportions of the British working classes hated the very institutions which had been meant to support them in leading a decent life; these institutions included the state benefits system, local municipal authorities, the school education system, and so on. Some of the political activists involved belatedly realised that the arrogance and high-handedness which frequently characterised such institutions made an enormous contribution to public support for Right-wing political parties like the Conservatives, who have taken major steps to privatise or abolish public institutions and services; instead some on the Left have proposed very different institutions which are meant to work much more collaboratively with the public (Gannon and Lawson 2013).

No serious anarchist would be surprised by that. Neither would they be surprised that a body such as the European Union (EU) has grown steadily more remote from its own publics. The EU started life in 1951 as the European Coal and Steel Community, and even then, was committed to the localising principle of subsidiarity, which is the principle that EU law (which overrides member states' domestic law) and all government which is not covered by the EU's supranational institutions should be implemented at the lowest and most local level possible, and if needed should be transferred upwards to higher levels only with local consent (Ward 2004: 88).

Not all the institutions of the EU have colluded in the process whereby the EU has become progressively more remote from its own citizens. The European Court of Justice has tried to preserve people's rights against their own governments. For example, in the case of *Marshall*, the Court ruled in 1986 that Southampton and South-West Hampshire Area Health Authority (Teaching) had breached the EU's Equal Treatment Directive by making a radiographer retire earlier than her male colleagues (EUR-Lex n.d.). In *Foster v British Gas* (1990) the ruling was that a privatised former state-owned utility was required to follow the Equal Treatment Directive, and in *Francovich* (1991), the Court decreed that individuals who had suffered harm because a member state had failed to protect rights under what was then European Economic Community law could sue their own government (Eur-Lex n.d.).

Certain EU institutions, such as the European Commission, nevertheless have done much to destroy the principle of subsidiarity; for example, they have accepted and implemented without hesitation and apparently without serious public consultation major ideas put forward by the biggest corporations in the European Union. These include nothing less than the Single European Act, one of the most important treaties within the world's biggest trading bloc. They also include the Channel Tunnel, the Sweden–Denmark road bridge, and the EU-wide road-building programme (Monbiot 2001a). The European Parliament, for its part, is the only elected body among all the EU institutions, and was created as an afterthought in 1979. It cannot initiate legislation—that is done by the so-called civil service of the EU, namely the European Commission—and although the European Parliament can reject or amend draft EU law under the Co-decision Procedure, it allows the bulk of EU law through under the Consultation Procedure, which gives it much less power (Føllesdal and Hix 2006: 535).

Anarchist ways of thinking and doing things, however, are far more widespread than current political discourse seems to recognise, and they continue to have more impact than is often acknowledged. Even at the height of the Industrial Revolution, the bulk of production was carried out not in vast factories but in small workshops; electricity had facilitated decentralisation, and so had mechanised transport (Ward 2004: 119). That is even a feature of today's so-called advanced economies, where one of the few serious studies of small businesses finds that the owners are not thrusting Thatcherite or Reaganite capitalists but people who are more like creative rebels against the idea of being either an employer or an employee (Ward 2004: 119). This again need be no surprise; any number of studies in industrial psychology show that satisfaction in and enjoyment of work—with clear implications for creativity and productivity—are centrally linked to autonomy at work and the freedom to make informed and authoritative decisions over issues arising at work. Just as importantly, the self-employed often detest the 'whole modern capitalist ethic' and express their commitments in terms of providing a good service and doing a good job (Thomson 1984, cited in Ward 2004: 49).

One of the world's most remarkable attempts to organise very large numbers of people on explicitly anarchistic lines is embodied by the Mondragón corporation in the Basque region of Spain. This was founded by a Spanish priest in 1956, and employs over 80,000 people in several different businesses, including the production of things like domestic appliances. In 2013, it had global sales of €15 billion, and was the tenth largest corporation in Spain. Mondragón is in fact a federation of about a hundred semi-autonomous cooperatives which contribute to joint initiatives and make larger decisions together; managers' salaries are capped at eight times workers' salaries. If workers have been made redundant by one Mondragón firm, they have often been re-employed by others within the federation (Bibby 2013; Tremlett 2013). Mondragón has 15 research and development centres, and its own university, mainly for business and management studies (Bibby 2013). Working schedules are adapted to give staff time for significant family and other such commitments, and it appears that over work matters the staff have considerable autonomy in making everyday decisions.

An area of life where anarchist thinking has had considerable impact is education, and anarchist philosophers have always taken education extremely seriously; Proudhon saw education for work as a matter for pride, because work was something to be proud of, a source of dignity and value—but he also held that education had to provide the young with wider accomplishments. Kropotkin went further, seeing education as essential for boys and girls; the Spanish anarchist Francesc Ferrer i Guàrdia (also called Francisco Ferrer) considered education for emancipation as equally essential; and his French counterpart Paul Robin set up a school in which boys and girls learnt all subjects, including cooking, needlework, and metalwork, and took part in all activities together (Ward 2004: 59). Robin's explicit atheism seems to have been too much for the French authorities of his time, but another French anarchist, Sébastien Faure, realised that the thing to do at that time was therefore to stay out of the official education system, and set up schools which had nothing to do with that system (Ward 2004: 59).

The greatest impact of anarchist educational thinking has probably occurred in the United Kingdom, where within a century anarchist ideas transformed almost all schools and especially primary or junior schools from near-prisons into places where teachers see themselves not as controllers but as guides and friends to the pupils (Ward 2004: 59–61, 73–74). Even here, however, there are differences between libertarians and those who see themselves as progressives; the former, for some decades after the 1960s, often ran successful free schools with no set curriculum, and the self-described progressives often worked within the formal system, but were often as controlling as those they replaced (Ward 2004: 59–61, 73–74). One change which anarchist thinking may have helped to bring about long before the European Court of Human Rights ruled against the practice in 1985 was the abolition of corporal punishment in British schools; in any case, the progressive abandonment of the practice may also have been facilitated by post-war cultural changes in northern Europe and Scandinavia.

Among the global achievements of anarchist movements were the worldwide protests in 1997 against the 29 countries and various giant corporations involved in the Multilateral Agreement on Investment (MAI). The MAI was leaked, and provoked widespread anger, which caused its abandonment. Needless to say, governments and corporates revived the MAI under the guise of the World Trade Organization (WTO); currently, the draft

Transatlantic Trade and Investment Partnership (TTIP) will extend even further the so-called right of businesses to sue any country whose laws allegedly restrict the 'right' to make profits; the tribunals involved will be entirely independent of any national law. These kinds of treaties amount to a 'charter for the corporate takeover of the world'; the profits in question would of course be imaginary or hypothetical ones (Monbiot 2000: 302–7). At the time of writing, the European Parliament, which represents over 500 million people, is debating the TTIP, and its members are receiving enormous numbers of protest mailings from constituents asking them to reject it.

Governments' reactions to the WTO protests also confirm anarchists' opposition to the very idea of the state. After the Seattle protests, the protesters gathered again at the WTO's later meetings in Gothenburg and Genoa respectively, but the Swedish and Italian governments—members of the European Union and signatories to the European Convention on Human Rights—turned both cities into fortresses with blockades and barbed wire. The police became violent, and protesters were killed. Today, cities which host WTO and Group of 7 (G7) meetings are put under near-lockdown. The Soviet Union could not have done it better. Anarchist ideas, therefore, are much more widely held than the dominant political discourses admit, and they merit more detailed attention than they often get.

Mutualism

The French word *syndicat* means a union—more commonly, a trade union—and anarchism became a mass movement only in the form of anarcho-syndicalism. In the early phases of industrialisation, trade unions were banned for long periods, and the British legal ban was lifted only in 1824, when the Combination Acts were repealed. Thereafter, unions grew steadily stronger, and the French national union body, the Confédération Générale des Travailleurs (CGT), adopted syndicalism before 1914; syndicalist ideas also spread through the Americas, Italy, and—as we have seen—Spain (Heywood 2007: 188–89).

Anarchist thinkers were attracted by syndicalism even though the latter involved what have been called crude theories of class. The syndicalists of the time, however, rejected conventional politics as corrupt and pointless, and held that workers' power should be expressed through boycotts, sabotage, and strikes leading to a general strike. They also had strong and relatively non-hierarchical grassroots movements, which was an added attraction for anarchists (Heywood 2007: 188–89). One problem for anarcho-syndicalism is the risk of focusing too closely on trade-union action at the expense of economic reform or revolution, but the example of the Catalonian movements shows that syndicalists can have much wider aims.

Anarcho-communism

This also requires the abolition of the state; the Italian anarchist Errico Malatesta agreed with Kropotkin over this, and according to Kropotkin, anarcho-communism is consistent with humans' natural capacity for cooperation. Partly in opposition to Charles Darwin, Kropotkin observed the extent of cooperation among different species of animals, and concluded that evolution strengthens sociability, which he also concluded is therefore an evolutionary asset.

For Kropotkin, an anarcho-communist society would have no state, and would instead consist of small, self-sufficient communities. Each of these would hold its wealth in common, and the sharing of work and benefits would strengthen social bonds among members; so would direct participation by all members in making decisions for the community concerned. Crucially too, each community would always be small enough to avoid the centralisation and depersonalisation which anarchists see as inevitable in larger communities (Heywood 2007: 190–91).

Individualist Anarchism

This is founded on the idea that the individual is sovereign. It had perhaps its most extreme expression in the work of the German philosopher Max Stirner, according to whom the individual is free to act just as they choose, irrespective of laws, social institutions, or conventions (Heywood 2007: 191). Other less-extreme forms of course exist, and some of them have had some political impact, especially during the last three decades, when neoliberal ideas have been purportedly dominant.

Libertarianism

Stirner's position has not had much effect on anarchism, and individualist anarchists have generally retained some conception of order and how to achieve that. The American novelist Henry Thoreau held that the individual must act according to their own conscience, especially in response to governmental wrongs; he himself disobeyed the US government because it upheld slavery and because it waged war against other countries. He spoke in favour of the abolitionist John Brown in 1859, and like various other American anarchists, he campaigned against slavery (Ward 2004: 65–66; Heywood 2007: 191). Other anarchists, like Josiah Warren and Benjamin Tucker, however, thought in terms of mechanisms or processes whereby some sort of market exchange would serve to reconcile conflicting interests. Warren, like the liberal John Locke, thought that mixing our labour with something made it our own property, and proposed a system in which labour time would be the medium of exchange, so that people could take advantage of the division of labour—which itself increases productivity (Heywood 2007: 193–94). More recently, Robert Nozick has restated a conception of individual rights such that our earnings are entirely ours by right, and that taxation is a violation of the individual's personhood (Nozick 1974, cited in Plant 2010: 48–50).

Anarcho-capitalism

In the last three decades of the twentieth century, free-market anarchism saw something of a revival. Most of its proponents were academics, though the novelist Ayn Rand, whose novels are associated with libertarianism or free-market anarchism, was not herself an academic (she died in 1982, penniless and totally dependent on state benefits, which she loathed and had railed against all her life). Among the proponents of anarcho-capitalism were Robert Paul Wolff, Robert Nozick, and Murray Rothbard. Nozick accepted the idea of a minimal state, the main function of which would be the protection of individual rights, and Wolff considered philosophical anarchism to be the only 'reasonable belief for an enlightened man' (Nozick 1974, cited in Plant 2010: 50–51; Wolff 1976, cited in Ward 2004: 66).

Rothbard, for his part, regards the individual and any property they may have as utterly sacrosanct, and insists that individuals may dispose of their property only by voluntary contract. He recognises that we may need protection against others and that we might need systems to resolve disputes, but he has total confidence in the market to meet all needs and proposes private 'protection associations' and private courts; according to him the market will weed out incompetent associations or unfair courts because customers will go elsewhere (Heywood 2007: 194–95). Such ideas are not as far-fetched as they might sound, and for example while the American West was being settled by immigrants from Europe in the nineteenth century, the settlers devised their own rules and procedures including dispute resolution, enforcement, protection agencies, and much else; the so-called Wild West was much less wild than the movies have made it out to be (Anderson and Hill 1979).

Anderson and Hill, however, may have neglected a background factor which may well have been decisive in the successes they describe. The immigrants and settlers they write about seem to have been largely white, English speakers of working-class origins, who in addition seem to have shared the Protestant faith. This would make it much more likely that they already held shared assumptions about the status of rules and institutions, such as the procedures, tribunals, and enforcement bodies they themselves created. These may well have included shared ideas about what it is to accept the authority of such bodies and procedures, and indeed of what it is to follow a rule at all. We can only guess how these settler societies would have worked if they had been composed of a mixture of groups from very different cultures, such as southern European Catholic peasant immigrants to the United States, Russian Jewish escapees from religious persecution, and so on.

In our own time, several governments have nevertheless adopted approaches which look libertarian or seem to express libertarian ideas. The United States, the United Kingdom, and Australia have large numbers of private prisons, and in many countries, services once regarded as the duty of the state—such as airport security or security for events like the Olympics—are now delivered by private companies. Even some military services, such as cover for US installations in Afghanistan and supplies for US troops there, have been handed over to private contractors. In several cases, the privatised services have been even worse than the public ones they replaced, and the US-based security firm Blackwater was involved in so many scandals, including the murders of unarmed Iraqi civilians, that it renamed itself Xe. US troops have also discovered that civilian contractors are not legally obliged to deliver supplies if they have to enter combat zones (Funnell et al. 2009: 225–60).

The state, therefore, continues to be heavily involved; it pays for the civilian contractors from public funds, and when it really matters—for example, over supplying troops in war zones—the state has to do the work itself. Secondly, very few, if any, of the libertarian theorists seem to have criticised the enormous expansion in state surveillance that has occurred in even the most self-conscious of democracies since the September 2001 terrorist attacks in the United States. Neither have such libertarians or anarchists criticised the constitutionality or legal nature of much of the relevant legislation, such as the USA Patriot Act (where 'USA' stands for 'Uniting and Strengthening America'), the Homeland Security Act, or the British Prevention of Terrorism Act 2005. Secondly, none of the main American libertarians has criticised the enormous power and influence private corporations have on government— to the extent of writing state-level laws and major national policies themselves for elected representatives to rubber-stamp (Sivaramakrishnan 2012c; Guha Thakurtha, Ghosh, and Chaudhuri 2014). Indeed, most of the American libertarians' energies seem to have been devoted to providing an ideological smokescreen for unrestricted market capitalism (Ward 2004: 69).

Federalism

Anarchist thinkers, as we have seen, reject the idea of the state because of the state's inherent tendency to extend and abuse its powers in progressively more imaginative ways without apparently ever relinquishing any of those powers. For example, in India a new land acquisition act passed in 2013 replaced the existing law, which the colonial government had made in 1894, but it retained the most sweeping powers of the old act—and therefore any central or state government official can still declare any land fit for public purpose, and the state can immediately take over the land in question. Similarly, the repeal of the Prevention of Terrorism Act was widely praised in 2004, but many of its provisions were later restated in other laws, such as the Unlawful Activities (Prevention Act) Amendment Act 2008 (Human Rights Watch 2010). This time, they were restated without expiry dates or review dates, and with only one day of parliamentary debate. The draft amendments had not been shown to the public at all (Human Rights Watch 2010). Anarchist analysts would consider this kind of conduct by a state typical.

There is, however, another set of reasons why anarchists reject the state. The state as we have it was created in a particular historical period, and for specific political purposes. The Peace of Westphalia, which many of the European monarchs of the time signed in 1648, was a deal between those monarchs and the Church. It delineated the respective spheres of authority of the Church and the monarchs, and gave the monarchs unquestionable rule over their defined territories; it is among other things the source of the modern concept of state sovereignty, particularly over territory. Today's states are the direct inheritors of that idea.

Anarchist philosophers have fiercely criticised the inherent tendencies of such states, or nation-states as they used to be called, to centralise power, to extend their powers indefinitely, and to conquer other states or regions. Proudhon, who greatly feared the unification of Italy in the nineteenth century, saw that Giuseppe Mazzini's slogan *'Dio e popolo'*—in English, 'God and the people'—was a gift to anyone who could seize the machinery of any centralised state; both France and what had been England had been brought under progressively greater central control. In France, Louis XIV had even said,

'L'état, c'est moi' (I am the state), and in England, Oliver Cromwell, who called himself the Lord Protector even though he was a commoner and not a hereditary aristocrat, continued the monarchs' extension of their powers over Wales, Scotland, and Ireland (Ward 2004: 78–79). Some of the anarchists' fears were almost prophetic. In 1920, three years after the Russian Revolution, Kropotkin said that imperial Russia would never be revived and that all attempts to unite the elements of the old empire, such as Finland, the Baltic states, Ukraine, Georgia, and the others, were 'doomed to failure' (Kropotkin 1920, cited in Ward 2004: 86). Today, among all the regions Kropotkin listed, only Siberia is still part of Russia.

In our time, we can see any number of examples of cooperation between states; the United Nations is the biggest and most obvious, but the European Union, the African Union, the Organization of American States, and the South Asian Association for Regional Cooperation are only some of the better-known ones, and international cooperation and dispute resolution are everyday matters without which the human world as we know it might all but cease to function. An anarchist response, however, could be that all of those bodies depend on their member states, and that the bodies are at the mercy of the most powerful states within them.

The anarchists have a strong point here. There has never been a single UN intervention in any of the five permanent members of the UN Security Council, and rarely have there been interventions in countries they protect and favour, unless those countries are threatened or invaded. Even the European Union, probably the world's most successful example of international cooperation since 1648, shows the problems the Westphalian idea of the nation-state creates. The public perception of the EU in almost all its 28 member states is of a remote, secretive authority which tells 510 million people how to live their lives, down to specifying food ingredients and standardised road signs, even though the EU's supranational powers are much more limited than many realise (Moravcsik 2002: 67). Critics, however, correctly point to areas where the EU has steadily extended its powers, but while the EU is secretive and remote from the public, it does not act very differently from member states themselves; the governments of those states draft almost all their own laws in secret (Føllesdal and Hix 2006: 534–37).

This supports Bakunin's arguments against the state and against associations of states. In 1867, he said that a United States of Europe could never come about under the given states as they existed at the time; the 'enormous disparities' between them and the extent of internal centralisation within them made such a development impossible—as did the scale of each state's militarisation. According to Bakunin, the state's own constitution will always amount to 'an explicit or implicit denial of domestic liberty' and would necessarily imply a declaration of permanent war or a permanent threat to the very existence of neighbouring states (Ward 2004: 84–85; Bakunin 1867).

In contrast, the main anarchist philosophers see regional affiliations and identities as offering an altogether better range of possibilities. The European Union is a confederal body and member states can leave, but almost no individual state in the world allows regions or provinces to secede, no matter how the state was created or founded in the first place. Politicians in the Indian state of Tamil Nadu openly and persistently demanded secession from India after India achieved Independence in 1947 (at that time the state was called Madras); the demands for secession only stopped in 1963, when the Union parliament outlawed secession. In Pakistan, leaders of the province of Balochistan did not want to be included when the new state was created in 1947.

In addition, successful secessions have often been preceded by terrible civil wars. The secession of East Timor from Indonesia involved attempted genocide by Indonesian troops and was ultimately overseen by UN troops, whose presence prevented even worse slaughter (Annan and Mousavizadeh 2012: 101–18). The secession of South Sudan from Sudan in 2011 also occurred after a brutal civil war; as so often, access to natural resources, in this case the South's oil reserves, may have worsened the war, and may even have been the main reason war started.

In view of the brutality of today's states—and not just those of today—and in view of what anarchists might well call the utter bankruptcy and chaos into which we have been led by states' attempts to maintain their power, irrespective of any ideology they claim to follow, anarchism might well offer something altogether better, which is also much more likely to be on a much more recognisably human scale. Anarchists sometimes seem to think that reasoned discussion can resolve all conflicts and disagreements, but their confidence in ordinary people's capacity for decency and kindness could well find confirmation in the way ordinary Europeans, even at great cost to themselves, are welcoming and helping refugees fleeing terrible turmoil in the Middle East and North Africa. Anarchist thinkers have also had much more impact on the ways we as ordinary people do things than those who run states or the mighty private corporations, or those who write ideologies, may wish to accept. Whatever else, anarchists are no mere utopian dreamers.

CHAPTER 5: ANARCHISM

Extension Exercise

1. Read this, on your own or with friends, and see if you are an anarchist.
   Graeber, David. 2000. 'Are You An Anarchist? The Answer May Surprise You!' Accessed 6 March 2017. Available at https://theanarchistlibrary.org/library/david-graeber-are-you-an-anarchist-the-answer-may-surprise-you
2. Read this: http://www.infoshop.org/AnarchistFAQSectionA5
   Take any two examples from the document and use the theory of anarchism to analyse why the author or authors of the document consider the examples to have been successful.
   Write about 800–1,000 words on this.

Further Reading

Chomsky, Noam. 2013. *On Anarchism*. New York: The New Press.

Guérin, Daniel, ed. 2005. *No Gods No Masters: An Anthology of Anarchism*. Translated by Paul Sharkey. Chico, CA: AK Press.

6

CHAPTER

Feminism

The condition of almost all of one half of humanity—women—is an obscenity. As great an obscenity is the fact that almost all the world's societies, political systems, and economic structures are such as to resist and prevent any significant change to this state of affairs. It hardly needs saying that poverty—or an economic and social structure which enforces and requires large-scale poverty—is an overwhelming factor here, not least because it keeps girls and young women from education. Among the 15–19 age group in India's lowest two quintiles by income, only half the girls have even completed the fifth standard in school (World Bank 2011: 14). The figures may have improved since the Right of Children to Free and Compulsory Education Act was passed in 2009, at which time they were shocking; the median length of time girls spent in school in India was 1.9 years, and for boys the figure was 4.9 years (Jha and Parvati 2008; Sivaramakrishnan 2012a: 169–70).

Even worse things are inflicted on girls and women. The World Bank notes this:

> More than 1.3 million girls are not born in China and India every year because of overt discrimination and the spread of ultrasound technologies that allow households to determine the sex of the fetus before birth. (World Bank 2011: 105)

Secondly, the indiscriminate mass rape of women by combatants, and by other men present, is now a standard weapon in war, and has included the deliberate transmission of HIV/AIDS (Aginam 2012).

Quite apart from that, women do the overwhelming bulk of the world's work, running family homes in addition to working outside the home; they spend at least twice as much time as men doing unpaid work in the home. Women's participation in the global labour force (not the work force, which refers to people in work) declined from 57 per cent in 1990 to 55 per cent in 2012, and women workers are paid between 10 and 30 per cent less than men for the same work (Morton et al. 2014: 6). That, however, says nothing about other forms of inequality, such as the ownership of wealth in the form of capital or land, though the World Bank recognises that:

> Women remain heavily concentrated into lower-paying jobs, including less-productive and less-profitable entrepreneurship and farming, than men. Occupational segregation is enduring, as are wage gaps. (World Bank 2014: 6).

It is also the case that women writers, scientists, and philosophers have never had the attention or the opportunities given to their male counterparts. Even the impact of particular women on our world has been grossly under-acknowledged; in the early 1840s, Ada

Lovelace (the daughter of the poet Byron) wrote what was probably the first computer programme, an algorithm for one of Charles Babbage's calculating machines; moreover, she saw that such machines could be used for purposes which went far beyond arithmetical calculations and nothing else. Other examples abound, but get grossly insufficient recognition; even if Marie Curie's discovery of the element radium in the late nineteenth century is famous, it is less widely noted that she was not allowed to deliver scientific papers to many famous bodies, or to take academic posts in at least one famous university. In political life, we are belatedly starting to take note of and give credit—if not yet due credit—to women's roles in historical developments such as the French and Russian revolutions.

There is, however, nothing new about feminism, about the knowledge of the condition and situation of women and the will to do something about that condition. One of the earliest known statements of feminism is by Christine de Pisan, an Italian who wrote her critique in the early fifteenth century (Heywood 2007: 31) In addition, countless other works around the world often say things about the position of women in society, even if they do so while expressing other concerns.

What we need to do is to understand the ways in which the present situation has been explained and challenged. That it needs to be challenged hardly needs saying, and has been said again and again; potentially, almost all of human society as we know it could be transformed. Emma Goldman's comment is both anarchist and feminist:

> First by asserting herself as a personality, and not a sex commodity. Second, by refusing the right to anyone over her body; by refusing to bear children, unless she wants them; by refusing to be a servant to God, the state, society, the husband, the family etc., by making her life simpler, but deeper and richer. That is, by trying to learn the meaning and substance of life in all its complexities, by freeing herself from the fear of public opinion and public condemnation. Only that, and not the ballot, will set women free.... (Goldman 1911)

Historically, feminism does not seem to have developed as a single ideology, though today it is much more like one and a very significant one at that; it could transform the world. The development of feminism, for its part, both parallels and illuminates historical periods. For example, what is taken to be the first text of modern feminism was written shortly after the French Revolution had effectively reshaped northern Europe by abolishing the French monarchy and stating the doctrine of universal human rights. The book in question was Mary Wollstonecraft's *Vindication of the Rights of Woman*, which was published in 1792.

Over the next half century or so, the demand for women's rights gained momentum as forms of democracy spread, particularly as the elites, however reluctantly, accepted the spread of the vote to other classes; the franchise was still, however, restricted to men, and although in industrial countries trade unions were very much part of the struggle for the vote, they were still largely male organisations. Women rightly demanded the vote too, and the franchise seemed to be a vehicle for the emancipation of all women from earlier restrictions and oppressions. It would, many of its advocates thought, cause all other forms of prejudice and discrimination against women to disappear (Heywood 2007: 231).

Since 1893, in contrast to what may well have been millennia of discrimination against women, women's vote has been achieved relatively quickly. New Zealand gave women the vote in 1893, Australia completed the process in 1911, and in 1920 the United States followed suit with the Nineteenth Amendment to its constitution. The United Kingdom equalised voting rights in 1928, and since then almost every country which has adopted democracy has almost unquestioningly started with equal voting rights for women and men. This was also the case in India. Some countries have taken gender equality in the electoral process very seriously. Tunisia, where the Arab Spring famously started in January 2011, requires that all parties field equal numbers of men and women in elections to the national parliament, and the names of male and female candidates are alternated on ballot papers, with each woman candidate's name coming before the corresponding man's name (*Hindu* 2011). The achievement of equal voting rights has often been called first-wave feminism (Heywood 2007: 231).

Second-wave feminism is more recent, and stems from the fact that by the 1950s it was clear that achieving the vote had not been enough to end the systematic structural and social disadvantages women face; instead, more fundamental changes were needed, and among the first pointers to these was Betty Friedan's book *The Feminine Mystique*, which was published in 1963. Friedan examined the lives of suburban American women, who to the rest of the world were living the American dream, with husbands in relatively secure jobs, comfortable homes in comfortable suburbs, children in good local schools, access to all the goods and appliances of American consumerism, and so on. Instead, Friedan found among large numbers of the women a sense of boredom, frustration, and depression resulting from their effective confinement to the roles of housewife and mother; many of the women's doctors too, prescribed antidepressant medicines for what was in fact a social condition. The American dream was spread and reinforced with immense power and effect by Hollywood movies, television programmes, and the rapidly expanding advertising business.

One implication of Friedan's work is that women need much greater access to education and careers than they have had so far, but others took the arguments much further; Kate Millett wrote the book *Sexual Politics* in 1970, and in the same year Germaine Greer published *The Female Eunuch*. Both books had a huge impact, with their fierce criticisms of the ways in which the oppression of women is not only educational and occupational but also has personal, psychological, and sexual dimensions. Millett and Greer argued that legal reforms and legislative changes were not enough, because they did not address much wider and globally powerful forms of oppression, the roots of which lay in whole societies, including their structures and political systems, and the attitudes prevalent across societies.

What Millett and Greer did was part of a process which greatly expanded our sense of the political by showing that what had previously been at best a minor part of public discourse, or had been kept to the private realm of the family, was a crucial element in the way whole societies work and should be a major focus of public concern. This kind of insight was perhaps best encapsulated by Shulamith Firestone and Anne Koedt, who in 1969 gave the title 'The Personal is Political' to a paper by Carol Hanisch; Firestone and Koedt were editing papers from a feminist conference for publication. Hanisch, for her part, was already very active in what had come to be called the women's liberation movement, and had organised protests at the Miss America and other contests. The movement succeeded in challenging many of the most basic assumptions of social and political thought at the time, and was a decisive advance in the spread of feminism around the contemporary world.

Feminism-inspired research has, among other things, exposed domestic violence which might otherwise have gone unknown, and has been complemented by work done in other fields in the 1960s and 1970s. For example, the psychiatrists R. D. Laing, Aaron Esterson, and David Cooper all challenged the assumptions and methods of mainstream psychiatry, and used detailed observation to show that the family, far from being a universally caring and nurturing context, was very often the site of terrible conflict and cruelty (Laing and Esterson 1970; Cooper 1974).

Since then, various analysts have said that a third wave of feminism has emerged, in which women feel sufficiently empowered to readopt some of the clothes—such as high-heeled shoes, and cosmetics such as lipstick—which second-wave feminists reviled, without feeling oppressed or constrained; this may be an expression of a general, perhaps postmodern, refusal to accept fixed identities, or the sex–gender divide, or other concepts which have featured in feminist and other debates (Rampton 2008). Many of the structural problems women face, however, have not been altered (Rampton 2008). In many ways, these problems have grown even worse, particularly for women in the developing world.

THE CONCERNS OF FEMINISM

Whether or not a third wave has emerged, and irrespective of the range of issues and approaches which inform feminism, certain concerns are common to all forms of feminism. They are:

- The public–private divide
- Patriarchy
- Sex and gender
- Equality and difference

The Public–Private Divide

One of feminism's great achievements has been to put firmly on the contemporary political agenda the fact that politics extends far beyond the purportedly conventional arena of elections, parliaments, governments, art, literature, and so on. Instead, any spaces where human power relations are involved, such as the workplace and the family, are also political spaces; what happens within such spaces, furthermore, is also shaped by the wider political forces in any society. For example, inequalities of wealth and power within the family, and the different male and female roles within the family, are themselves not natural but are the result of political and economic systems and structures (Heywood 2007: 235). The consequences could be very far-reaching; many industrial countries have recognised that state-funded childcare enables women to resume working, when a traditional family structure would prevent them from doing so either completely or until children were much older. Some countries have legislated to grant paternity leave for varying lengths of time too.

In addition, the earlier traditions of political understanding grossly undervalued, demeaned, and even obliterated the contributions women have always made to keeping even traditional societies functioning at all. These contributions still include the overwhelming bulk of childcare and the care of the elderly or the sick. They also include the bulk of early-years and elementary schooling and nursing care in hospital, or other organised forms of healthcare.

Patriarchy

The feminist critique of patriarchy is founded on the argument that all social structures and systems, and all political systems, are patriarchal. Patriarchy literally means rule by the father (it is a neologism derived by combining the Latin word *pater*, meaning father, with the Greek word *arche*, meaning rule, although other analyses give it entirely Greek roots). According to several feminist arguments, the power division between men and women, which according to them has obtained throughout almost all human history, systematically oppresses and disadvantages women; it operates throughout society, in politics, work, the family, legal and judicial systems, and so on. According to these arguments, gender is the single most important division in human life, and is even more important than class.

Of course, societies vary in the nature and extent of patriarchal oppression of women, and in most of the global North, the obvious signs of patriarchy are much less clear than they were before women got the vote, before legislation outlawing gender discrimination was passed, and so on. In many other societies, patriarchy is still extremely crude and often violent. About 80 million women, mainly in Africa, still face female genital mutilation or clitoridectomy, and it may be impossible to count the tens or hundreds of millions who face forced marriages—in contrast to genuinely arranged ones—as well as female foeticide, and explicit sexual discrimination, oppression, insult, or violence throughout their daily lives. South Asian countries are, on the evidence, the places where female foeticide and widespread sexual violence against women are particularly common. Among the Group of Twenty (G20) countries, India ranks last, behind Saudi Arabia in this regard (Baldwin 2012). In addition, the practice of forced marriage among South Asian communities has led countries with substantial South Asian-descended populations to declare the practice a criminal offence. In June 2014, England and Wales followed the Scottish example with new law; the law also applies to UK nationals who are outside the United Kingdom, and the British foreign ministry, the Foreign and Commonwealth Office, has a unit tasked with preventing forced marriages and helping victims thereof.

Daily sexual harassment and violence in the form of groping are still widespread even in the global North, and the spread of the Internet, which affords anonymity, has shown the scale and extent of hate directed against women. For many feminist theorists, these kinds of conduct are all expressions of patriarchy, as are the feelings many women victims have that they cannot do anything about it or will not be taken seriously if they try to complain, or face even worse brutality if they fight back physically.

Kate Millett took the arguments even further; patriarchal societies are hierarchical in several ways, with men dominating women and older men dominating younger men; patriarchy can coexist with, and is part and parcel of, other systems of power and status. There is a vast amount of evidence to support this. For example, the concept of *droit de seigneur* was widespread in mediaeval Europe; when the tenant of a feudal lord or landowner got married, the lord of the manor could claim the right to have sex with the bride first (various historians argue that more often than not the feudal master accepted a payment or tax in lieu of sexual access to the bride, but that does not change either the patriarchy or the sexism involved). Similarly, Manu decrees how many wives men of different Hindu castes may have; a Brahmin can have four, men of lower castes three, two, and so on. Manu says nothing, however, about multiple wives for Dalits (H. Singh 2014: 71–73). The sixteenth-century poem *Radhika Santwanam* is, among other things, a searing response by a woman to male polygamy.

Sex and Gender

The purportedly traditional view is that these are natural divisions resulting from our biological nature; according to this theory, we are male or female, therefore we have natural powers and roles as a result, and therefore society has to be organised according to the biological differences between males and females. This kind of argument can be called an argument from biology, because it bases a theory of society on its conception of human nature as a biological fact or biological given. For example, women can bear and suckle babies, and men cannot do so; therefore, women must rear babies, men must have other roles in the family, and so on.

The feminist challenge to this theory is that these expectations and roles are largely social or cultural and are not biological in origin. Women do not need to be mothers, or to take on the traditional roles of motherhood; child-rearing can be shared whether by the parents or by other members of the family, and aspects of it can be and often are taken over by the state (Heywood 2007: 237). Secondly, while sex differences may be biological, gender differences are not, and are largely social; we are brought up to be boys and girls, men and women. One very powerful critique of the way we are socialised to be of a particular gender is Simone de Beauvoir's book *The Second Sex*, which was first published in 1949. One consequence is that it is more accurate to speak in terms of gender than sex, and a further consequence is that gender analysis enables us to examine far more of our lives and social structures and systems than the idea of biological sex as the defining difference between men and women does.

Equality and Difference

This remains one of the most contested areas in feminist thought. While feminists can reach wide agreement, with considerable political and social impact, on ending the oppression of women and discrimination against them, it is much harder to say what is to count as the achievement of equality, or even if comprehensive equality is intelligible. In a sense, first-wave feminism has achieved formal legal and constitutional equality in almost all democracies, and throughout the world women have the opportunity to vote even in the most traditional cultures. Similarly, laws forbidding discrimination on the grounds of gender are found in almost all democracies. Yet these formal conditions have completely failed to bring about substantive equality anywhere in the world. In addition, it is not clear that the existing world is so wonderful that women must achieve equality in, say, combat roles in war, or in the notably coarse and ugly world of everyday politics, or in doing back-breaking manual labour in often extremely dangerous and illegal conditions, and so on. Equality as an undifferentiated concept makes no sense unless we also consider what it is in respect of which we want equality. The question is, 'Equality in respect of what?'

FEMINISM AND OTHER IDEOLOGIES

Feminism cuts across all other ideologies, partly because many ideologies been propounded by men, and because political parties or movements which express them have been overwhelmingly controlled and run by men. Nevertheless, different forms of feminism have been clearly informed by assumptions, and sometimes explicit commitments, which are derived from or part of other ideologies.

Liberal Feminism

Through the twentieth century, the general condition and position of women improved unrecognisably in most Western countries. The changes were brought about by the vote, by women's access to education (often as a result of legislation), by vast changes in divorce law, by the legalisation of abortion, and by vast improvements in women's access to safe and reliable methods of contraception—which enabled them to control their own fertility (Heywood 2007: 236).

The changes, however, were not uniformly spread throughout Western countries. The Republic of Ireland, for example, was founded in 1921 as a result of bitter sectarian divisions between Catholics and Protestants while Ireland was a British colony, and was culturally and by law totally opposed to both contraception and abortion; in the Republic of Ireland, abortion remains illegal unless the life of the pregnancy endangers the mother's life; that condition includes victims of incest or rape, who would need to show that the pregnancy was a danger to their own lives. Spain and Portugal, for their part, were ruled by fascist dictatorships from 1936 to 1975 and 1974 respectively, and were both marked by rigid and conservative forms of Catholicism. All three societies changed significantly only after they joined what was then the European Economic Community (which since the Treaty on European Union was signed in 1992 has been the European Union); Ireland acceded in 1973, and Spain and Portugal did so in 1981.

Most of the relevant changes resulted from claims to rights, such as the right of access to education, to contraceptive advice and services, and the like. In employment law, for example, the United Kingdom's Equal Pay Act was passed in 1970, and the Sex Discrimination Act followed in 1975. As we have seen, in 1986 the European Court of

Justice significantly advanced women's rights by ruling, in the *Marshall* case, that the employers involved had breached the European Economic Community's law by making Helen Marshall, a radiographer, retire earlier than her male colleagues. That decision is binding throughout what is now the European Union.

In ideological form, these are typically liberal changes, even if they have very substantial economic and other practical consequences. They usually involve claims to rights, or to the creation of new rights, within existing democratic systems; they often involve legislation intended to ensure that women and men are treated fairly and equally under existing procedures and have, for example, equal access to education, and to all occupations and professions. Liberal feminism, therefore, is broadly reformist in character. It relies on an individualist conception of society, and in general does not seek or demand radical changes in economic or political structures or systems. It can also accept that certain areas of life can be separate for men and women respectively. Betty Friedan wrote as recently as 1983 that the family is central to women's lives (Heywood 2007: 243). Secondly, this liberal approach runs the risk of failing to address existing patriarchal attitudes; in some parts of India, women have been employed as bus drivers, but most of them leave the job soon because male colleagues often behave very badly towards them (Sreeraj 2015). In the US military, improved reporting and recording systems have shown that sexual assaults by male personnel on female colleagues are much more common than the military had previously recognised them to be; even the United Nations has publicly noted the extent of the problem, though of course the aggregate figures cover male sexual assaults on males as well (McLaughlin 2015). Any changes in attitudes may well need other kinds of approach besides the purely punitive.

An approach based on liberalism, however, has an inherent conceptual problem. Liberalism, as we have seen, is by definition suspicious of the state's capacity and tendency to intrude into the private space, and therefore legislation affecting the family is something liberal feminists have always found a problem or potential problem (Heywood 2007: 244).

Socialist Feminism

Socialist feminism, unlike liberal feminism, locates women's position in the context of the structural inequalities which shape almost all societies. Where liberal feminism largely neglects class-based inequalities among women themselves in respect of access to education, the professions, political participation, and the like, socialist feminism is founded on the argument that gender equality cannot be achieved without a revolution in the control of the means of production. The argument has some weight; for example, in commodity-producing systems women are expected to—and largely do—stay at home to bring up the children and run the house so that their respective husbands can go out to work as the family's sole or main earner.

That in turn means that women are required by the economic system to abandon occupations, careers, and higher studies so that men can have long working lives. It also means that women in capitalist societies form a free work force, doing colossal, perhaps incalculable, amounts of work without which the same economies might well collapse. The socialist-feminist response is that the answer is certainly not wages for housework, which have been proposed and amount to a form of liberalism, but a complete transformation of the entire system of production relations. In addition, being the main earners gives men economic power over women within the family. This power can also be transmitted across generations, for example by patrilineal inheritance, or by the hypocrisy involved in men's having, say, far more opportunities for sexual liaisons outside the home than women do; this is often reinforced by cultural assumptions about women's femininity or the idea that the home is a woman's space, and among the patriarchal assumptions which sustain such ideas are moral codes imposing monogamy.

Socialist feminism goes even further at times, for example by analysing the ways in which the enormously profitable cosmetics and fashion business turns women's bodies into commodities to be exploited for profit. As Laurie Penny argues, women's flesh itself has become a vehicle for highly profitable businesses which themselves propagate patriarchal ideas of women's entire lives; Anne Taylor Fleming concludes that what is in progress is a culture war that is taking place 'atop the female body' (Penny 2011; Fleming 2012). Socialist feminism extends socialist thinking by introducing such significant additional issues, and by requiring socialism to address patriarchy as a social and cultural matter as well as a key element in capitalist economic systems. This greatly strengthens the revolutionary or transformative potential of socialism.

Radical Feminism

Radical feminists regard patriarchy, not class or any other organising principle, as the central problem in existing human society. One result is that women have been portrayed as inferior to men, and that their natural sexuality has been suppressed by highly oppressive male systems of conditioning (Heywood 2007: 248). The radical feminist response has been to advocate various forms of independence from men and male-dominated organisations. There is evidence to support the likely benefits; for example, in the various British school education systems, girls get better examination results in girls-only schools than they do in mixed schools.

In radical feminist thought, gender is therefore the deepest of all divisions in society, and patriarchy pervades society, perhaps even all societies. Susan Brownmiller, for example, holds that men dominate women by physical and sexual abuse (Heywood 2007: 249). In addition, forms of everyday sexual harassment are very widespread and occur around the world (Bates 2014). Secondly, official agencies around the world, such as the police and the judicial system, have long been documented as not taking women's complaints of physical, including sexual, abuse seriously. One result is that the extent of sexually motivated violence against women is very seriously underreported. Brownmiller also holds that all men benefit from the fear and anxiety that the very possibility of sexual violence generates among all women.

FEMINISM—CURRENT PROSPECTS

Despite enormous advances in legislation and vast improvements in women's position in many societies over the last century or so, the overall global position of women has not improved nearly as much as it could have done, and in some respects has even worsened. Extreme and even less extreme fundamentalist movements in all faiths and in many countries have openly asserted not only rigid divisions in gender roles but have attempted to confine women to the home; some of the movements concerned have even banned women's education.

Secondly, within feminist theory, it hardly needs saying that fierce and significant controversy continues, and that what is said in this space is often highly illuminating. Many of the issues have to do with what it is to be a writer at all, particularly of fiction, and Toril Moi for example has provided very clear expositions of some of the questions involved (Moi 2009). Among other things, Moi notes here that the impact of poststructuralist literary theory on the ways we locate or characterise women's writing has been immense, but that this has caused its own problems; she remarks on the difference between Simone de Beauvoir's account of how society creates the feminine gender (and of how those processes can therefore be changed) and Judith Butler's apparent elimination of any sense of human agency in the process of gendering, because strong strands in poststructuralist theory regard authorship as irrelevant or meaningless (Moi 2009).

While Moi's concerns are mainly with literature, the implications of the issues she identifies are obvious. If becoming a person of a particular gender is a social process about which we can do something, then we see the whole social world indescribably differently from anyone who sees human agency as a fiction or as non-existent. In addition, Moi has more recently expressed severe criticism of the extent to which feminist theory has become so 'abstract and overgeneralised that it no longer says anything relevant about women's lives' (Moi 2015, quoted in Bergstrøm 2015). That is not an issue I shall address here, but the important thing is that Moi has put it on the public agenda.

Needless to say, this matter is not easily resolved, and Maitrayee Chaudhuri has shown additional difficulties facing anyone who attempts to give an account of feminism in a formerly colonised country such as India, where—as in many other former subject cultures—issues which are marginal or insignificant in the West are central in the non-West (Gandhi 1998, cited in Chaudhuri 2012). Chaudhuri concludes that Indian feminists have to 'confront the question' of Western feminism, precisely because India's path to modernity has been, as Chaudhuri says, mediated through colonialism—as have Indian encounters with nationalism, democracy, socialism, the free market, and other ideas and institutions. That in turn means that we have to articulate the contexts in which ideas are produced, circulated, and received as an essential element in our coming to grasp those ideas and their implications (Chaudhuri 2012).

Thirdly, the central issue of material inequality, of women's structural disadvantage in the system of production relations, seems to remain largely unaddressed at present. This may be a result of the apparently global dominance of an ideology, namely neoliberalism, according to which—as we have already seen with Hayek and his followers—human agency is irrelevant to market outcomes, which are themselves as inexorable as natural laws (or so neo-liberalism sees them anyway). It may be impossible to change that state of affairs without vast changes in our modes of production and therefore our entire political economy, but without that kind of change, we as humanity may well not face up to the task of bringing about global improvements in women's situation and condition. That failure will only compound our continuing failure to accept that women are full members of the human species.

CHAPTER 6: FEMINISM

Extension Exercise

1. Use the theory from the Feminism chapter to identify the forms of feminism (if any) which are expressed respectively in the five High Court judgments this article analyses:
   Kumar, Alok Prasanna. 2017. 'Surrogacy and the Laws on Maternity Benefits'. *Economic and Political Weekly* 52 (3): 10–11.
   Available on the Companion website [https://study.sagepub.in/as_IPI]
2. Read the article below thoroughly, including the author's explanatory footnotes, and write down a list of the main issues which the author argues face those who write about feminism in India: Chaudhuri, Maitrayee. 2012. 'Feminism in India: the Tale and its Telling'. *Revue Tiers Monde* 209, 19–36. Accessed 29 January 2017. doi: 10.3917/rtm.209.0019.
   You may find 8–10 points. From your own list, choose *one* and state what you yourself can do to alter the situation for the better.
3. If this article is available, read it and summarise it in about 300 words:
   Rinkunas, Susan. 2016. 'What Will Women's Health Care Look Like Now?'. *The Cut/New York Magazine*, November 9. Accessed 7 March 2017. http://nymag.com/thecut/2016/11/what-will-womens-health-care-look-like-under-trump.html
   Make sure you include the key factor in reducing abortion rates.
4. Read this article:
   Penny, Laurie. 2016. 'The New Chauvinists Try to Defend Women—But Who Will Defend Us from Them?'. *New Statesman*, 13 May. http://www.newstatesman.com/world/2016/05/new-chauvinists-try-defend-women-who-will-defend-us-them
   Write down the author's main criticisms of conservative feminism. You can take about 100 words for this.
   (You may need to link to the article through Penny's own site: http://laurie-penny.com/2016/07/).

Further Reading

Adichie, Chimamanda Ngozi. 2015. *We Should All Be Feminists*. New York: Anchor Books.
Beauvoir, Simone de. 1993. *The Second Sex*. London: Everyman. (or another edition of this book).

Each of these is a great work; each shows us how diminished we all are by our current ways, and how much we have to gain from the transformation of our world to one in which gender relations are genuinely equalised, in every aspect of our lives private and public—around the world.

7

CHAPTER

Ecologism

That human activity in all its forms has had an enormous impact on all of life on Earth is no longer seriously doubted. The United Nations Intergovernmental Panel on Climate Change (IPCC) has concluded that the evidence of the human contribution to global warming is 'unequivocal'—and that abandoning the use of fossil fuels altogether will have a negligible effect on the global economy (IPCC 2013: 4, 15).

One of the relevant human impacts is the effect of introduced species of plants and animals into local environments; this can be inadvertent or unintended, with one example being the European zebra mussel, a species of shellfish which arrived in North America in the ballast tanks of ships. Ships often pump out and replace the water in their ballast tanks, and one result has been that this particular mussel has covered the bottom of American rivers and lakes and also blocked municipal and industrial water pipes (Vitousek et al. 1997). Vitousek and his colleagues note six ways in which humans cause global environmental changes, all of which had already been well documented at the time they were writing: the increasing concentration of carbon dioxide in the atmosphere, alterations to the global biogeochemical cycle of nitrogen and other elements, the production and release of persistent organic compounds such as the chlorofluorocarbons, widespread changes in land use and land cover, hunting and harvesting of natural populations of large predators and consumers, and biological invasions by non-native species (Vitousek et al. 1997).

While there is no evading what may be the greatest problem humankind now faces, or our need to change our ways quickly, modern ecology as a field of study is not very new. It started in the second half of the nineteenth century, as a form of biology which examined the 'total relations of the animal both to its organic and its inorganic environment' (Haeckel 1866, cited in Heywood 2007: 255). The word 'ecology' itself is derived from the Greek word *oikos*, which means the household (or habitat). That word is also the source of our word 'economy'. Today, ecologism is a fully fledged but complex ideology; all its versions, however, share the belief that nature is an interconnected whole which includes all species, including humans and the inanimate world (Heywood 2007: 255).

Ecologism itself is divided into two main strands, shallow and deep ecologism, terms coined by the Norwegian philosopher Arne Næss (Heywood 2007: 260). Shallow ecology is sometimes called environmentalism, and its proponents see ecological issues largely in terms of human needs and activities; it would mean continuing to do most of the things we already do, but modifying them so that we reduce or minimise the harm we cause to the environment. Cars which cause less pollution, refrigerators which do not use chlorofluorocarbon coolants or CFCs, and so on, are examples of a shallow ecological approach. The critics of this approach also call it weak ecologism.

Deep ecologists, on the other hand, reject shallow ecologism for continuing to place humans at the centre of its concerns, that is, above all other forms of life, and for, in effect, maintaining and protecting the way of life in most industrial societies. That also implies that shallow ecology preserves the inequalities which exist within and between countries. The United States, for example, accounts for half the world's annual consumption of energy and natural resources, but has only 6 per cent of the world's current population. It is physically impossible for the Earth to support that kind of consumption for all human beings.

According to deep ecologists, one of humanity's main purposes is to sustain nature. This means humans have no privileged place or status. Secondly, taking deep ecology seriously would require enormous changes in entire ways of life. For example, we might have to restrict or end commercial farming for meat production, for which we have destroyed very large areas of forest, and in which we use substantial amounts of chemicals to fatten animals artificially, and to ensure breeding for maximum output; several scandals have also emerged about the terrible treatment meted out to animals in the commercial production of meat. It is also the case that the animals we feed for meat production consume disproportionate amounts of grain for comparatively small amounts of yield in the form of edible meat. We might also, for example, have to limit our use of cotton, a crop which needs large amounts of water and cannot be grown in many climates without substantial human intervention to ensure sufficient water supply, which can mean the destruction of other plant species; that could apply to other crops too, many of which are now grown commercially in countries into which they were imported in the first place. We would almost certainly have to reshape entire transport systems, such as those involving internal combustion engines and air travel, and may have to reorganise whole economies so that we consume less, commute less, and even ship goods around the world to a far smaller extent than we do now.

The distinction between shallow and deep ecologism is, nevertheless, not always clear. For example, railways constitute an excellent way of transporting freight and people, often in very large quantities and numbers and often over very large distances. They can be far less damaging to the environment than, say, road transport, but nevertheless depend on fossil fuels or electricity generated from fossil fuels. In addition, high-speed railways require very expensive technology, the manufacture, construction, and use of which can cause significant environmental and other costs, in addition to the economic uncertainties around projected passenger numbers and the additional policies that would be needed to encourage the use of high-speed trains rather than cars or passenger planes (Deakin 2010; Chester and Horvath 2010; Friends of the Earth 2011). In any case, irrespective of whether any particular issue or policy comes under shallow or deep ecology, if we do not change our ways—and quickly—we may be left with no option but the enormous changes required by deep ecology.

Some countries have already acted on the matter of global warming. On average, about 40 per cent of Germany's electricity comes from renewable sources, though on 8 May 2017 the figure was as high as 85 per cent (Hanley 2017). Sweden aims to have a carbon-neutral economy by 2040, and looks as though it will meet that target; in 2015, 57 per cent of its power supply came from renewables, and four of the country's 10 nuclear reactors are currently being phased out (Sims 2016). On the night of 9–10 July 2015, Denmark produced 140 per cent of its electricity needs entirely from wind farms; those two days were exceptionally windy, and the surplus was transmitted to Germany, Norway, and Sweden. Denmark has the capacity to generate three quarters of its electricity from wind farms, and plans to add to its current capacity (Hill 2015; Neslen 2015). Germany—as a result of the 2011 Fukushima nuclear disaster in Japan—also plans to phase out and close down all its nuclear reactors by approximately 2050. The apparent delay may well have to do with the problems faced by any country over the storage of the radioactive materials which are used to fuel nuclear reactors.

Each of the strands of ecologism in turn draws upon elements in socialism, anarchism, feminism, conservatism, and even fascism. As a result, there is a wide range of ecologist or ecological analyses of our present condition; all of these therefore provide different kinds of policies and proposals for a sustainable future, but they all have in common the conviction—for which there is overwhelming evidence—that our current way of doing things seriously threatens the survival of humanity and quite possibly all life on earth.

In addition, air pollution in India is so severe that reducing fine particulate matter in the air to the current Indian regulatory standard would increase the life expectancy of 660 million people in the worst affected areas by 3.2 years; in China, air pollution is estimated to contribute to 1.6 million deaths a year, or 17 per cent of the annual figure (Greenstone et al. 2015; Rohde and Muller 2015). In January 2017, the Greenpeace Environmental Trust published a report which, among other things, draws on work by the Global Burden of Disease research programme to estimate that air pollution causes just under 1.2 million deaths a year in India, and causes the country's gross domestic product (GDP) to be 3 per cent lower than it would be otherwise; smog, haze, and other atmospheric phenomena resulting from air pollution are now a familiar cause of school and industry closures, and of transport shutdowns in India (Dahiya, Myllyvirta, and Sivalingam 2017: 2). Greenpeace also uses data from state pollution control boards to conclude that almost no places in India comply with World Health Organization and National Ambient Air Quality Standards (NAAQS) and that air pollution is the cause of a public health crisis in the entire country (Dahiya, Myllyvirta, and Sivalingam 2017: 1).

MAIN IDEAS OF ECOLOGISM

That we live in an environmental crisis is no longer seriously disputed, despite the fact that several powerful corporations and very rich individuals continue to fund campaigns and media denials of climate change; among these are the American fossil-fuel billionaires, the Koch brothers, who have donated nearly $80 billion to bodies which deny climate change (Union of Concerned Scientists n.d.; Greenpeace n.d.). In recent times, the problem was first brought to global attention in 1962, when Rachel Carson's book *Silent Spring* was published; the book focused on the damage which our increased use of pesticides and other chemicals in agriculture was doing to human life.

Since then, a very great amount of work has been done on what we now call climate change; as human activity is the major causal factor here, the process has also been called anthropogenic climate change or human-induced climate change. These terms are all consistent with a key principle in ecologism, namely that human life has to be understood as part of the whole system of all life. Ecologists have often criticised or rejected other ideologies for placing humans at the centre of their theories and therefore neglecting the impact of human activity on the planet; they have also criticised many other ideologies for ignoring limits to production and consumption, or for assuming that there are no limits to what we can produce and consume. For example, in view of our current dependence on petroleum products and other fossil fuels, what are we going to do when we have used all these up? At present, we have no apparent alternative source of energy for the uses to which we put petroleum and its derivatives; these derivatives include plastics and other polymers.

Ecologists, then, reject theories which are anthropocentric; these put humans at the centre of their respective analyses. Instead, ecologists argue, we need an ecocentric perspective, one which sees life as an interconnected whole, in which the various elements are also interdependent. This replacement of anthropocentrism, or human-centred outlooks, by ecocentrism is a principle running through the main ides of ecologism. These are:

- Ecology
- Holism
- Sustainability
- Self-actualisation

Ecology

This has developed as a branch of biology, and its basic principle is that all forms of life, whether plants or animals, depend on systems of living and non-living things. These systems are called ecosystems, and examples would be a pond, a forest, or a field. Ecosystems are not, however, closed systems. Ponds and lakes are often fed by other sources such as rivers or underground watercourses, and these are also warmed by the sun. According to ecology, ecosystems have an inherent tendency towards equilibrium or homoeostasis, and when left to themselves they are self-correcting or self-regulating; the term 'balance of nature' seems to cover both ideas.

Yet such concepts raise other problems. For example, many natural processes take too long a time for us to be sure that they have a natural tendency towards equilibrium, and other large-scale events such as violent storms or earthquakes can make it impossible for us to tell whether or not any one ecosystem would have regulated itself over a period of time. Secondly, ecosystems often interact with other ecosystems in very complex ways; a poor monsoon can mean that rivers carry much less by way of nutrients into the sea than they otherwise would, and ocean life is therefore affected—with consequent effects on local ecosystems, such as particular species of fish and their food chain, and so on. Ecology has, however, become a very substantial and varied field of research, and has contributed greatly to scientific knowledge.

Holism

Holism involves a rejection of exploitative attitudes towards the natural world, that is, of attitudes which see nature as no more than an economic resource for human use. Holistic thinkers also reject those philosophic or scientific approaches which regard the whole of nature as a machine, the workings of which can be identified and then controlled to serve human purposes. They particularly attribute those kinds of instrumental views to the French philosopher René Descartes (1596–1650) and to Isaac Newton (1642–1727), despite the fact that Newton spent much of his time in the study of divinity. Among the particular areas of Descartes' work which holists criticise would be his separation of the mind and the body, his system of two-dimensional mapping, and his conception of logical reasoning; Newton's ideas of straight-line motion, frictionless surfaces, and mathematical explanations, or explanations using analytical mathematics, of all mechanics would also be a problem for holists.

We must remember, however, that holism does not require us to reject all science or anything like it. For example, many areas of medicine have long recognised the importance of diet, occupation, social contexts, and customs and habits as essential elements in both treatment and longer-term healthcare. In addition, holistic thinkers can point to developments within the physical sciences themselves, such as the demonstration in relativistic physics that acceleration and retardation affect the speed of time when that is measured in the respective frames of reference of the observer and the observed.

Holistic ecologists, however, have often gone much further, arguing for example that religions such as Hinduism, Taoism, and Zen Buddhism regard all things whether living or not as part of a divine creation (Heywood 2007: 263). Some green thinkers make no distinction between the animate and the inanimate, and even see all things as being alive. James Lovelock, perhaps the best-known proponent of such a theory, calls this the Gaia hypothesis, after the Greek word for the Earth (our word 'geology' also has the same source); Lovelock, a biophysicist, holds that the Earth is an intelligent living system, which will respond to changes humans cause to it and will even punish us if we cause too much harm to it (Lovelock 1989). Lovelock rightly points out that this is not a new kind of theory in the sciences, and that James Hutton, often regarded as the founder of modern geology, likened the Earth to a superorganism (Lovelock 1989). The theory may not be as far-fetched as it might seem to be at first sight; for example, the sun has warmed up by over 25 per cent since life is thought to have begun on Earth, but the composition of the Earth's atmosphere has hardly changed at all, and there is a case for saying that human activity has affected the atmosphere more than solar warming has done (Heywood 2007: 263–64).

Sustainability

It is here that ecologism goes beyond analysis and criticism and offers prospective solutions or ways of proceeding. These start by rejecting the idea of infinitely increasing consumption and affluence. Instead, sustainability theorists remind us starkly that we are rapidly destroying many of the resources or natural capital which we are exploiting to support our current ways of life, including economic production. This has been called the tragedy of the commons, meaning that unlimited access to resources which seem to be available to all has a devastating collective impact on those resources. We have already noted the effects of pollution; another serious problem has been the destruction of forests for logging or—as in the case of Brazil—for the creation of grassland so that cattle can be reared for commercial meat exports, mainly to the United States, Russia, and China. In Brazil, close monitoring by environmental activists has led to better enforcement of legal controls and to some replanting of forests which had been cut down (Richardg 2014).

Sustainability therefore requires that we use only renewable and replaceable materials and resources, and that we actively replace and renew whatever we use. This could mean abandoning the use of fossil fuels altogether, because we cannot replace them. Like holism, the idea of sustainability amounts to the rejection of an entire economic tradition, according to which individuals are motivated to maximise their own utility, particularly in financial terms. According to sustainability theory, we can survive only if we recognise that we are part of a very complex biosphere, and if we ensure that our actions do not upset or destroy the balance of the biosphere (Heywood 2007: 267).

That means we need a completely different philosophy of economics, and in fact proposals for alternatives have been made for almost a century now, not least by scientists. The physicist Frederick Soddy, who discovered isotopes, argued from 1922 onwards that there were physical limits to growth, as well as ethical limits in that beyond a point, GDP growth would not be worth whatever it displaced, presumably meaning people as well as environmental assets and features (Lindley 2015). The economist J. C. Kumarappa held that exchange must include human values, and Herman Daly saw the economy as a 'wholly-owned subsidiary of the environment'; we need to limit throughput because of its high external costs, and to employ more people, presumably instead of replacing them with machines; Daly also advocated an incomes policy (Lindley 2015). The economist Nicholas Georgescu-Roegen opposed weapons production or war production; he called his approach bioeconomics and argued in favour of organic agriculture together with the use of solar energy or nuclear fusion energy; another economist, Joan Martinez-Alier, holds that economic sustainability requires social justice (Lindley 2015; Gowdy and Mesner 1998). Matthis Wackernagel, a qualified engineer, and William Rees, a professor of public policy, devised the term 'ecological footprint', which has gained increasingly wide use (Lindley 2015).

Perhaps the most famous figure in this area is E. F. Schumacher, who argued in his 1973 book *Small is Beautiful* that production needs to be reorganised; in addition to creating goods and services, it must also create social bonds which encourage cooperation and overcome egocentrism. This, which also has an anarchist element, runs completely counter to mainstream economics by recognising a spiritual dimension in economic activity, and it has been called Buddhist economics (Lindley 2015; Heywood 2007: 268). Today, some of the things Soddy and Kumarappa said may seem almost prescient, but mainstream economic theory—almost all of it classical or neoliberal—seems not to have responded to the challenges environmental economics poses; this is probably because the latter rejects or shows the problems in one of the central conceptions in classical economics, namely, the idea that we are all rational calculators of our self-interest and apparently little else.

If Schumacher is right, then it would not be enough to continue producing and consuming more and more but to do that more slowly. Instead, we would need to accept that the current idea of economic growth is both misconceived and deadly dangerous, because it ignores or cannot accommodate the idea of what we shall do when our finite resources run out. According to Schumacher and his followers, we need to return to much smaller communities, to revive craft skills, to consume less, and, above all, to restore and replenish all the resources we consume. Sections of certain Green parties—for example, in Germany—hold to this view in designing their policies.

Environmental Ethics

A range of moral theories underlies ecologists' challenges to the dominant economic theories. The main theme here is that we have to think about the effect our actions will have on the biosphere not only today but in the future; it means thinking of generations yet unborn and of doing all we can to ensure that animal and plant species will survive into the future.

This kind of approach has been called environmental ethics; it is a form of deep ecology, and encompasses all of life on the planet, over a very long and perhaps indefinite period. This is also a form of biocentric equality, because according to it we humans are neither superior to other species nor privileged in any way; Arne Næss says all living beings have an 'equal right to live and blossom' (Næss 1990: 28). In practice this would mean, for example, abandoning monocropping, in which we grow single or dominant crops, sometimes over very large areas, because these endanger and sometimes destroy biodiversity. Similarly, we would have to stop introducing non-native species of plants and animals into particular environments, both in view of the evidence we already have and because we cannot predict the outcome when we do introduce such species.

Self-actualisation

The rejection of the dominant economic and political models also raises philosophic questions about the conceptions of human nature involved. According to most, if not all, ecologist theories, our whole idea of human development is dangerously unbalanced, in that we have what looks like an unlimited capacity for technical knowledge or knowhow, but almost no answers to questions of why we do the things we do and why we live the lives we lead.

This in turn has led many ecologists to propose wide-ranging theories of how best we must live in relation to one another and to the natural environment. For some ecologists, elements in Buddhism and other Eastern philosophies are the source of the idea that humans are part of a wider reality, a single whole made up of all other humans and all other living things, even the entire universe. This may sound vast or far-fetched, but such thinking could have significant effects on what we do; for example, scientific research may have to investigate wider effects on animate and inanimate things, and we would have to consider the likely environmental effects of new policies or technologies before rushing them into production or service. The value of the idea of self-actualisation may well lie in its critique of almost all our current ideologies and economic systems, both for the environmental damage they cause and for the ways they restrict and even crush other ideas of what it is to be human.

ECOLOGISM AND POLITICS

Many ecologists reject conventional ideologies, but others draw upon existing ideologies or embody some of those in order to devise ideas of how to treat the natural environment better, and thereby create better lives for all of us. Needless to say, existing ideologies express very different kinds of concerns and policies over the environment.

Fascist and Right-wing Ecologism

It is no surprise that fascist movements have often asserted a form of explicit ecologism. As we saw in Chapter 1, early twentieth-century ecologists were disturbed by the rapid industrialisation that had taken place in the preceding century. That process had caused huge social upheaval and had transformed entire societies; it had created very large industrial cities and had caused terrible pollution, and had also abolished what fascists saw as the stabilities of the earlier agricultural order.

In response, former peasant leaders like Walther Darré strongly supported the German Youth Movement in the 1930s. Darré was Hitler's minister of agriculture from 1933 to 1942, and combined a theory of Nordic racial superiority with an idealised vision of rural life. The result was a form of blood and soil theory which was thoroughly fascist; indeed it was Darré who coined the phrase 'blood and soil'. Similar ideas of closeness to nature and the land have reappeared in contemporary environmentalist movements, though most of the people involved today would probably try to ensure that their thinking was free of fascistic implications or undertones.

Conservative Ecologism

In many ways a conservative outlook goes well with a commitment to ecologism. Such an outlook involves caution about rapid change or change based on grand theories, lest the apparent solution to a problem turn out to be worse than the problem itself. For example, rapid industrialisation created pollution, degraded the environment, and caused social rootlessness when it happened in Europe. Conservative ecologism therefore requires that we literally conserve rather than destroy. For example, new techniques in mechanised farming may give much greater short-term yields, but it usually also needs larger fields, which means farmers need to destroy existing hedgerows—but that in turn can accelerate the loss of topsoil through wind erosion; wheel tracks in fields can also contribute to erosion (Boardman 2013).

Conservative ecologism, however, faces the same problems that we have seen in conservatism as a whole, in particular those of how to reconcile the operation of market forces with the desire to conserve. For example, tax reductions for ecologically sound or sustainable methods in business would be typically conservative measures, and some capitalist businesses are starting to recognise that their long-term profitability can only be ensured in the context of environmentally sound practice (Heywood 2007: 273). Eco-conservative economics, however, gives us no yardstick for deciding which market-driven changes to accept and which to reject or resist; we could do that only if we were sure about the sources and origins of our traditional practices and institutions—but that would involve just the kind of close examination of social and political history that conservatism generally eschews.

Secondly, market-type solutions have their own problems. For example, emissions trading schemes such as those agreed in the 1997 Kyoto Protocol, or carbon-trading schemes, enable wealthy countries to buy poorer or less industrialised countries' pollution quotas and then to carry on polluting. Similarly, imposing fines on countries or businesses which damage the environment—also called the 'polluter pays' principle—is consistent with eco-conservative philosophy, but the first problem here is that such damage can take a long time to emerge, and that the activity which causes it can continue for a long time before we see the damage. The second problem is that some—if not most—environmental damage is irreversible. We simply do not know if we can completely clean up many of the forms of pollution and other damage we have caused, and in any case, it would be impossible to revive animal or plant species which we have rendered extinct. Thirdly, market competition can mean that businesses which implement environmentally sound practices could lose short-term profits and incur shareholder wrath if their competitors carried on as before.

Ecosocialism

Ecosocialism, or socialist ecologism, starts with the argument that capitalism is inherently destructive of the environment, because for capitalism human labour power and the natural environment are no more than resources to be exploited for profit, or more precisely, for surplus value. Many successful Green politicians too, started as members of far-Left or other Left groups in their younger days.

The relation between socialism and ecologism is nevertheless a complex one, even if for both ideologies capitalism is the main problem. To start with, socialist alternatives are often expressed in terms of increasing production and consumption. These are undoubtedly powerful messages in view of the increasing inequalities and spreading mass poverty we face all round the world, not least since the financial collapse of 2007–9. Similar issues arise among governments; India and China, for example, have succeeded in gaining global recognition of the injustice involved in the claim that developing countries must deny themselves the benefits of industrialisation and mechanisation. This of course poses enormous challenges to the domestic systems in developing countries as well, and the link between environmental degradation and poverty is well established (Khoday and

Perch 2012). There is, however, no possibility whatever that all the seven billion people currently on the planet could consume energy and natural resources on the same scale as the United States does.

Secondly, the ecological record of the major state-socialist and communist countries—namely, the Soviet Union and China—is disastrous, as they took an economic approach so instrumental that the economist Richard D. Wolff has called them state-capitalist and not state-socialist systems (Wolff 2012). Conceptually, however, arguments for an affinity between ecologism and socialism have a point. Marx recognised the environmental damage capitalism causes, and more recently Andrew Collier has developed an account of this affinity (Collier 2004: 150–62). Marx was always alert to the damage capitalism by its very nature does to the environment, and he says that we remain in 'continuous interchange' with nature—but he adds that estranged or alienated labour subordinates our productive lives into no more than means for our existence (Marx 1844: 31). Marx might, however, have been more of a shallow ecologist than a deep one, as he saw the environment as our environment rather than something of intrinsic worth, and he seems not to have considered humans to be part of an overarching natural system; nevertheless, a capitalist outlook sees the environment as just another object for exploitation (Collier 2004: 31–32, 159–61).

We must remember that many very eminent campaigners would reject the application of labels to what they do, but that some of the things they do or advocate are identifiable in the broad categories I am describing here. The categories are nevertheless only guidelines. For example, one of India's most famous environmental campaigners, Vandana Shiva, rejects the suggestion that she is an ecofeminist, because she considers that the label is too neat and excludes other significant concerns of hers—for example, her rejection of the Hindu caste system and other forms of religious exclusion (Shiva 2003, cited in Barsamian 2003). Shiva also, rightly, points to her long record of struggle against the monopolist nature of intellectual property rights and against biopiracy, a notable example of which was the failed attempt by the US corporation W. R. Grace and the US Department of Agriculture to patent an antifungal product derived from the neem tree (BBC 2005). The point here is that many successful environmental campaigners do what they do without necessary making explicit commitments to ideological positions. Those who do address theoretical or other such issues in relation to the environment, nevertheless, often articulate highly interesting positions. For example, Rupert Read has argued that ecologism is the 'true heir' to both socialism and conservatism (Read 2013).

Ecofeminism

Ecofeminism is a distinct strain or strand of feminism, and raises significant challenges to our current systems of politics and economics, in particular to patriarchy (Heywood 2007: 276–77). The main argument here is that men and male-designed and male-dominated institutions are the major threat to nature. The sexual division of labour—which is not solely the result of capitalism—enables men to dominate women and the natural environment, and one implication is that if we put an end to patriarchy we would end both those forms of exploitation.

That set of arguments is based on an assumption that the differences between men and women are not so great as to make the required equalisation impossible and therefore a misconception. One strain of ecofeminism has it that male and female humans are radically different, and that women are naturally, perhaps inherently, closer to nature because they bear and suckle babies; according to some versions of this theory, women find personal fulfilment when they act in accordance with nature rather than against it (Heywood 2007: 277).

That could be a form of the argument from biology, which we encountered in Chapter 2, on conservatism. Its supporters have often noted that many ancient cultures and religions saw nature and the Earth as female deities; today, the Gaia hypothesis also does this. Politically and socially, a society based on an essentialist form of ecofeminism would be one in which caring, nurturing, and sustaining the natural environment replaced or at least took precedence over what that form of ecofeminism considers the male tendency towards competition and hierarchy.

Ecoanarchism

Many anarchist thinkers have taken environmental matters very seriously; Peter Kropotkin was one, as was William Morris, one of the early figures in the cooperative movement. More recently, Murray Bookchin has argued that ecological balance is the best foundation for social stability (Heywood 2007: 275). Substantial evidence could be adduced for this, such as the wars that occur over natural resources for commercial exploitation; the terrible genocide in Rwanda in 1993–94, and the protracted wars in the neighbouring Congo over coltan, an essential ore for computers and mobile phones, are only a few of the many examples thereof. The illegal United States-led invasion of Iraq in 2003 was acknowledged by the British government's former chief scientific officer, Sir David King, to have been a resource war about oil—but the interviewer to whom he told this in 2009, James Randerson, did not follow up the point, and did not respond when David Edwards and David Cromwell asked him why he had not done so (Edwards and Cromwell 2012: 113–15). Similarly, severe climatic events such as prolonged drought or very severe heatwaves caused by global warming (which could also cause very severe winters) might cause substantial migrations as very large numbers of people find that their immediate environments cannot support them any longer. These could in turn cause severe political tensions.

In contrast, ecoanarchist thinkers hold that when left to itself, nature will find its own balance, just as they think human societies will when freed of the oppression and domination they experience under conventional forms of state and government. Another affinity between anarchism and ecologism lies in the commitment to decentralisation, to smaller communities, and to local participation in public matters. These would imply a life or lives led in a much closer or immediate relation to nature than is available to us in today's societies (Heywood 2007: 276).

Ecoanarchists may nevertheless differ from other ecologist or environmentalist movements because they reject the idea of the state. Many Green movements regard the state as the only body powerful enough to implement environmentally sound laws and policies, and seek an active role for it. One of their main criticisms of the state is not that it is the state but that in its present form it is suborned by very powerful business interests or other groups into colluding with global environmental damage if not destruction.

ECOLOGISM TODAY

This has much wider public support than it is generally acknowledged to have. The larger political parties, especially on the Left, have adopted various Green policies relatively routinely, and in Germany the Green Party leads the governing coalition (with the Social Democratic Party, the SPD) in several of the provincial assemblies or *Länder*; this is particularly important in Germany, because the federal upper house or *Bundesrat* is made up of members deputed from the *Länder*, and under the German Constitution this chamber can approve or reject any legislation proposed by the federal government. In France, the Greens and the Socialist Party did so well in the 2011 cantonal elections that they formed the governing coalition in several of the 96 *départements*, which constitute the third tier of the French state; as in Germany, the national upper house (in France, the Senate) is elected from a range of lower-level assemblies, and therefore got its first-ever broad-Left majority.

At the national level, the German Greens led the way by winning 28 seats in the federal lower house, the *Bundestag*, in the 1983 general election. They won 47 seats in 2002 and 55 in 2005, becoming coalition partners with the SPD in both the resulting governments. The former co-chairman of their parliamentary faction, Joschka Fischer, was Germany's foreign minister and vice chancellor to Chancellor Gerhard Schröder from 1998 to 2005. In France, in 2011, a Green alliance with the Socialist Party and other Left groups won a majority in the Senate for the first time since the Fifth Republic was founded in 1958. In the United Kingdom, the Greens attracted widespread attention by winning 15 per cent of the vote in the European Parliament elections in 1989, and they won their first seat in the House of Commons when Caroline Lucas was elected for the Brighton Pavilion constituency in 2010. We need to note, however, that the proportional or hybrid electoral systems used in almost all Scandinavian and continental European countries—as well as Scotland and Wales—give Green parties a far better chance of effective representation than the simple majority system used in British and Indian general elections.

In everyday matters, in almost all industrial countries households have long been required by their local councils to separate waste for recycling by the councils; for example, glass, paper and cardboard, and recyclable plastics, all have to be separated by householders for separate collection by councils. Councils also provide separate facilities into which people can put different kinds of household waste, and many now have separate facilities for the disposal of old computers and mobile phones, or e-waste, which contains highly toxic and dangerous substances. Practice, however, varies, and in the United Kingdom some councils take only a limited range of plastics for recycling. The rest may well go into very expensive and possibly environmentally harmful landfills.

Public authorities in many democracies are also now required to prepare environmental impact assessments for all projects above certain threshold values, and certainly for all larger public works, but public awareness of this fact is limited, and access to the reports may be restricted under the laws of various countries. In at least one case, which is given in the exercise accompanying this chapter, the public authority concerned submitted an assessment prepared for an area on the opposite coast of the country.

Those kinds of measures, although a good thing, still fall far short of deep ecologism, which would require wholesale economic changes and is bitterly resisted by powerful corporate interests, who in many countries are overwhelmingly the biggest source of politicians' election campaign funds. The mainstream news media too, are overwhelmingly corporate-owned, and consistently underreport or suppress the seriousness of the global environmental crisis. This has been called the ultimate media betrayal (Edwards and Cromwell 2006: 154–71).

Other developments, however, may well be occurring out of sight of the news media. The field of environmental economics is expanding, and some statements of it recognise the issues it poses for existing economic orthodoxies; for example, the idea of externalities which lie outside any one economic activity or transaction is a problem, because everything we do has some impact on the environment, and yet in an ecological sense there are no such things as externalities.

A strong argument for this, which includes excellent evidence to support her detailed rejection of one of the main tenets of orthodox economics, namely the idea that we are rational economic beings, has been put by Kate Raworth. In the same book, Raworth goes on to propose a radically revised economics which recognises the interconnected environmental effects of all human activity (Raworth 2017).

Other kinds of analytical methods include environmental audits, in which the energy uses, or greenhouse-gas emissions, of any activity or policy are identified, just as the financial costs might be. These can be quite shocking, and online systems exist whereby we can calculate the particular environmental costs of, say, journeys by air and the like. Some notable authorities have produced sobering analyses. In some industrial countries, the costs of running a car fall steadily while public transport gets more and more expensive; yet even coach travel, a form of road transport using the internal combustion engine, could be used to such great effect in the United Kingdom—a comparatively small country in global terms—that every coach would not only take 50 cars off the road but reduce highway or motorway car traffic by a mile's length of cars, and would carry up to 13 times the number of people at any one time (Monbiot 2007: 149–50). Another factor often ignored in standard economic analyses, presumably because economists can define it as an externality, is the cost of road congestion and delays; the Royal Academy of Engineering estimated the cost in the United Kingdom alone at £15 billion per year in 2005 (cited in Monbiot 2007: 152–53).

Any number of such analyses can be found, but the governments we elect seem as incapable as ever of reaching agreement on what could rapidly become a global catastrophe, if we are not in the middle of one already. Conceptually, the challenge remains: we almost certainly need a completely new metaphysics of value if we are to avert that catastrophe. Few or none of us would survive it.

Conceptual Problems

Campaigners and campaigning groups are very well aware of the differences in their various approaches, and several have produced wider statements of our predicament and what we need to do about it. Substantial conceptual or philosophic problems, however, do arise, and some of these have been clearly outlined. For example, Andrew Vincent points out that the Green agenda goes beyond human concerns, in contrast to the customary concerns political theory shows, such as government, justice, the state, and so on (Vincent 2001: 183).

Vincent states the familiar distinction between shallow and deep ecology, which he calls ecocentrism and anthropocentrism, respectively. Even within these, we find differences. One strand of ecocentrism sees nature as having intrinsic value and as being a comprehensive system, while another sees our having a sound relationship with nature as requiring a change in moral sensibility. This is the result of what Vincent here calls a mature psychology rather than of our being convinced by moral arguments or obeying moral imperatives (Vincent 2001: 195 n.7). One implication is that we need to develop an entirely different sense of ourselves within the environment.

Anthropocentric approaches themselves vary considerably too. Deep anthropocentrism is indifferent to nature, and lies outside Green arguments, though Green activists and indeed all who are concerned about the environment would no doubt be directly opposed to it. In contrast, what Vincent calls pliant anthropocentrism introduces environmental concerns into the existing body of political thought (Vincent 2001: 184). The aim of pliant anthropocentrism would therefore be to devise a conception of being human which is appropriately alert and sensitive to the natural environment and our impact on it; we would be human-centred without being instrumental towards nature (Vincent 2001: 184). It hardly needs saying that both sets of approaches see humanity as living inseparably from nature, though the concepts of interdependence vary greatly across both main approaches.

As Vincent shows, the concept of nature is crucial to this whole issue. One concept takes nature to be, so to speak, driven by patterns, or perhaps by an inner logic, which is distinct from human action. Another sees humans as being a part of nature. This latter view raises the problem that if we are fully within nature as a part of it, then the process resulting from our existence and our actions, including the environmental damage and degradation we cause, are themselves part of nature; this implies that we should not do anything about our current conduct towards the natural environment. The tension here is between reducing human culture to a natural phenomenon and anthropomorphising nature so that we see it mainly or even only through our concerns and purposes (Vincent 2001: 187–93).

Vincent concludes that Green political theory is close to incoherence, but the global environmental crisis is still very much the case. If there is some light coming through the smog, it might be found in the increasingly direct approaches being taken by some of the industrial or formerly industrial countries, particularly some in western Europe and Scandinavia; I have mentioned some of these above. The change in sensibility that Vincent and others discuss may already be taking place.

CHAPTER 7: ECOLOGISM

Extension Exercise

Read this text and do the exercises set on it:

Monbiot, George. 2014. 'The Pricing of Everything'. *Guardian*, 24 July. Originally SPERI Annual Lecture, Sheffield Political Economy Research Institute, University of Sheffield. http://www.monbiot.com/2014/07/24/the-pricing-of-everything

1. Specify the three main problems Monbiot identifies and—in your own words—summarise one example he gives of each problem.
2. Specify Monbiot's proposals for addressing those problems.
3. Read this article:
   Glasson, Ben. 2012. 'Gentrifying Climate Change: Ecological Modernisation and the Cultural Politics of Definition'. *M/C Journal* 15 (3).
   http://www.journal.media-culture.org.au/index.php/mcjournal/article/view/501
   Highlight similar points the author makes to those Monbiot makes.
4. Is the position Monbiot criticises a form of shallow or deep ecology?

Further Reading

Vincent, Andrew. 1993. 'The Character of Ecology'. *Environmental Politics* 2 (2): 248–76.

Baxter, Brian. 2000. *Ecologism: An Introduction*. Washington DC: Georgetown University Press.

Read, Rupert. 2013. 'How Ecologism is the True Heir of Both Socialism and Conservatism'. *LSE British Politics and Policy Blog*, 22 June. http://blogs.lse.ac.uk/politicsandpolicy/how-ecologism-is-the-true-heir-of-both-socialism-and-conservatism

8

CHAPTER

Poststructuralism and Postmodernism

Poststructuralism and postmodernism are terms which have had very widespread use in the last half century or so. As has happened in the case of Marxism, however, these terms are very often used without much knowledge of their origins, their specific details, and their implications. I shall focus on the main figures in both, starting with poststructuralism, and try to show what the work of those thinkers might mean for us.

POSTSTRUCTURALISM AND DECONSTRUCTION

Poststructuralism may well be the more accessible of the two outlooks. It arose primarily in France in the late 1950s, in response to certain methods which were then widely used in social sciences, such as anthropology and sociology, and which were often called structuralist. For example, between 1947 and 1950 the American sociologist G. P. Murdock investigated 250 different cultures around the world with a view to showing that all societies had families as part of their social structure (Murdock 1965: 1–6). Marxism has its own structuralist forms, which are particularly associated with Louis Althusser, even though Althusser's later work showed significant departures from his earlier thinking, which was based on the principle that all societies are decisively shaped by their respective economic structures. Among other social scientists who did not conduct empirical studies, forms of structuralism were common for several decades in the twentieth century. The American sociologist Talcott Parsons' work is structuralist in form, and one of his major works, which was first published in 1937, is called *The Structure of Social Action*.

The strongest challenge to structuralism in the last half century was launched in 1966 by the French philosopher Jacques Derrida, whose lecture at Johns Hopkins University that year bore the title 'Structure, Sign and Play in the Discourse of the Human Sciences'. The lecture was a direct critique of the French anthropologist Claude Lévi-Strauss, whose work in ethnology was world-famous and who had written several books based on a structuralist method. One of those was on what Lévi-Strauss saw as a taboo on incest, which he considered a ban common to all societies and therefore a structural element. Today, following the publication of large numbers of research studies on child sexual abuse all round the world—with much of the evidence being that this is carried out within the family—we would probably test Lévi-Strauss's conclusions much more rigorously, but his book *Elementary Structures of Kinship*, which was published in 1949, was typical of its time.

Therefore, Derrida's 1966 lecture had a great impact on the humanities and, later, the social sciences. Derrida's main argument is that structural explanations are incoherent; according to him, what he calls the centre of any structure—by which he seems to mean the organising principle or idea of a structural explanation—is not itself part of the structure (Derrida 1978: 278–79). Derrida goes on to say that philosophers have replaced one such structure by another as they have created one system of ideas after another, with the centre taking different names in different explanatory systems; examples are essence, existence, substance, consciousness, God, and so on (Derrida 1978: 279–80).

The argument, however, goes even further, as Derrida concludes that the centre of an explanatory system is what he calls a non-presence, not a thing or a place (a locus) but a function which takes different names in different systems. Here Derrida uses concepts drawn from the French linguist Ferdinand de Saussure, who called names signifiers and objects or things the signified. If the central idea of an explanatory system cannot be signified, that is, if there is nothing to be named, then the term 'signifier' also ceases to have any use. The result is that all explanations become systems not of signs but of discourse, by which Derrida seems to mean social or cultural fields (Derrida 1978: 282–84).

This clearly undermines all structural explanations in the humanities and social sciences, and Derrida points out that Lévi-Strauss shows some recognition of this. In *The Elementary Structures of Kinship*, Lévi-Strauss sees nature as universal and even spontaneous, and social structures as varying from one culture to another. He acknowledges, however, that the prohibition of incest is both cultural and universal, because according to him that prohibition occurs in all cultures (Derrida 1978: 282–84).

Yet Lévi-Strauss does not abandon the nature/culture distinction, and uses it as a heuristic device or an aid to investigation even while he is aware that it may be incoherent. He even goes on to say that founding or foundational myths in any culture are themselves transformations of other myths in the same societies (Lévi-Strauss 1949, cited in Derrida 1978: 286–88). Furthermore, this seems not to matter to Lévi-Strauss, who likens the resulting ethnographic or anthropological analysis to the work of a linguist who can work out the grammar of a language without needing a complete record of all the words that have ever been used in that language.

Yet if the idea of an identifiable central idea within any structure collapses, then so does the idea of that or indeed any structure of ideas. That need not stop our investigations in the humanities or social sciences, but it does mean that what we say in those investigations has a very different status from the one we thought it had. According to Derrida, what we say does not have to refer to things which are, so to speak, present. The signifier does not have to refer to a signified, and meaning becomes a matter of the position of what we say in relation to other utterances in a field of discourse. This kind of step is radical enough, even though Derrida's argument is in part a response to empiricist theories of knowledge, according to which all knowledge is ultimately gained from experience (Culler 1997; Hume 1969: 52). Derrida then went even further, because from then on he held that the humanities had to proceed by identifying the internal divisions and fragmentations in all texts; texts themselves have no identifiable centre or core (Barry 2002: 68).

Deconstruction

According to Derrida, the move away from structuralism had already taken place by the time he lectured on it in 1966; he calls the move a rupture or an event, and examples of the move are decolonisation, civil rights movements, a new wave of feminism, and the like. The approach which Derrida says replaces structuralism is one he calls deconstruction. This does not mean dismantling something or destroying it; instead it means identifying the multiple themes, elements, and inheritances within a text, so that we attain a richer sense of it. This can also mean learning about what has been left out of a text. For example, William Shakespeare's play *Julius Caesar* makes no mention of the possibility that that Brutus was Caesar's illegitimate son; the play remains a great work, but concluding that Caesar might have been Brutus's father will almost certainly make us see the play very differently.

Deconstructing a text, then, does not mean deconstructing it in the way we might dismantle a machine. It does mean, however, identifying the potentially indefinite range of things that went into the creation of the text. These may be biographical details of the writer's life, or things they experienced, or other texts or works which their own works resemble, or which they seem to evoke—possibly without even realising that themselves—or events in the world at the time they were writing, and so on.

This has two main consequences. The first is that the reader is in a sense creating the text by engaging closely with it. The second is that almost anything can be relevant to the reader's engagement with the text, that is, to their reading of the text; so no final or definitive reading of the text is possible. In the stronger version of poststructuralism, this means that reality itself is textual. No reading of the text can transcend the text by moving *towards* something, towards what Saussure would have called a signified, outside the text. Derrida says, famously and bafflingly, 'There is nothing outside of the text' (Derrida 1976: 158). In his original French text, he writes, *'Il n'y a pas de hors-texte.'*

For a long time, Derrida's writings were much more favourably regarded in English-speaking literary studies than in philosophy. This may well have been because scholars of literature are usually very accustomed to analysing literary works by making appropriate reference to biographical detail, historical or political events, other works or genres of work, and so on. They are also very accustomed to showing that particular words, or passages, or whole works, can be read in different ways—in effect, to showing that the meanings of texts are not fixed or frozen. Secondly, analyses of works of literature—or other aesthetic creations—are not usually themselves works of literature. In philosophy, on the other hand, when we analyse a work we create another philosophic work.

Problems in Poststructuralism

It is easy to forget that Derrida's main target is Saussure's theory of linguistics and the work derived thence, particularly Lévi-Strauss's structural anthropology or ethnology. Secondly, Derrida writes throughout in language which is both highly abstract and rarely settled; it is often fluid and allusive, if not elusive (Barry 2002: 64–65). This makes Derrida and most of his followers very difficult to read, but that in turn can cause us to forget another and much more serious problem in Derrida's work.

That problem is that nobody has ever seriously claimed that any text is a self-sealed entity, or that other factors such as biographical or other issues must be excluded from our reading of a literary text or other aesthetic work; indeed scholars of literature have almost always included such factors in their analyses of particular works or bodies of work. Secondly, structuralist theories themselves have never been immune to modification, revision or even abandonment. Thirdly, Derrida seems not to recognise that we need to show the pertinence or relevance of any wider factors we adduce in our analysis of a text. We need to show what effect, say, an event in the author's life, or a political or social event, or the weather, or anything else, had on the text.

The political implications of Derrida's form of poststructuralism are also far-reaching. He may well be right that in the mid-1950s the world was abandoning or had abandoned many seemingly permanent certainties. European imperial dominance had ended, and the post-war exposure of the Nazi programme of genocide had undermined the European sense of cultural and racial superiority that had developed during the age of empire. In the arts and architecture too, challenges to established conventions or systems had already had an impact, from atonal music through modern visual art to architecture (Barry 2002: 66–67).

Yet many of the changes were driven by demands for inclusion in many of the systems which characterised modernity, such as political independence, equal rights for men and women, and an end to racism and racial discrimination. The relevant movements were not movements for the abolition of political and social systems and structures, but for their expansion and improvement. Derrida did, in response to this kind of criticism, express some commitment to a broadly Leftish politics of emancipation. It is, however, far from clear how such a commitment can demonstrably follow from his major writings.

Michel Foucault

The other famous poststructuralist is Michel Foucault, who made his name with his three-volume *History of Sexuality*, in which he argued against the idea that sex is a natural phenomenon, a phenomenon which modern people have or claim to have liberated from periods of repression. Instead, Foucault argues, reducing sex to a single such concept obscures the great complexity of sex, that is, the combination of biological and anatomical elements, cultural practices and meanings, psychological factors, and so on, which are involved. This reduction also obscures the great variety in sexual practices and orientations among humans not only around the world but within what we might think of as single cultures (Culler 1997: 5–6). Foucault claimed to have been analysing the historical development of the idea of sexuality, but by doing so, he also showed why we need to be cautious, or even suspicious, when things are presented to us as natural phenomena, or as simply given (Culler 1997: 7).

This was a decisive moment in the development of Foucault's thinking; he came to see that what had been presented to us as a dichotomy or opposition between natural sexuality and social controls on it was instead a matter of complicity. According to him, social forces have even created the phenomenon they seek to control, namely human sexuality. This also means that apparent acts of rebellion, such as free-sex movements, are nevertheless still working within the terms set by the existing social forces.

Foucault goes on to argue in his later work that the whole of the history of ideas is a search for knowledge as a form of power. In his 1970 book *The Order of Things*, he says he cannot give an account of the transition between different historical periods and their respective systems of knowledge, such as the eighteenth-century move from classical thought to modern thought; so instead he focuses on the period he knows best, namely the modern one (Foucault 1970: xiii).

According to Foucault, the system of thought, or *episteme*, of the modern period gives humanity the central position, but Foucault adds that this centrality is illusory and that when the current *episteme* gives way to the next one, the modern idea of humanity will disappear 'like a face drawn in sand at the edge of the sea' (Foucault 1970: 387). Foucault says this also applies to history and the history of knowledge; as humans, we in our modern form are constituted by our *episteme*, by our field of discourse. Even though we might think of modern knowledge as being made up of permanent and universal structures and systems, Foucault tries to show that this way of thinking about knowledge is also illusory.

Foucault reserves his strongest criticism for the period he calls the Enlightenment, by which he seems to mean a modern or modernist project in which we subject everything to reason and attempt to ground the whole of human life on knowledge gained by rational inquiry. He puts this more strongly in his later book *The Archaeology of Knowledge*, in which he says the main result of that attempt is that we come to think of the Enlightenment as the progressive spread of ideas of universal validity (Foucault 1972: 138–40, 1987; Merquior 1985: 78; Sivaramakrishnan 1995: 33–34). For Foucault the key issue is therefore that of power, which he sees as the informing principle of all human thought and action; everything we do is an expression of the search for power.

Problems in Foucault's Work

To many scholars in the humanities and social sciences, Foucault's conception of power as the informing principle of all human conduct seemed to be as much of a comprehensive explanatory idea as Marx's insight into the way social structures are shaped by class seen in terms of production relations. Foucault's work, however, shows its own wide range of problems.

One obvious problem is that of the implied claim that a book (or any other artistic creation) is a self-contained entity. It is true that in the 1920s critics such as I. A. Richards used to present texts to students without the authors' names, in an attempt to free the students of preconceptions about the texts concerned, but as a general method of literary evaluation, this was fiercely disputed even when it was introduced (Barry 2002: 29–31). Although Richards and others like F. R. Leavis, the founders of what came to be called New Criticism, encouraged and inculcated the practice of reading texts closely, their methods have of course never been the sole approach to any aesthetic work, and it is not clear how important a target those methods need have been for Foucault.

The second problem is that of the tranquillity with which, according to Foucault, we occupy the already existing discourse. It is simply not credible that people lived in or occupied all previous states of affairs, or our present world, with no disquiet or disturbance at all. Even in the realm of philosophy and political thought, Foucault seems to have forgotten that Socrates so disturbed the Athenian order—or rather, the minds of those who held power in his time—that he was condemned to death and accepted the punishment. As for our own time, the claim that we are untroubled about our world is barely credible; it is nonsense.

Foucault's comparative neglect of the history of philosophy has further consequences. He explicitly takes the German philosopher Immanuel Kant to be the crowning or emblematic figure of the Enlightenment's spread of reason as the universal method for the acquisition of knowledge, but he seems to be unaware that Kant himself, equally explicitly, places clear limits on the scope of reason—and that Kant does so in order to make room for faith (Kant 1933: 29; Sivaramakrishnan 1995: 37–38). In addition, Foucault, apparently without realising it, re-enacts the much earlier series of exchanges between Kant and Hume, and he also fails to see that Kant clearly denies the possibility of a human self which transcends the particularity of time, space, and sense experience (Kant 1933: 135–69, 323–30, 380–83; Norris 1993: 77–78). This may be because Foucault never specifies sufficiently what he means by a transcendental self.

Power

Foucault seems to offer the idea of power as a universally explanatory concept, by arguing that the search for knowledge is an expression of the search for power. This can be very persuasive; we have gained an enormous amount of knowledge in the course of our attempts to control the world. Medical advances constitute an obvious example, as do advances in all applied sciences. Foucault, however, takes power to be an all-pervading principle or motivation, which means that we cannot tell if an action is motivated by the search for power or not. Even Foucault's account of power as a universal principle therefore becomes not an illuminating or liberating explanation but an attempt to exert power over us, that is, over his readers or listeners (Dews 1987: 166).

This too shows Foucault's lack of attention to a very substantial, indeed enormous, amount of previous work. Foucault criticises our Enlightenment-derived thought for taking the given at face value, but he neglects the fact that colossal advances in the sciences, and enormous changes in society, have occurred precisely because we have, so to speak, looked beneath the surface of things and have questioned established orders and practices. Secondly, Foucault makes no mention of Hegel, perhaps the greatest critic of Kant and a philosopher who argues in detail that the given is itself a created or constructed entity (Hegel 1979: 58–79). In sum, Foucault never shows why our existing uncertainties, methods of inquiry, and critiques are inadequate or insufficient (Sivaramakrishnan 1995). Perhaps above all, like Derrida, he seems to be unaware that he reasons at great length and in great detail in his attempt to convince us to abdicate reason and reasoning (MacIntyre 1990: 49–55). But we cannot reasoningly abdicate reasoning.

Political Activity

Like Derrida, Foucault came to see that his thinking could well imply that we must abdicate all political activity. Yet he was a committed political activist, and later in his life, he recognised that political activity requires a commitment to some form of publicly identifiable and binding truth, or at least a commitment to a space in which we can argue freely towards agreement on what to do and how to organise our societies. Foucault also recognised that the search for truth might result in political commitments of various kinds, but he never reconciled his various suggestions that politics is a matter of class conflict with his other arguments against any conscious formulation of aims and plans (Dews 1987: 144–70; Sivaramakrishnan 1995: 38).

Foucault's philosophic work, then, is riddled with gaps and incoherences; it is possible, if not likely, that he attained his intellectual status in the 1980s because his work was, like Derrida's, very warmly received in English-speaking departments of literary studies, and later in English-speaking anthropology and sociology.

POSTMODERNISM

Postmodernism has had a much wider impact on society than poststructuralism, which—insofar as it amounts to an ideology—has largely been a feature of the academic humanities. Postmodernism, in contrast, has been expressed in architecture, the visual arts, music, the theatre, and many other areas of life. Indeed there is a case for saying that postmodernism has been as much a part of contemporary life as it has been a way of thinking in the humanities. Postmodernism may therefore be more accessible through architecture and the arts than through its philosophic proponents, who if anything can be even harder to read than Derrida and Foucault.

In architecture, postmodernism has often been cited as a direct counter to modernism. In modernist architecture, form or shape was supposed to follow function, and modernism is associated with the use of new materials, such as reinforced concrete, steel, plate glass, and forms such as right angles and austere flat surfaces; some modernist architects set out to create buildings in accordance with the functions of modern industrial society, and designed skyscrapers, giant factory spaces, concrete apartment blocks, and so on. The work of the Bauhaus school, which flourished between the two world wars, is perhaps the most famous example of this kind of approach. Among the main modernist architects are Le Corbusier (whose real name was Charles-Édouard Jeanneret-Gris), Mies van der Rohe, Frank Lloyd Wright, and Oscar Niemeyer. Le Corbusier designed the centre of the Haryana state capital, Chandigarh, in the 1950s, and Niemeyer designed the Brazilian national capital, Brasilia. Le Corbusier pioneered the use of stilts or pilotis as supports for apartment blocks, and once said a house was a machine for living in.

In the visual arts, modernism is associated with, for example, cubism, in which objects and living beings are represented by cubes of different sizes and in different colours; Georges Braque was known for this. Abstract modernists often used severe right-angled shapes in different colours, sometimes separated by black borders of varying widths, as in the work of Piet Mondriaan (who later spelt his name Mondrian). A strong element of technique was involved, with Pablo Picasso, for example, going through several phases and using a great range of artistic techniques over his long working life, and with sculptors often adopting new steel-working technologies. Some of the artists involved, and their architect colleagues, had explicitly socialistic commitments; among the Russian constructivist sculptors was Vladimir Tatlin, whose most famous work is a steel frame supporting a revolving cylinder, cube, and cone, all made from glass. The work, nearly seven metres in height, was a monument to the Third International, and during the 1920s many of the constructivists conducted sessions for workers in the factories of the then-new Soviet Union. Among the Bauhaus architects, Hannes Meyer had had part of his upbringing in an orphanage and had served an apprenticeship as a stonemason; he was openly socialistic.

Modernism also appeared in the theatre and in music. In the 1920s, Arnold Schönberg introduced atonality, by discarding the idea of harmonic keys for the use of all twelve notes in the Western scale in any composition (though Schönberg was not by any means the first to use atonality in Western music), and plays by Samuel Beckett and Eugène Ionesco are notable for the starkness and minimalism of both their settings and their language. James Joyce's novel *Ulysses,* a much bigger work, it is often regarded as a major modernist creation.

The postmodernist challenge to these forms of creation relied primarily on the idea that form does not have to follow function; the shape of something does not have to be determined by its purpose, and in architecture a movement developed which made, for example, structural elements open to view; many contemporary airport buildings are examples of this. In the arts, the idea of systematic or coherent creation was replaced by the juxtaposition of elements from different styles and contexts. The theory is intellectually as difficult as poststructuralist theory, but postmodernism has been much more explicitly located in the political and historical context of the late twentieth century. The term 'postmodern' seems to have been used first by the French philosopher Jean-François Lyotard in the title of his 1979 book *The Postmodern Condition*, and the word 'postmodernism' may well have attained its intellectual status as a result of the American culture critic Fredric Jameson's book *Postmodernism, or, the Cultural Logic of Late Capitalism*, which was published in 1991; the work became almost the defining commentary on postmodernism.

According to Jameson, modernism shows a confidence in technical knowledge to improve the quality of society and of people's lives. Despite the fact that many modernists were egalitarians, critics of modernism saw modernism as inherently elitist and arrogant, with a reliance on technical or other experts to decide the layout and appearance of towns, cities, and houses. In literary studies, the New Criticism was also called elitist for excluding those who had not the educational background to engage in very close analysis of literary texts with no reference to anything but the texts. In addition, much modernist work is hard to engage with; the artwork is often totally abstract, the music often seems accessible only to trained musicians, and so on. Despite that, abstract sculptures and paintings became progressively more familiar in everyday life, especially in public spaces. Nevertheless, high modernism came to be associated with a wide gap between high culture and popular or mass culture.

Postmodernism, especially from the late 1980s onwards, posed several challenges to the dominance of modernism, but the movements in art that initiated the theoretical challenges may well have dated from 1962, when the term 'pop art' was coined to describe the use of images and materials from everyday life, advertising, and popular consumption and culture in artistic creations; Andy Warhol's work may well have been the most famous example of this kind of practice, and the critic Clement Greenberg thought the decline in modernist confidence started at that time (Pissarro 2009). Practitioners and followers rejected, in particular, the distinction between high culture and popular culture, and also rejected the idea that works of art had to be created within rules and conventions of, say, perspective, harmony, proportion, and the like. Once again, architecture provided the most visible or obvious rejection of modernism. Many architects abandoned any link between form and function, and many of them stopped concealing key structural elements of their buildings.

The new approaches were not confined to single buildings or complexes; giant transnational corporations started to set up very large offices in provincial towns, probably because land or rents were cheaper there, and in the world of work, old class divisions seemed to disappear as old industries vanished and were replaced by new forms of employment and business. These processes also started to undermine ideas of locality and neighbourhood, and the global spread of television—and more recently the phonecam and the Internet—created a new currency of the image, with the attendant risk that everything will become just an image or a simulacrum (Jameson 1991). What it might be a simulacrum of, however, becomes more and more of a problem; examples might well be found in the apparently universal availability of fast food, or the endless reproducibility of musical and other performances, often in multimedia formats.

Jameson is very clear about the ideological demands and difficulties we face as a result; analysts of the political Left and Right have both inveighed against postmodernism, but railing against postmodernism for undermining the apparent high seriousness of other explanations causes its own problems. In particular, we would then fail to devise a sufficiently serious response to postmodernism, by failing to see its historical location as a phenomenon which reinforces and intensifies the processes of late capitalism. We would also be at risk of failing to pay sufficient attention to the very aesthetic creations which might be understood as postmodern or even postmodernist. Marx, as Jameson reminds us here, took capitalism very seriously indeed.

Locating postmodernism as a historical phenomenon will of course be made all the more difficult because many of its theorists reject or attempt to undermine the idea of historical location itself, but much of postmodern architecture has a 'virtually unmediated relationship' with business in respect of commissions and land values, and is also dependent on multinational and transnational business (Jameson 1991). Secondly, the collapse of the distinction between high culture and mass culture conceals the fact that today's mass culture itself involves the instant commodification of aesthetic production, and potentially involves the instant commodification of all artistic creations. The system of production relations therefore requires all creators—all artists of all kinds—to produce more and more apparently new works, from books through movies to fashion, cars, and the smallest of lifestyle accessories, at what Jameson calls ever greater rates of turnover. In addition, institutional support in the form of foundations, grants, and corporate sponsorship is increasingly available for works produced in this system—but only in this system, and especially for successful artistic creators, or at least those who have gained popularity for any reason at all (Jameson 1991).

It is certainly true that postmodernism in its many manifestations has accompanied, or has been accompanied by, a flourishing range and variety of artistic activities and creations, but when artistic creation is propagated by the major mass-communication agencies, such as the increasingly conglomerate-owned mass media and media conglomerates, it becomes just another commodity. Then this commodification of artistic production and the apparent abdication by major architects of any public purpose combine with claims of aggregate economic growth to create a very smooth slick of language and images; we have already seen, in Chapter 3 on liberalism, that the financialisation of the world's economy has created notional holdings 'worth' a dozen times the world's total output. The terms in which the financial holdings are expressed are part of the slick. This condition can be extremely beguiling. Jean Baudrillard sees the whole world as nothing but representations; according to him, we started with realism, and moved to distorted representation. Then our representations came to conceal emptiness, and we ended up with signs which relate to no reality at all. Everything becomes virtual reality; Baudrillard famously, or notoriously, said the Gulf War of 1990–91 never happened and was only a series of television images.

The slick, however, conceals a much uglier state of affairs. The figures are themselves simulacra, but they are not simulacra of nothing; the claims about the aggregate growth of economies, employment figures, and so on, conceal the fact that the growth has been largely driven by enormous rises in the purported value of non-productive assets, such as land, stocks and shares, gold, and so on. Secondly, claims about employment figures too often avoid the fact that the purportedly industrial economies have seen huge rises in the numbers of low-paid, dead-end, casualised jobs of the kind done by hundreds of millions around the world. Other unpleasant facts still stand too; at the time of writing, India, for its part, ranks 135th out of 187 countries on the UN Human Development Index and has 700 million permanently malnourished people.

The global financial crash of 2007–09, whence we are yet to recover—and which has seen entire economies go to the wall under the shibboleths of the current financial orthodoxy—has undermined much of the system of economic relations (they can hardly be called production relations) which has so intensified postmodernism in our time. Yet poststructuralism and postmodernism have posed serious challenges, and in their own way may have helped us towards a clearer understanding of our condition. For example, it is not a disaster that Derrida undermines the idea that there is such a thing as a transcendental signified, or one meaning that holds all the others in place, be that God, reason, truth, or the laws of nature (Belsey 2002: 78). Instead, if we take meaning to be the effect of language and not its cause, then these foundations lose their transcendental status (Belsey 2002: 78). Even if it is not clear what it would mean to 'take' meaning to be—rather than to show the ways we mean things in our life and language—the poststructuralist challenge has enabled us to think afresh about things we might otherwise have taken for granted.

In addition, the corporate systems which underlie the postmodern commodification of production and consumption—indeed, of whole lifestyles—can be thrown into chaos by political events of a very recognisable, if often terrible character. Following the illegal United States-led invasion of Iraq in 2003, McDonald's lost enormous amounts of trade in the Middle East and North Africa, because their globally and instantly recognisable logo and their globally inescapable advertising had all but turned them into the national symbol of the United States. We might sympathise with the bald eagle which has been the official symbol of the United States for two and a half centuries, but for postmodernism it might not be at all implausible for McDonald's to be the US government and for its logo to be the representative symbol thereof.

That shows yet another problem with poststructuralism and postmodernism. What would it mean to take their rejections of systems of knowledge seriously? A postmodernist anaesthetist, for example, might not bother to measure our weight and consider our age when deciding how much anaesthetic to give us before an operation; they might just say, 'We think that's about enough', and stick the needle into us. The ground crew who refuel aircraft might also reject the power-seeking apparatus of Enlightenment-derived science and stop the refuelling whenever they felt like it, and those from whom we buy fruit and vegetables might abandon their scales for the feel of the weight of whatever they sell us. Our banks, of course, could cease to do any arithmetic in respect of our accounts, and simply estimate the figures.

Perhaps too many of those who advocate either poststructuralism or postmodernism, or both, have simply overreached themselves. Furthermore, one of the least tenable claims of postmodernism is that it is new. Even as modernism was rapidly becoming something of a dominant ethos in the arts, artists of the period were doing things which we might well call postmodernist. They were experimenting with the juxtaposition of high culture and mass culture, abandoning the rules of musical composition, perspective, and almost everything else in artistic creation (Callinicos 1989). In addition, postmodernism has been severely criticised for colluding with or even being an expression of neoliberalism, in which individual preference is the sole principle of action—and even more dangerously, for opening the door to fascism, because it removes the very idea of reasons for our actions and therefore of accountability for them. It also has to see all moral and political positions as equivalent (Crowder 2004).

The point here is that we may be—and we very often are—confused about what a state of affairs is, about how things stand, and about what to do about them if they present a problem. As a result, we may question the stories we have been told, or question entire societies and systems of thought, but that does not mean we must stop trying to make sense of our world. Similarly, it is not an answer to a badly designed, or badly run, or corruptly run, system or even an entire state or society to say that all actions and all systems are no more than expressions of and vehicles for power. In late December 1981, Derrida was arrested as he was about to board a flight out of Prague, where he had been lecturing to members of an internationally known artistic and academic dissident group. Czechoslovakia was still a communist country, with a notably more rigid government than those of certain other communist countries. Derrida was charged with drug trafficking (what seemed to be drugs had been planted in his bag), interrogated for eight hours, and held in a cell in a prison. He had been framed by an over-eager security official who wanted to do something dramatic against a dissident group, and who had no idea that arresting Derrida, of whom he had never heard, would cause an international outcry. Derrida was released after some days, but the episode shocked him so much that he began to see that there might be some point to the very idea of the rule of law.

One question arising thence is that of how postmodernism achieved the status it did. Its currency may have owed much, as Jameson shows, to the fact that it is a genuine ideology, a range of ideas which themselves systematically mislead us; ironically, postmodernism itself excludes the possibility of systematic explanations. Secondly, both poststructuralism and postmodernism may be right to challenge dominant systems of ideas, but their rejection of the possibility of reasoning inquiry and reasoning judgement neglects the fact that making judgements, knowing and deciding what things mean and what to do, may need no Archimedean point or fulcrum; it is something we learn to do as we learn language and human life. Without it, our lives would probably be unintelligible as human lives.

CHAPTER 8: POSTSTRUCTURALISM AND POSTMODERNISM

Extension Exercise

Read the following article:

Bérubé, Michael. 2009. 'Post Hoax, Ergo Propter Hoax'. *American Scientist*, January–February. http://www.americanscientist.org/bookshelf/pub/post-hoax-ergo-propter-hoax

1. Summarise this article in 10–12 points. Single points of one or two lines each will be sufficient.
2. The title is an adaptation of a Latin saying. Find the Latin saying, and write down the saying and its standard translation.
3. Write a short paragraph (4–5 lines) expressing your argued response to the author's concluding paragraph.

Further Reading

Dews, Peter. 2007. *Logics of Disintegration: Post-Structuralist Thought and the Claims of Critical Theory*. London: Verso.

The above is a reissue of a truly outstanding book first published in 1987. Accessible without ever avoiding intellectual difficulty.

Eagleton, Terry. 1996. *The Illusions of Postmodernism*. Oxford: Blackwell.

A very accessible critical analysis by a major figure in English critical studies.

Norris, Christopher. 1990. *What's Wrong with Postmodernism? Critical Theory and the Ends of Philosophy*. London: Harvester Wheatsheaf.

A noted work. It is clear and authoritative, and takes poststructuralism and postmodernism seriously to show where they lead; it also shows that among certain thinkers within postmodernism, a constructive critical position has not been abandoned.

9

CHAPTER

Theocracy and Fundamentalism

Theocracy means rule by a priesthood or rule in accordance with religious principles, but fundamentalism involves an insistence on the literal truth of a particular book or set of principles as the only basis for any given faith.

THEOCRACY

There are comparatively few genuine theocracies in today's world; the Vatican City State is one. Another was Iran from 1979 to 1997; between 1979 and 1989, Ayatollah Ruhollah Khomeini, the supreme religious and political leader, was the main and often the sole source of religious and political authority. Of course, all over the world there are religious movements which would like to create or impose theocracies, but in some democracies such movements are banned from standing for election. India, for example, prohibits the Rashtriya Swayamsevak Sangh or RSS from contesting elections, and in fact banned the RSS altogether between February 1948 and July 1949. In the United States, many of the various groups broadly described as the New Christian Right in the United States have considerable influence on politicians and on the whole political climate at all levels, even though few of the groups' members stand for election.

Another example of explicitly theocratic rule was the period of the Taliban government in Afghanistan, which lasted from 1996 to 2001. Here, the whole of society was organised by the Taliban on strict religious lines, in accordance with a particular version of Islam; the Taliban banned women's education, required all women to wear the burkha and men to grow beards, and strictly regulated relations between the sexes. Transgressions of any law were tried by religious courts, and punishments were in accordance with the priests' interpretation of a particular Islamic code.

Iranian theocracy, however, was more complex, even though the theocracy Islamised all aspects of Iranian life. For example, all women in Iran had to wear the headscarf and chador, restrictions on polygamy were lifted, public floggings or executions were carried out for adultery, and homosexuality incurred the death penalty (Heywood 2007: 299). In addition, the elected national assembly was called the Islamic Consultative Assembly, and all laws it passed had to be ratified by the Council of Guardians, which was composed of six religious lawyers and six secular ones. This council ensured that all laws conformed to their interpretation of Islamic principles; in any case, political power lay with the Council of the Islamic Revolution, a body made up of Khomeini and fourteen other senior clerics; this body was dissolved when the first parliament was formed in August 1980.

The theocracy permeated the whole of Iranian life; government policy was communicated to the public at Friday prayers in Tehran, but Iran has long traditions of political, cultural, and religious diversity, including a Jewish population of about 9,000, who have lived there for over 3,000 years. After Khomeini died in 1989, the much more moderate Akbar Hashemi Rafsanjani rose from the speakership of the national assembly to be elected president. The more conservative Mahmoud Ahmadinejad was elected to the presidency in 2005 and won a second term in 2009, though he did so amid widespread allegations of electoral fraud. In 2013, the current president, Hassan Rouhani, was elected, and immediately changed the whole tone of Iranian politics, especially in foreign affairs, adopting a much less confrontational tone and manner than this predecessors had done. He became the first Iranian head of state since the Shah to speak directly with a US President; in September 2013, as he was on his way to Kennedy Airport after the United Nations General Assembly, he and Barack Obama had a 15-minute telephone conversation.

Secondly, Rouhani has maintained talks with the five permanent members of the UN Security Council plus Germany (the P5+1) over Iran's nuclear programme. Iran does remain a theocracy, and it is virtually certain that Rouhani's main policies have the approval of the country's highest religious authority, Ayatollah Ali Khamenei, but it is equally true that Iran has not attacked any other country for 240 years.

Theocracies, therefore, vary in their specific forms and may change over time, but political position and status within them depend on position and status within the religious hierarchy. In strict theocracies, almost all areas of life are run on specified religious lines, but some theocracies are less rigid than others, and some theocratic leaders are often thoughtful and subtle in international dealings.

FUNDAMENTALISM

All religions, and many political movements, have and perhaps always have had fundamentalist tendencies or factions. Secondly, there is nothing new about fundamentalism; the German Anabaptist priest Thomas Müntzer (1489–1525) and the Swiss-French Protestant Jean Calvin (1509–64) were both fundamentalists, and Calvin, who was highly active in politics, created a theocracy which wielded great power in the Swiss city -state of Geneva (Heywood 2007: 282).

Some fundamentalist groups, however, have withdrawn from society to lead lives which are self-contained and peaceable, and one such group is the Amish community in the New England region of the United States. Today's Amish are descended from seventeenth-century German Protestant farmers, and they lead the same kind of lives as their forebears did. The grow all their own food, build their own houses from materials they have made themselves, use horses and horse-drawn wagons for transport, and use no electricity. They speak the kind of German their ancestors spoke, and are completely self-sufficient. They have virtually no contact with anyone outside their villages, and as they take nothing from any public authority they are exempt from US taxes whether federal or local.

It might therefore be more accurate to talk in terms of fundamentalisms rather than fundamentalism as a single ideology, and they seem to arise in several different cultures (Heywood 2007: 293–94). Very few fundamentalist groups, moreover, call themselves fundamentalists. Far more often, they describe themselves as evangelists, after the Greek word *evangelion*, which means 'good news', or as revivalists or conservatives or traditionalists (Heywood 2007: 281). In general, individuals' position in a fundamentalist state or movement is connected to their position in the religious hierarchy, but almost none of the major fundamentalist leaders has been a conventionally successful priest making their way upwards through the hierarchy of an established religion. This has to do with the main themes of fundamentalism.

Religion and Politics

This combination is central to almost all forms of fundamentalism except the most reclusive ones; in effect, fundamentalist movements are politico-religious movements, and explicitly set out to take control of the political space so that they can impose their version of their faith. All but the most reclusive fundamentalist movements are intensely involved in politics; most, if not all of them, actively aim to achieve political dominance and to transform the whole of political life in accordance with their own religious doctrines and principles. Fundamentalism, like fascism, obliterates all distinctions between public and private life.

This obliteration is in part a response to the global spread of different forms of broadly liberal democracy, which allows freedom of religious belief and observance but usually restricts these to the private sphere and can even rule certain practices within faiths illegal; several democracies have created laws which allow followers to act in ways which their faith would prohibit. For example, 98 per cent of American women who identify themselves as Catholic and have ever had sex have used a non-natural form of contraception—a practice banned by the Church of Rome (Guttmacher Institute 2012).

Modern democracy also has the effect of secularising society by reshaping the various forms religious observance itself takes. In India, the law requires those organising large religious festivals to cease the public use of loudspeakers and conclude events like processions by 10.30 pm. Very often people themselves reshape their religious practices; in the United Kingdom, despite a continuing decline in church attendance, particularly within the Anglican denomination, a majority of people still turn to the church for baptisms, weddings, and funerals. In India, although reliable figures might be hard to obtain, substantial numbers of people do not observe their particular faith very strictly and often breach many of its tenets, even though they continue to hold the usual religious ceremonies for naming babies, and for weddings and funerals.

Fundamentalist movements see such tendencies and developments as utterly destructive and even degenerate. For them, the restriction of religion to a private space allows the public space to be pervaded by materialism, corruption, and immoral conduct, and the answer is to take over the whole of life—institutions of state, social practices, the economy, and everything else—and start afresh (Heywood 2007: 285–86).

Fundamentalist Versions of Religion

Although most religious fundamentalists refer to themselves by other labels, a fundamentalist outlook means what it says; it requires that we return to the basics or fundamental principles of a faith. Sometimes this means asserting the literal truth of a holy book; many American Protestant fundamentalists believe in creationism, the doctrine that God created the world in six days, as the Book of Genesis states.

That kind of focus on the fundamental principles in a holy book is of course possible only if the faith in question has a book; nevertheless, the attempt to assert fundamental principles is found in all fundamentalisms, and Hinduism has its own share of people and groups who assert those and even impose them on others. Typically, such movements state very few principles, so that they can assert their message quickly and clearly; in addition, the message is often part of a very strong assertion of identity. Fundamentalism often has a powerful psychological appeal as well, and many fundamentalist leaders are highly charismatic characters (Heywood 2007: 289).

Antimodernism

All forms of modernism, whether activist or retreatist, are deeply hostile to modernity, and usually see it as the source of moral decay; for them, examples would be the loss or weakening of religious authority, the spread—however partial and incomplete—of women's rights, the very existence of workers' rights and trade unions, and many other features of modernity. Fundamentalist movements often find modernity so morally repulsive that they hark back to some past golden age of moral stability when traditions were unquestioned and everybody knew right from wrong. Almost all fundamentalist movements, however, are extremely adept users of all the latest technologies. Even in the early 1970s, US evangelists used television—making their own programmes for dedicated Sunday-morning prime-time slots—so effectively that they became known as televangelists and had followings of millions. More recently, groups like Al Qaeda and Islamic State in Iraq and Syria (ISIS) have used social media very successfully to recruit from all over the world. Their techniques include making very sophisticated promotional CDs and constructing highly professional websites.

Militant fundamentalist groups are also very good at acquiring and using weapons. This shows both that such groups are often very well funded—as are non-militarised movements like the New Christian Right—and that when it comes to imposing their will, they have no problem using some of the most terrible instruments of modernity. When they are at war, fundamentalist groups have often captured large stocks of lighter weapons, such as rifles and machine guns, from forces they have defeated, or they have gained access to weapons stores in areas where the official military or militias are badly run or corrupt; the weapons can include rocket launchers (Harte and Smith 2014). One sample of ISIS weapons came from 21 countries, including the US, Russia and former Soviet republics, China, and Serbia; ISIS themselves are now using oxyacetylene torches to remove manufacturers' markings or even to add new serial numbers so as to make tracking harder (Harte and Smith 2014). Some tracking organisations, nevertheless, have identified the geographical progress of particular types or weapons or even individual weapons (Conflict Armament Research 2014).

Militancy and Violence

A number of today's fundamentalist movements are explicitly vigorous, militant, and even very violent (Heywood 2007: 291). Secondly, many of them hold to a Manichaean world view, one which divides the world into good—meaning their own idea of the good—and evil. In addition, most fundamentalisms are religious in nature, and religious conflicts tend to be terribly violent, with a long history of hate and mass slaughter.

Fundamentalist movements rarely hold office, but some—like the New Christian Right in the United States—have very great influence, and some engage in calculated violence by inspiring individual members to acts of violence which can have enormous effects. In 1948, Gandhi was assassinated by a Hindu fundamentalist; the Israeli Prime minister Yitzhak Rabin was murdered by a Jewish fanatic in 1995. The Egyptian president Anwar Sadat was assassinated by Islamic fundamentalists in 1981, and in 1984 Sikh extremists murdered Indira Gandhi. In the United States, clinics which perform lawful abortions have been firebombed, and at least one doctor working in such a clinic has been murdered.

Among acts by movements, the Al Qaeda attacks in the United States killed over 3,000 people, and the resulting United States-led illegal invasion of Iraq and its aftermath has probably resulted in over a million deaths, not to mention lasting political violence in much of the Middle East. In 2001, the then-president of the United States George W. Bush said in a speech to both houses of the United States Congress, 'Either you are with us, or you are with the terrorists'; that reaction to the 9/11 attacks was a Manichaean utterance, and may well have stemmed from Mr Bush's own born-again Christian fundamentalism.

Even without violence, fundamentalist movements can create a climate of fear. In 1983, a fundamentalist Protestant family called the Mozerts brought a civil action against their local municipal school authorities, Hawkins County Public Schools, in the American state of Tennessee, over a picture they had seen in a civics textbook for fourth-grade pupils, that is, for children aged eight or nine. The picture showed boys cooking for girls, and the Mozerts argued in court that this was a violation of the divine order of things. The case was finally concluded in 1987, when a federal court ruled that exposing the picture to the children did not amount to an attempt by Hawkins County to indoctrinate them.

The consequences, however, showed the power and influence of the New Christian Right. First, the Mozerts removed their children from the public education system and put them in a private school with a very strong fundamentalist ethos. That meant their children would grow up in isolation from children whose families practised the same faith in less extreme ways, and from children of other faiths or no faith. Yet in a democratic polis, an essential aim of education is the development of pupils' and students' capacity to make autonomous and informed judgments on the issues facing them and their fellow citizens, and to maintain an informed respect for and tolerance of diversity;

they cannot do this if they go to school in isolation from one another, in schools vastly distanced from one another by class, faith, or geography (Brighouse 2006: 129–30, 84–92). Secondly, although the municipal authorities had won the case, the book's publishers, Holt, Rinehart and Winston—a famous and long-established firm—removed the passages concerned from subsequent editions of the book (Brighouse 2006: 85). There seems to be no published evidence as to whether or not the publishers received any actual threats.

Fundamentalisms and Other Ideologies

The parallel between fundamentalism and fascism is obvious. Both regard the present as decayed and corrupt, and both conclude that the only way ahead lies in strictly following a small number of very explicit and rigid principles; for both, dissent is betrayal and must be expunged, violently if needed. Fascist doctrines, however, stress the idea of a pure and glorious past, while fundamentalism looks more towards some gloriously purified future. This is often called a millenarian outlook, and according to some fundamentalist theories, the glorious future will come about only after some terrible event, like a virulent disease, or a world war, or a global natural disaster, has made humans see the light and repent of their previous ways. This kind of outlook is sometimes called apocalypticism (Heywood 2007: 292–93).

Another ideology with some apparent similarity to fundamentalism is conservatism, which is also committed to a traditional order from the past. Serious conservatism, however, is cautious about change but does not reject it. Secondly, conservatism rejects the adoption or imposition of grand theories of morality, politics, or society. Most fundamentalisms impose a comprehensive theory involving all three, and cannot tolerate difference or dissent.

Fundamentalisms and Religious Differences

Most of the politically active forms of fundamentalism are openly and often bitterly hostile to other faiths and often inflict terrible violence on followers of other faiths; some fundamentalist movements consider those who follow other faiths to be subhuman. Fundamentalist movements, nevertheless, have as much of a problem with other forms of their own faith as they do with other faiths; for many fundamentalists, less rigid followers of the same faith, or followers of another sect within the same faith, are an even greater enemy than those who follow another faith or have no faith. Examples are not difficult to find; in theory at least, ISIS is committed to exterminating something like 200 million followers of Shia Islam, precisely because the ISIS view that any diversion from its idea of strict Koranic practice amounts to a denial of the Koran's perfection (Wood 2015).

For fundamentalism, disagreement or dissent amounts to betrayal or apostasy, that is, to denial of precious and all-important principles. At worst, that can mean that fundamentalists use violent methods to eliminate less rigid and more tolerant versions of their own respective faiths; for example, ISIS have reportedly killed recruits who have started to question the ways imposed on them by ISIS and have tried to return to their own countries. This may be an inevitable consequence of the very nature of fundamentalism; a fundamentalist outlook reduces major religions to a small number of very simple propositions, but this means that fundamentalism can have no response to the complex problems of everyday life, and that it reduces often weighty bodies of religious thought to minimal and rigid rules.

That everyday life can pose religious problems is obvious, as we have seen in the case of contraceptive use among American Catholic women. Similarly, those Indians who—perhaps illegally—would not let their own houses out to people of other castes or faiths in India may have no problem leasing other people's properties in other countries irrespective of the owner's faith or dietary habits, or perhaps even over letting their own overseas properties out irrespective of the tenants' faith and customs (significant elements of anti-discriminatory law may well be involved here too). Fundamentalism seems to have no response to such complexities, largely because it has no space for any kind of moral complexity or uncertainty, or for any doubt about what the right action might be in a complex and uncertain situation.

Contexts for the Rise of Fundamentalism

The reasons for the emergence, the spread, and the hold of fundamentalism vary across faiths and cultures. It seems particularly to arise in societies which face what they, or groups within them, think are serious crises of identity or meaning; these can include the prospect of significant changes to the social structure or social order, even though such changes or challenges can take very different forms.

In the United States, Christian fundamentalists—overwhelmingly white Protestants—were very troubled by the expansion of the public sphere in the first three decades after the Second World War. In that period, the Supreme Court ruled against prayers in schools because these violated the constitutional right to religious freedom; the federal government greatly expanded urban development programmes and funding for public education at every level; some of the latter funding was specifically for those who had served in the war (the Servicemen's Readjustment Act of 1944 provided a wide range of benefits, including funds for university education). Many traditionally religious Protestants felt that their ways of life were being threatened, and their anxieties were intensified by the invention of the contraceptive pill, which became widely available in the early 1960s. The pill enables women to control their own fertility, and to do so entirely of their own volition and—if they wish—without anyone else's knowledge; the US Protestant traditionalists were among many groups around the world who feared that for a range of reasons this form of women's empowerment would undermine what they thought of as the traditional family.

In the United States, further deep social change was started by the Civil Rights Movement in the early 1960s; traditionalists and conservatives in the United States saw these as threats to the social and economic order. The extensive network of laws and policies enforcing centuries of racial discrimination and oppression against African-Americans was ruled unconstitutional, and the Voting Rights Act meant African-Americans had a right to be on the electoral register. These developments were so bitterly resented by sections of the American political Right, who include American Protestant fundamentalists, that even in the 2008 presidential election, groups of them attempted to challenge the validity of African-Americans' voter registration at the ballot box.

Secondly, many of the former slave states, most of which have strong and active fundamentalist groups and politicians, have devised voting registration procedures which make it particularly difficult for African-Americans to register to vote. The United States has no election commission, and the party in power in each state devises its own voter registration procedures, conducts the election, and counts the votes. Several Republican-held states continue to pass laws which in effect make it even harder for African-Americans to register on the electoral roll, and in 2013 the Supreme Court overturned the federal government's attempt to enforce federal monitoring of such changes in states which have a history of racial discrimination. Claims that electoral fraud was taking place on such a scale that the states concerned needed tough procedures for electoral registration have been comprehensively exposed as false (Weiser and Norden 2011: 19–24; Kennedy and Palast 2008; Sivaramakrishnan 2012b).

The extent of the US political Right's bitterness over the Civil Rights Movement and the ensuing legislation has not always been fully recognised, though more recently various analysts have provided sharp reminders of it. For example, in 2016 the explicit racism of the US Republican Party's primary election campaign and the general election—the presidential election, which the Republican Donald Trump won—is a revival of the fear and hatred white voters in the American Deep South have felt not only since the civil rights laws (including the right of all Americans to vote, irrespective of race or colour) were passed in 1964, but also the Democratic Party, at its national convention in 1948, committed itself to ending 'all racial, religious, and economic discrimination' (cited in Fountain 2016). Fountain adds, with several examples, that Republican presidential candidates like Ronald Reagan have long used covert references—'dog-whistle' phrases in US political parlance—to indicate their support for a return to the old racist ways (Fountain 2016). For example, Republican politicians' talk of states' rights refers, at least on the surface, to the 10th Amendment to the US Constitution; under this amendment, all powers not specifically given by the Constitution to the federal government are reserved to the states or the people. The coded message here is that if they are elected, such politicians will use the 10th Amendment to repeal the civil rights legislation, which of course is federal law and which when passed overrode the southern states' own racially discriminatory laws.

One important implication is that an event which has often been called the crucial catalyst for the New Christian Right was much less decisive than many have taken it to be. That event was the 1973 US Supreme Court ruling in the case of *Roe v Wade*, in which the court gave all women in the United States a right to an abortion in the first three months of pregnancy. The ruling itself passed almost unnoticed among Christian conservatives in the United States, most probably because the majority of them were Protestants and saw abortion as an issue for Catholics. Some denominations, such as Southern Baptists, even passed a conference resolution confirming the 'possibility of abortion under such conditions as rape, incest, clear evidence of severe fetal deformity, and carefully ascertained evidence of the likelihood of damage to the emotional, mental, and physical health of the mother' (cited in Balmer 2014).

In fact, nationwide religious opposition to the *Roe v Wade* decision did not gain momentum until 1979, when leaders of what became the New Christian Right saw that opposition to that decision might serve as a convenient cover for something that even they did not dare express openly in public—namely their extreme racism. They were also deeply frightened by an 8-1 Supreme Court ruling which abolished the tax-exempt status of universities which openly barred African-Americans from admission; that ruling was made in 1983 (Balmer 2014). Thereafter, however, the New Christian Right made the most of the opportunities *Roe v Wade* had given them, and even made a propaganda film showing allegedly dead babies left on the shores of the Dead Sea. The purported corpses were plastic dolls (Balmer 2014).

The New Christian Right has certainly been a major force in US politics, as we have already seen. Presidents Ronald Reagan and George W. Bush were both fundamentalists, and on his first day in office Bush issued an executive order banning US-aided non-government organisations in other countries from using even their own non-US funds in any of several ways even remotely connected with abortion; such agencies could not even refer women to abortion advice services elsewhere (Center for Reproductive Rights 2003). Yet, as Randall Balmer says:

> Although abortion had emerged as a rallying cry by 1980, the real roots of the religious right lie not the defense of a fetus but in the defense of racial segregation. (Balmer 2014)

Within the United States, the New Christian Right dominated the Republican Party by the mid-1980s, and, if anything, its hold on the party has only strengthened since then. In addition, many states have legislated to restrict access to contraception and abortion services; several states have also attempted to ban the teaching of evolution in publicly funded schools (Pew Research Center 2014). As to other Supreme Court rulings, it remains to be seen whether the New Christian Right can gain the same momentum from the 2014 decision in *Obergefell v Hodges*—when the court ruled that the ban on same-sex marriages in Ohio, Michigan, Kentucky, and Tennessee was unconstitutional—as they did from the *Roe v Wade* ruling. Societal attitudes to the public expression and legitimation of same-sex relationships have changed very greatly in the last half century or so, and on this issue the US religio-political Right may simply not get the same support they might have done earlier. Therefore, we should not be surprised that during the 2016 US presidential election campaign the Republican candidates moved closer and closer to openly racist statements, most probably because their former smokescreen, namely a hardline puritanical sexual politics, may have lost the effect it used to have.

One central element of the US New Christian Right's aims seems to be winning electoral control of as many state assemblies as possible, and of course winning majorities in both chambers of the federal legislature, the US Congress. As all those institutions already exist, that is an understandable strategy, but it marks a significant difference between the New Christian Right and certain other fundamentalist movements. Osama bin Laden apparently did not expect to see the establishment of a caliphate, an Islamist territory, in his own lifetime; al Qaeda operated (and presumably still operates) as a network of relatively autonomous cells in many regions of the world (Wood 2015). ISIS, however, clearly intends for theological reasons to establish its command over territory, that is, to create a state it can call a caliphate; this is enormously important to the movement, because within its own territory it could implement the whole of its own version of Islamic law. That would include public institutions—even a consumer protection office—and a system of public welfare organised on lines which according to ISIS are specified in the Koran. Leaders of fundamentalist movements are often extremely knowledgeable about their foundational texts (Wood 2015).

Colonialism

Another context for the rise of fundamentalism is the effect of colonialism or imperialism on former subject cultures. Postcolonial societies often retain a deep sense of inferiority in respect of their former oppressors, and movements which seek to reassert a precolonial identity (whatever that might mean) can be very attractive. The character of colonial rule is a significant factor here. Quite apart from maintaining political and economic domination, the colonials may well have intended to inculcate a sense of cultural inferiority. It has emerged publicly that enormous amounts of British documents showed the extent of malice and racial prejudice colonial officials had towards non-white subjects of the Empire; in addition, the use of torture against such subjects was recorded. It has, furthermore, emerged that British officials—under orders—destroyed millions of the relevant documents as colonial territories moved towards independence (Cobain 2013).

Secondly, many former colonial countries have quickly become corrupt and often brutal dictatorships. For example, in Egypt the repression inflicted by Hosni Mubarak's regime was one of the main reasons for the resurgence in the 1990s of the Muslim Brotherhood, which had been founded in 1928. The Brotherhood soon gained a reputation for being almost an alternative local administration in several parts of the country, and was above all not corrupt. In 2013, two years after the Arab Spring forced Mubarak to leave office, the Brotherhood won Egypt's first democratic elections, but were soon overthrown in a military coup; the military junta which removed President Mohamed Morsi, who was also elected, remain in office at the time of writing, and Morsi has been tried and sentenced to death, but has appealed the sentence.

In other postcolonial countries, the failure to reform colonial institutions of state and the retention of vast areas of highly repressive colonial law have both contributed to the state's failure to fulfil many of its promises, and have thereby given fundamentalist movements added momentum. The government of India did repeal the colonial Armed Forces Special Powers Act in 1949, but reintroduced it for six months in 1958; the Act remains in force, and has been imposed in several states with no apparent prospect that it will be lifted, let alone repealed. In addition, any rise in fundamentalism in one faith tends to encourage similar developments in other faiths. Electoral success, nevertheless, is a powerful motivating factor; the 2014 general election victory by the BJP may well have emboldened various state governments to extend a form of assertive Hinduisation; for example, in 2015 the Maharashtra state government banned the slaughter of cattle, though not water-buffaloes. Here too, economic oppression cannot be ruled out, and a class/caste element in the policy —which now has counterparts in several other Indian states—has also been publicly identified (Karat 2015).

Neocolonialism

A specific form of this has contributed to Islamist or Islamic fundamentalism, which globally seems to get more current attention than other forms of fundamentalism. The Ottoman Empire, which had been founded in 1299, finally collapsed in 1922, and the world's then-largest colonial powers, Britain and France, divided much of the Middle East and North Africa arbitrarily, with no regard to tribal occupation, nomadic routes, or other existing customs and practices. In addition, Dutch colonials in East Asia and French colonials in North Africa had long banned the then-vigorous Islamic sciences and Islamic medicine, even on pain of death. One result was that religious authority came to be the preeminent authority in Muslim-majority societies, despite fierce challenges from within over a long period (Sardar 2008: 57–83; de Bellaigue 2015). Further political humiliation came with the Western-enforced creation of the state of Israel in historical Palestine, after which the rights of the Palestinians stated in the Balfour Declaration in 1917 were simply ignored (Karmi 2007; Pappé 2006).

The newly created countries, as I have already noted, often turned into monarchies or dictatorships; it is very likely that many of the governments there served as instruments or proxies for the United States and the Soviet Union during the Cold War, but the resulting repression and corruption in the region only strengthened the appeal of Islamic fundamentalism. For a time, nationalist leaders like Gamal Abdel Nasser in Egypt offered the promise of better, but Nasser's attempts to create a pan-Arab sensibility and a form of Arab nationalism both failed.

Of course, these developments need not have result in strengthened fundamentalism alone. For a time, between 2011 and 2013, the several popular uprisings which came to be called the Arab Spring seemed to raise the prospect of renewal based on democracy rather than fundamentalism, but among the states concerned only Tunisia has managed to hold two successive democratic elections; in the second, held in 2014, the moderate Islamist party Ennahda was voted out in favour of the liberal-secularist Nidaa Tounes party, by 86 seats to Ennahda's 69; there are 217 seats in the Tunisian parliament. In much of the rest of the region, protest has been brutally repressed, and in both Syria and Yemen terrible civil wars continue, with the involvement of several other countries; several hundred thousand civilians have been killed and perhaps 10 million displaced.

Democracy

It may seem surprising that democracy can provide a context for the rise of religious fundamentalism, but fundamentalist movements around the world are bitterly hostile to democracy or—as in the United States—have enormous problems over even reasonably functional democracy.

One reason for the fundamentalist fear of democracy is the undoubted prospect democracy offers of material improvement for marginalised or oppressed groups and classes; as we have seen, the abolition of the entire body of racist laws in the United States southern states (also called the Jim Crow laws) in the 1960s was probably the decisive motivator for what became the New Christian Right.

Secondly, democracy, in almost all the many forms of it which obtain today, almost always brings about a secularisation of everyday life, in everyday ways; for example, in much of India, urban authorities require religious festivals to switch off loudspeaker systems by 10.30 pm. In the United Kingdom, an Anglican state, many churches have for a long time refrained from ringing their bells early on Sunday mornings. Broadly speaking, the democratic state, sometimes through its courts, decides the limits of specific religious practices and for the rest leaves it to people to decide how they will practise their faith within those limits—and citizens are free to not to practise any faith or even to deny all faiths. Democracies as we have them give people the freedom to think and decide both public and private issues, and that principle obtains irrespective of how well or badly any given democratic state upholds it. This potentially undermines all religious authority. Fundamentalism, by its very nature, has to reduce all of life to a few rigid prescriptions, and has to exclude from membership of humanity all who even begin to question those, for whatever reason they do so.

CHAPTER 9: THEOCRACY AND FUNDAMENTALISM

Extension Exercise

Read this paper:

Al-Atawneh, Muhammad. 2009. 'Is Saudi Arabia a Theocracy? Religion and Governance in Contemporary Saudi Arabia'. *Middle Eastern Studies* 45 (5): 721–37.

1. In about 500 words, using the chapter above and material from the set paper, write down an argument as to whether Salafism or Wahhabism, as currently established in Saudi Arabia, is fundamentalist.
2. In about 500 words, again using material from the chapter above and the set paper, write down an argument as to whether contemporary Saudi Arabia is or is not a theocracy.

10
CHAPTER

Technocracy and Managerialism

These mean different things. Technocracy means rule by the experts; the Greek word *technê* means a craft or an art, and there are many examples of technocratic ideologies even in ancient writings. The Athenian philosopher Plato (429–340 BCE) advocated a form of technocracy with his idea that only those fit to be trained to rule should rule. Today, the word 'technocracy' more commonly connotes rule by those with technical or professional qualifications, such as scientists or engineers; the term itself was coined by an American engineer, William H. Smyth, in 1919 (Gunnell 1982: 393). We shall also see, however, that people with genuine technical expertise often import their own moral and other presuppositions and assumptions into their work, often without realising that they are doing so. I shall examine technocracy first.

Managerialism, for its part, is much more recent, though it has been called a fully fledged ideology (Willard 1993). In its widest form, its main principle is that a training in management enables anyone to manage anything without any substantive knowledge of the activity they are managing, that is, without being a practitioner of the given activity. Managerialist doctrines make significant claims to generalisability and to predictive authority, and managerialism raises serious questions in philosophy and political theory.

TECHNOCRACY

The idea of technocracy has a very long history. Plato proposed a special form of education for philosopher-rulers, whom he called Guardians. Those considered fit to become Guardians would have a specially designed education, which would be followed by 15 years' experience working in institutions of state before they could start to take more powerful positions (Plato 1956: 231–311). The other classes, whom Plato divided into two more in rank order, would be subordinate to the Guardians and would work under their direction.

Main Themes

Plato likened the Guardians to ships' captains, who with their training in navigation and ship handling, as well as their knowledge of the winds, tides, and seasons, are experts in commanding their crews and sailing their various routes (Plato 1956: 249–51). This is potentially an attractive idea, and there is no doubt that we have relied on experts of one kind or another since ancient times. Among such experts are doctors, navigators, builders and architects, scientists of all kinds, engineers, farmers, and of course tradespeople such as plumbers and electricians; we might well not be able to survive without plumbers, electricians, and mechanics.

One result of the existence of technical expertise is that the relation between the technical expert and the wider polity—of which technical experts are of course members—is a very difficult one to characterise. The idea of technocracy has been part of optimistic and even utopian visions of society, though for several decades now has more often been seen as a form of political pathology or as the informing principle in dystopic accounts of society, including powerful novels and films (Gunnell 1982: 392).

Very few, if any, societies have been totally technocratic, though novels like Yevgeny Zamyatin's *We*, published in 1924, have characterised dystopic and tightly controlled societies run by technocrats and ideologues, and probably the most famous example of this kind of novel is George Orwell's *Nineteen Eighty-Four*, which was first published in 1949. Technical experts, however, have often had a colossal impact, for example in the framing of nuclear policy, agricultural policy, and many other areas of great public importance.

In fact, there is nothing new about the idea that technical knowledge, usually involving the use of machines, can be used to create a new society in which technical education and the use of machines would enable us to have far greater amounts of leisure time. Philosophers such as Tommaso Campanella and Francis Bacon raised such possibilities in the seventeenth century, and among those who developed or maintained such themes were Jean-Jacques Rousseau and Henri de Saint-Simon in the eighteenth century. Saint-Simon, in particular, proposed that an elite class made up of scientists, engineers, industrialists, and planners would provide technical knowledge which would enable us to solve social problems and thereby create a rational social order (Gunnell 1982: 394).

Main Problems

Technocracy, however, raises several problems. The first is that of whether political and social issues are problems of the same kind as technical problems. In a famous paper, Renford Bambrough points out that Plato's sea captain may know all about handling ships in different conditions and sailing different routes in different seasons, but that other people, such as political leaders, or shipowners and merchants, decide which routes are to be sailed, which cargoes are to be carried, whether to send ships to trade or to war, and so on (Bambrough 1956). It is true that those decisions may very probably involve technical factors, but ultimately they are never based solely on technical factors, and it is not at all clear how anyone can become an expert in all matters of the political space, or of all businesses and all trades. Indeed it is not clear, as I shall try to show in the section on managerialism, if there can even be a body of knowledge of the kind Plato thinks his Guardians can have.

A second problem with technocracy is that technocrats—or rather, those who possess technical knowledge or expertise—are also people brought up and living in human societies and cultures; that is, they live and work in contexts which involve and express ideas of appropriate conduct, manners, and so on, and they have careers to make, advance, and often protect in face of technical, organisational, and political issues of which they might not approve or which might threaten their positions. One result is that technocrats often—and sometimes deliberately—make technical decisions which are already permeated by moral and political factors; many even carry out much of their professional work in ways which are heavily influenced by such factors, and may not even realise the ways these factors shape their decisions; experts themselves do not operate in what Abraham and Sheppard have called a social vacuum (Centeno 1993: 311–12; Abraham and Sheppard 1997: 141). This matter, needless to say, can only be examined in respect of particular examples or case studies, though wider questions do arise thence.

Three Major Risks of Technocracy

We need not be surprised that technical experts have often had very great influence on major policies and decisions. The relation between the technical expert and the rest of the body politic, including citizens, elected representatives, and public servants, is never going to be easy, but unless we as citizens engage seriously with the experts we run at least three major risks.

Unquestioning Acceptance of Technical Expertise

The first risk is that we could make enormous mistakes by relying unquestioningly on those who possess technical expertise. Indeed, political power often seems to gravitate towards technological elites (Gunnell 1982: 397). This seems to hold even when the concept of technical expertise is expanded to include those in higher managerial positions who may not themselves be qualified in the sciences or applied sciences. For example, Indian public-enterprise managers have been described as being solely interested in whether the economy could be run in an 'efficient, disciplined and rational manner' and as making no normative comments whatsoever about ideologies such as socialism or capitalism (Waterbury 1992, cited in Centeno 1993: 311).

The risk of the technocratic approach here is that technical experts come to dominate our public institutions and political processes; at worst, their expertise would be inaccessible to the public and would be put beyond accountability to us, and we might well be excluded from holding the experts to account even for their grossest and deadliest errors.

The Subordination of the Political Space

A second risk is that the technology—or rather, the technological expert—becomes in effect autonomous, and the political space therefore becomes structurally subordinate to decisive factors and forces over which the public and public institutions and representatives have no control (Gunnell 1982: 397).

That kind of takeover may not happen often, but it has certainly caused serious concern. No less a person than the US president Dwight D. Eisenhower, in his valedictory address in 1961, warned of the dangers posed by this; it was he who devised the term 'military-industrial complex', and in the same speech he stated that public policy could itself become the 'captive of a scientific-technological elite'. He added that the danger would persist (Eisenhower 1961; Gunnell 1982: 397–99).

One compensating factor here may be that while many have identified such dangers, technical experts do not have a single overriding interest or set of concerns or interests which make them into a single class. Rather do the organisations in which they work become the holders of power based on technical expertise, but these organisations themselves have to vie and compete for power and influence in the political space, even if they do wield enormous political and financial power (Gunnell 1982: 399–401).

One difficulty in this kind of analysis, however, is that it neglects or even conceals the extent to which it often embodies ideological commitments, some of which have occasionally been brought to light. For example, in the late 1950s the Ford Foundation effectively established technical rather than institutional change as the guiding principle in Indian agriculture; this even resulted from a specific plan (RUPE 2003). Therefore, institutional change (which may well have expressed very different ideological commitments from those propagated and imposed by the Ford Foundation), such as the redistribution of land, or the reshaping of public institutions to provide farmers good support and advice services, was sidelined in favour of seed technology, chemical fertilisers, and pesticides, with rich farmers in irrigated areas receiving subsidies, generous credit terms, price incentives, and so on. This had World Bank approval (RUPE 2003). The selection of already successful farmers for the trials—a practice called cherry-picking—was no accident, as it would have been essential to show success, especially in the early stages (Sivaramakrishnan 2012a: 155–57; Stone 1983). The impact on India's agricultural policy has been immense. The Ford Foundation policy was soon

> ...adopted by the Indian government, with far-reaching effects. Agricultural production of rice and wheat in the selected pockets grew immediately. Talk of land reform, tenancy reform, abolition of usury, and so on were more or less dropped from official agenda (never to return). But the initial spectacular growth rates eventually slowed. On the average agricultural production all-India has grown more slowly after the Green Revolution than before, and in much of the country per capita agricultural output has stagnated or fallen. Today even the Green Revolution pockets are facing stagnation in yields. (RUPE 2003)

Technology as a New Ideology

The third major risk is that science and technology themselves come to constitute what Gunnell calls a new legitimating ideology in its own right; this then conceals or masks certain forms of social domination; at worst, technique takes over humanity itself (Gunnell 1982: 397). That sense of the spread and power of technology as a pervasive ideology which does not just permeate our thinking but comes to constitute our entire sensibility has been articulated in great detail by famous philosophers of recent or relatively recent times, most notably by members of the Frankfurt School, such as Max Horkheimer, Herbert Marcuse, and Jürgen Habermas. We need not go into detail over what amounts to an enormous body of work, but one of the most accessible and well-known arguments for this position is Herbert Marcuse's *One-Dimensional Man,* which was first published in 1964 and became one of the guiding and even inspirational texts for the student movements of the late 1960s (Marcuse 1964; Gunnell 1982: 406–10).

The philosophic issues arising here are certainly important, but we do not need to go into them in detail. It is important not to take the applied sciences as forming a single body of knowledge or as taking a single type of approach, and an analysis of technocracy is therefore best done in the light of particular examples. Secondly, some ideologies not only provide much more space for the idea of technical expertise as a political factor in itself but also create the idea of politics itself as a form of technical activity (Gunnell 1982: 41). The ideology which does this to the greatest extent is liberalism, and a good example is provided by the framers of the US constitution, who were almost textbook examples of ideological liberals. They even seem to have seen the creation of their new republican state as a technical task, the main point of which was to create institutions and procedures for the limitation, regulation, and possible reconciliation of competing or otherwise incompatible interests—and nothing else. This outlook takes the constitutional structure to be separate from the rest of society, but as a result, it takes for granted the validity of the competing claims which it has to regulate or reconcile, and offers no conceptual resources for us to examine the concepts which those claims embody or express (Gunnell 1982: 415).

This has a further and very significant result in respect of technocracy, because one of the key issues that arises in the relation between technocratic specialists and those in the wider polity is that of the struggle over the very methods by which we determine the validity of the questions and the answers in the exchange between technocrats and those in the wider polity (Centeno 1993: 313). We must also remember here that the technocrats, or those who claim technical expertise, may not be confined to the sciences or applied sciences. Senior officials in international financial institutions, and their like-minded colleagues in many parts of the world, especially in developing countries, take typically technocratic or instrumentally rational attitudes, which include questioning or rejecting the validity of the questions put to them from outside their own purported fields of authority, even if the questions are put by those in a democratic polity to whom the technocrats are supposed to answer (Centeno 1993: 313–14).

The nature of the engagement between possessors of technical knowledge and the wider public is perhaps most accessibly illustrated by means of an example. This British example comes from before the passage of the Freedom of Information Act 2000, but it clearly shows the kinds of issues that arise, even though at the time of the research, the British licensing system for pharmaceuticals was the most secretive in the Western industrialised world (Abraham and Sheppard 1997: 141). The researchers conducted semi-structured interviews with 17 members (one was not a scientist) or former members of the Medicines Commission, a body tasked under the Medicines Act 1968 with evaluating all applications for the licensing of new drugs. The 17 interviewees made up a fifth of all who were serving on the Commission or had served on it in the previous 10 years (Abraham and Sheppard 1997: 141–42). The researchers also interviewed a range of groups of patients and a selection of nursing staff.

Expert Responses

Among the main findings, all but two of the 17 Commission members interviewed considered that there was a clear demarcation between science and social judgement (*sic*), but seven said that the risk–benefit analysis which was part of the decision on licensing new drugs had no scientific guidelines and was therefore a matter of interpretation. At least in private, the experts said that scientific testing and epidemiology could not provide clear knowledge about the risks and benefits of medicines, and that although new drugs were licensed for a particular dose, the clinical trials for the first two years tended to show that the patients were 'grossly overdosed', after which the Commission and the manufacturers would reach agreement on the dosage, often cutting the conventional dose to a tenth of its previous level. None of the experts seem to have mentioned commercial pressures as a factor in the initial overdosing, though some did say that the publication of licensing details would be resisted by manufacturers on commercial grounds (Abraham and Sheppard 1997: 148–49, 151).

As for public participation in the licensing process, almost all the experts opposed it, because they considered the public ill-informed, and also thought the media contributed to public misunderstanding about the safety of medicines. Four of the experts would consider some public participation, but only within a technocratic decision-making process, and only one thought that citizen involvement would be part of a dynamic and educative process of the kind that occurred when AIDS activists campaigned for more appropriate drugs testing and regulation in the United States in the mid-1990s. Only one thought the secrecy enabled the concealment of bad decisions, but one went so far as to say that once a drug was on the market, the public became 'part of an experiment' (cited in Abraham and Sheppard 1997: 149–53).

Non-expert Responses

The non-experts were made up of nursing staff and of patients who were either receiving treatment or not. All three groups expressed much greater caution and scepticism about prescribing practices and about the 'assurances' given by pharmaceuticals manufacturers about the drugs they produced. Just as importantly, the patients' groups emerged as being nothing like passive consumers of the drugs they were prescribed; they wanted, but were struggling for, a much more active role in managing their treatment. They knew that many general practitioners know little about the specific clinical trials for drugs, and they did not think the shortcomings of the drug licensing system would be redeemed by, say, having a general practitioner on the licensing committee. Crucially, only the patients knew that the licensing committee did not conduct any independent testing of drugs, but only reviewed the data which manufacturers sent them (Abraham and Sheppard 1997: 145, 152–53, 160).

A further element in the Abraham and Sheppard findings is political in a wide and highly pertinent sense; the authors cite one of the experts as saying that if a scandal arose over a given medicine, then the central-government minister would usually shift the blame to the relevant expert body in what seems to confirm earlier conclusions that the role of the technocrat in modern societies makes the technocrat less of a ruler than a figure to shield political elites from public pressure (Abraham and Sheppard 1997: 148). This seems to hold despite the fact that the United States, for example, had what was (at the time of the research) a far more transparent process for drug licensing than the United Kingdom did (Abraham and Sheppard 1997: 148, 142–43).

If we can draw wider conclusions from this example, the first of those is that the experts are very much located in political, legislative, and commercial contexts, and that even if they know this, they are extremely sceptical about the public's capacity to understand the technical issues at all, let alone participate in the licensing process. They seem to be the group most committed to maintaining their technocratic authority. That authority, however, does not extend to the risk–benefit evaluations of new drugs, and it seems not to enable the experts to state where the politicians or other lawmakers are responsible for bad decisions on drugs policy or licensing.

Secondly, if the experts consider the public ignorant and incapable of informed judgement, the experts themselves—going by their own statements—seem to be equally ignorant about the very public they claim to be protecting (if not serving, as in this case they are a public body constituted under an Act of Parliament). Another issue arising from the Abraham and Sheppard paper is that it is not clear if the expert committee concerned were aware that they might also be serving as a shield or screen for the pharmaceuticals industry, in effect preventing the development of informed and authoritative public scrutiny of the very drugs the public themselves consume.

Thirdly, the public are both less irrational and much more willing to be involved as serious participants in the whole licensing and treatment process than the experts seem to think they are. Informed public participation in a public space which takes serious public issues seriously could well, of course, generate not only better mutual knowledge between experts and the public but generate far greater public confidence in the experts.

Since the Abraham and Sheppard paper was published, a lot of work has been done on situations and systems in which experts and non-experts engage in participative evaluation or participatory appraisal; this has accompanied increasing public engagement in and with science, particularly in the United States and other Western democracies (Chilvers 2008: 421–23). The public, however, tend still to be excluded from what Chilvers calls core appraisal tasks, because a strict separation is usually maintained between scientific analysis and public deliberation (Chilvers 2008: 446). This in turn excludes analysis of the ways in which scientific or related forms of knowledge are created and validated, and Chilvers notes that this is a failing in many current studies of participatory appraisal (Chilvers 2008: 447). Plato might have thought he had settled the matter of specialist training and knowledge as the foundation of political judgement and the conduct of political life, but instead his argument opened a question which is still very much with us.

MANAGERIALISM

In general, we may have a range of reasons for not doubting technical experts' knowledge, which is usually supported by training, certification, licensing within particular professions (which also have the power to cancel licences to practise), and so on. Managerialism, however, raises serious questions about its own scope and ambitions, and about its own claims to being a body of knowledge at all.

The first thing we need to note is that managerialism is significantly different from public-sector or public-service bureaucracy, even though managerialism and public-service institutions often show similarities, and even though many public institutions, especially in the Anglophone world, have adopted managerialist methods, almost always with disastrous consequences, on which a very substantial body of research work already exists (Morley and Rassool 2000; Cheliotis 2006; Sivaramakrishnan 2012a: 18–21).

The difference between managerialism and public bureaucracy in democratic systems is, however, that no matter how well or badly public bureaucracies work, their work is given to them by lawmakers on behalf of the electorate. It makes no difference that the legislation often leaves the specifics to the bureaucracies. The point is that in principle and by definition public authorities are publicly accountable, even if their accountability is very often perverted and corrupted by political processes, or by the wealthy and the powerful, or by officials and the public themselves.

Managerialism, on the other hand, as I shall show here, is radically different. For its very existence and survival, it has to claim a special kind of knowledge which puts it beyond accountability except as defined by itself; managerialism in many forms even puts those definitions beyond public evaluation.

The central idea of managerialism is the idea that, as I have mentioned above, anyone can be trained to manage anything. It has even happened that someone who had run a bus company was put in charge of a National Health Service general hospital in the United Kingdom, and the consequences for the whole hospital have been documented by doctors who worked there at the time (Riddington Young et al. 2008: 27–86).

Managerialist ideas themselves have quite a long history. The French philosopher Auguste Comte (1798–1857), who for a time was secretary to Henri de Saint-Simon, and the sociologist Émile Durkheim (1858–1917) were so impressed by the success of what they took to be the methods of the natural sciences that they proposed similar methods for the social sciences. According to them, empirical observation would reveal law-like patterns in society in the way the sciences were discovering law-like patterns in nature. The resulting law-like generalisations could then be used for the positive improvement of society, and would replace the old and largely negative critical philosophies. Comte and Durkheim in effect invented the modern term 'positivism'.

Such thinking was not confined to a small number of academics or other scholars. For example, Karl Marx took the work of Saint-Simon, who was himself a philosopher and political economist, very seriously; partly drawing on Saint-Simon, he noted that as the new industrial economies expanded during the Industrial Revolution, fewer and fewer of the new industries or factories were owned and run by single people or single families. Instead, joint-stock companies were rapidly becoming the standard form, and the stock-holders or shareholders left the actual running of the businesses to an emerging class of managers. Very few of this managerial class were rich enough to own either factories or large volumes of shares in them, so in strict terms they were as much members of the proletariat as the factory hands and labourers, but they occupied an intermediate position between the labourers and the owners, and Marx revised his earlier analysis to include managers as a distinct class within capitalism.

In the twentieth century, several attempts were made to develop a science of managerialism, or at least something that looked like a body of managerial knowledge. In the United States, Frederick W. Taylor almost single-handedly invented time-and-motion studies by observing workers on building sites and in factories. In the 1930s, Frank Gilbreth took Taylor's thinking even further, and attempted to apply such methods to every human action.

In 1941, James Burnham, who had been a very eminent figure in the Communist League of America and a successor body called the Socialist Workers Party, wrote a book called *The Managerial Revolution*; his argument was that in industrial societies, when large groups of people did similar things—like buying burgers at big sporting events—the regularities involved could be predicted in law-like ways. In the 1950s, the sociologist Daniel Bell argued in his book *The End of Ideology* that as societies became more industrialised, the ideological differences between them would diminish to the point of insignificance, because the main issues would have to do with how best to manage these increasingly similar systems (Bell 1974).

Main Features or Characteristics

Efficiency

Managerialist theory sets great store by efficiency, such as maximal output for minimal input in the least possible time. In practice, this usually means efficiency is expressed in economic or financial terms. The methods used usually involve purportedly neutral observation, which—according to managerialist theorists—enables us to identify patterns and regularities. We can then identify the causal relations involved and therefore predict the outcome of any particular managerial intervention. Finally, we can replicate these outcomes by making similar interventions in other systems and situations.

The Claim to a Body of Knowledge

Over the last 120 years or so, managerialism has developed a substantial body of literature, and various forms of managerial education and certification have emerged around the world; many famous universities have world-renowned business schools. The underlying theory is that such schools transmit a body of managerial knowledge which enables anyone trained in it to manage any organisation or activity.

This claimed or assumed body of knowledge also generates a form of class consciousness among those who are certified to possess it, and we have already noted Marx's recognition of the emergence and importance of a managerial class. This managerial class has to maintain a distance, which sometimes amounts to total separation, from the practitioners of the activity being managed. The financial rewards can be very substantial indeed, and in the upper ranks of private-sector management often include shares in the businesses concerned.

Problems

The main problems in managerialism fall into two broad categories, the conceptual and the empirical.

Conceptual Failures

Targets

Managerialism almost invariably expresses its own effectiveness, and the quality of the work managed, in terms of targets to be attained. This results from managerialism's own self-definition as a body of knowledge separate from and superior to the knowledge possessed by practitioners of the activity being managed. Otherwise, the managers would have to engage with the practitioners' judgement and experience, and would lose their claim to a special body of knowledge. Therefore, managerialism requires its own index of effectiveness, and most commonly this is a single figure in the form of an output or sales target, earnings, examination pass-rates, and so on.

This, however, reduces often very complex activities to single indicators or indices; it is thoroughly reductivist. In addition, it has to be imposed on the practitioners concerned, and reduces their knowledge and judgement to an irrelevance. Furthermore, expressing managerialism in economic or financial terms alone relies on the assumption that these are the only ways to evaluate any activity.

Neutral Observations and Descriptions

In order to be universalisable, managerialism needs to claim that its body of knowledge or expertise is independent of any context or contexts. This requires two further assumptions. The first is that any regularities or patterns we identify in activities or organisations are unaffected by the observer. The second is that we can describe people's activities in neutral terms. This immediately raises a problem, because when we know we are being watched, we tend to act differently, and yet if a manager or anyone else observes us systematically—and probably for long periods—without our knowing we are being watched, all kinds of moral problems arise. Some countries have recognised this in their laws, and have put restrictions on the observation of people, whether at work or in certain other contexts, even if the extent of electronic surveillance by official bodies today remains largely unaddressed.

The second issue, namely the idea of neutral observation as a managerialist technique, is derived from certain understandings of the natural sciences, or rather from ideas various social scientists have had of the natural sciences. Max Weber, for example, described workers who were lining up to be paid as a line of people assembling to receive pieces of metal. This, however, makes no sense without the idea of contracts for paid work, the idea of institutions such as contract and the relevant laws, and the understanding the workers and their employers have of what contracts of employment mean. Weber himself came to realise this, and concluded that social-scientific explanations had to provide descriptions as well as an understanding of the observed actions or other social phenomena.

Yet managerialism, by its own self-definition, cannot accommodate agents' or practitioners' own accounts of what they are doing; if it does that, it loses its own claim to superior status. The problem is that without the agents' own ideas, any account we give of their actions is unintelligible; we cannot explain, say, a monk's life without an account of the religious ideas involved and the monk's own account of how those ideas inform the monk's life, including their relations with others, such as lay people (Winch 1958: 21–32). This does not mean the monk has sole or unchallengeable authority over an account of what they are doing; we are all familiar with situations in which people interpret what we say or do in ways which surprise or even shock us but which we sometimes have to recognise are accurate interpretations. This is also very common in artistic or aesthetic creation, and a writer or director might well have to respond with something like, 'I hadn't thought of that, but now I can see that my work implies X or Y' (Cavell 1976: 230–37). The point here is that any account of action which excludes the agent's own ideas of what they are doing is unintelligible. It is only an account of movements and not of action.

It also follows that under managerialist theories, we cannot tell the difference between accidental and intentional achievement. If someone who knows nothing about computers or programming happens to sleepwalk to a terminal and write a functioning program, or even happens to write one while tapping randomly at a keyboard, they have not achieved anything by intention; indeed it is not clear what the term 'achievement' would even mean here (MacIntyre 1962: 55–61). The sleepwalker, however, may have met a managerial target. For managerialism, the target is all that matters, not how it is achieved. An accidental achievement is still an achievement, according to managerialism (Fay 1996: 114).

It would, furthermore, not be an answer to replicate the conditions in which somebody achieved or did something in the expectation that they or other people in a similar situation would replicate the actions involved. On 30 January 1968, the day of the Vietnamese Lunar New Year or Tet, the Việt Cộng launched a completely unexpected military offensive against US bases in South Vietnam; the offensive was a military disaster, but it had a shock value far beyond its military context and results. Yet dozens of research institutes around the world spent years trying to simulate the conditions in which the Tet Offensive had been launched, with a view to predicting when and where military commanders or governments would do such a thing again. Some researchers may still be engaged on that task. The point is that failures of prediction in complex human situations are not technical failures; they can result from any number of accidental factors, such as unexpectedly severe weather, political and social events which have unexpected effects, radical conceptual innovations, or very significant discoveries (MacIntyre 2007: 95–100). Above all, however, failures of managerialism occur because people's conduct is simply not predictable in formulaic ways, and the reason for that is that we are intentional beings.

The incoherence of managerialism's purported body of theory or knowledge therefore means that attempts to apply it result in decisions whose outcomes cannot be predicted and which are therefore arbitrary. In practice, the decisions seem to depend as much on the personality of individual managers as on any supposedly rational training or any body of managerial theory (Simkins 2000: 324–27). Just as dangerously, the incoherence of the theory means managerialism has no criteria for relevance. Anything, however trivial, in the lives of those being managed can be used as evidence to evaluate their performance. This has clear parallels with fascism and other forms of totalitarianism. The fact that a handful of very large private corporations are starting to abandon annual performance appraisals does not change the character of the process (Cunningham 2015).

Empirical Failures

The failures of managerialism are legion, and have been covered in detail elsewhere (Sivaramakrishnan 2012a: 1–47; MacIntyre 2007: 88–90). Those are, of course, only the failures which have become public knowledge; we shall probably never know how many others have been covered up or lied about, or the victims of which have received payments under gagging clauses. For our purposes here, a small number of examples will suffice, including those which show how managerialism affects even the most everyday details of our lives.

The British National Health Service, which has had a very demanding range of managerialist targets imposed on it over a period of several years, provides many such cases. One monitoring system required Accident and Emergency (A&E) departments in hospitals to attend to all new patients within a set time. The target time was almost the sole index of performance, and became so important that some A&E departments started keeping ambulances waiting outside, because the waiting time was measured from the moment the patients came in through the door; other responses to the target regime involved sending patients to other departments, such as diagnostics, so that they did not appear in A&E department records (Gubb 2008: 442–43).

In another British example, in 2008 Surrey Police decided to concentrate on everyday practical policing rather than meeting managerially imposed conviction targets. The pressure to meet those targets had been so great that officers had started charging children with criminal offences for marking chalk lines on pavements for their games. The senior officer who announced the decision said the force had realised that ordinary people who called the police wanted ordinary practical solutions to the problems involved, because public confidence in the police to deal with relevant everyday matters was more important than achieving misleading targets (*Daily Telegraph* 2008).

Managerialism also has a toxic effect on major national policies, even if the managerialist terms in which these are expressed are not necessarily used with that intention. Yet managerialist language enables failures to be concealed, when the use of plain language would have enabled far more accurate and thorough evaluation of policy. For example, in India the Raghuram Rajan Committee, which reported to the central government in 2013 on the allocation of central government funds to the states, put some of its main proposals in exclusively managerialist terms. The report attempted to include factors such as education, female literacy, household amenities, and the like in the way it calculated the proposed allocations, but it concluded with a thoroughly managerialist formula based on the concepts of absorption capacity and performance (Prakash and Goyal 2013).

Absorption capacity means the capacity of states to use the funds allocated, which is often a serious problem in Indian public policy (Sivaramakrishnan 2012a: 87–88). Performance here means the aggregate outcomes of the policies which use the funds allocated; one index might be, say, health figures in terms of morbidity or changes in the incidence of illness, but that would fail to show, for example, how many Dalits or Muslims visit local health centres, or even if disadvantaged groups had any health centres within reach. In addition, the report puts performance in terms of economic growth (Prakash and Goyal 2013).

The report assumes an input–output logic of precisely the inductive kind which makes the establishment of causality impossible. Secondly, it omits the crucial fact that performance involves both process and outcome; its proposed indices cannot accommodate, for example, the way powerful or dominant groups—most often in India, caste groups—capture implementing bodies or regulatory bodies to the exclusion of others, often those who need good implementation most (Prakash and Goyal 2013). Prakash and Goyal term the thinking behind the report techno-managerial, and they would have been equally right had they simply called it managerialist.

Another highly significant Indian policy in which managerialist terms enable inherent and serious flaws to be concealed has to do with education. The Right to Education Act 2009, which is partly based on a constitutional amendment, gives every child the right to free and compulsory education between the ages of six and fourteen. The Act has certainly led to increases in school enrolments, especially in states where enrolments had long been low, but at the same time, some of the states concerned stopped appointing qualified teachers, and systematically replaced them with unqualified parateachers on far lower salaries and far worse terms. The parateachers, however well-intentioned, are on the evidence not paid enough to stay (Rao 2009). They would presumably be sacked if they obtained professional teaching qualifications. The result is that targets for enrolment, and for the appointment of staff, can be reached, but that putting the outcome in terms of targets enables the governments concerned to conceal this calculated subversion of the Right to Education Act.

Conclusion

Within managerialist theory, there are some signs of change, though how far these will affect managerialism in practice is far from clear. Rakesh Khurana, in a detailed history of management training in the United States, argues that management has failed to fulfil the promise its own proponents have repeatedly made, namely that it would become a profession with an identifiable body of knowledge and its own licensing and certifying bodies (Khurana 2007). Bob Locke, for his part, argues that management schools have failed to recognise the effect of significant cultural differences in management styles, for example, those which obtain between Japanese and US management methods (Locke 2009). In addition, Kothari and Kothari have pointed out that Indian management schools have focused so much on teaching a certain version of corporate-orientated management theory that they have neglected highly successful forms of management in India, especially in the semi-formal sector. The number of businesses in this sector could number tens or perhaps even hundreds of millions, and their methods are highly suitable for the cultures and the specific contexts in which they work (Kothari and Kothari 2011).

That, however, leaves unaddressed—perhaps intentionally—the nature of managerialism as it stands. The American management professor Bob Locke does not mince words:

> **Managerialism**—What occurs when a special group, called management, ensconces itself systemically in organizations and deprives owners and employees of decision-making power (including the distribution of emoluments)—and justifies the takeover on the grounds of the group's education and exclusive possession of the codified bodies of knowledge and know-how necessary to the efficient running of organizations. (Locke 1996, cited in Locke 2009)

It could of course be that even within managerialism, claims to universality are being abandoned. It remains to be seen if the other incoherences I have identified will also be admitted, but whether or not they are, the one question no form of managerialism seems yet to have acknowledged is that of why a particular activity is being carried out at all. That kind of question raises moral and political issues, but its neglect—or deliberate exclusion—can have truly terrible consequences. One person who showed a remarkable talent for management and managerial organisation was Adolf Eichmann, an administrator in Nazi Germany who organised the Final Solution, the mass extermination programme whereby six million people, almost overwhelmingly Jews, were slaughtered on an industrial scale. During his trial, which took place in Israel in 1961, Eichmann was asked how he could implement such a plan for mass slaughter without ever questioning it. He replied in German, '*Befehl ist Befehl*'. In English, that would be 'An order is an order'. His statement summed up managerialism.

CHAPTER 10: TECHNOCRACY AND MANAGERIALISM

Extension Exercise

Read this article:

Lynch, Kathleen. 2014. 'New Managerialism: The Impact on Education'. *Concept* 5 (3): 1–11. http://concept.lib.ed.ac.uk/index.php/Concept/article/viewFile/271/255

Using the article, write short notes on these:

1. The main internal changes that occur when managerialism is introduced into an organisation.
2. The moral values which managerialism also introduces as an unstated element, and the ones these values or concepts replace.
3. Do the stated values of managerialism put an end to hierarchies within organisations?

Further Reading

Bucchi, Massimiano. 2010. *Beyond Technocracy: Science, Politics and Citizens*. Dordrecht: Springer.
Noted analysis of the tensions between technical experts and the public on a range of issues including nuclear energy, genetic engineering, and stem-cell research.

Locke, Robert R., and J-C Spender. 2011. *Confronting Managerialism: How the Business Elite and Their Schools Threw Our Lives out of Balance*. London: Zed Books.
Sharp analysis of managerialism's dependence on neoclassical economics and finance theory, showing the effect on business schools and the consequences for organisations, with empirical evidence of the resulting problems, inefficiencies, and loss of productivity.

11

CHAPTER

Nationalism

> Nationalism is the starkest political shame of the twentieth century, the deepest, most intractable and yet most unanticipated blot on the political history of the world since 1900. But it is also the very tissue of modern political sentiment, the most widespread, the most unthinking, and the most immediate political disposition of all at least among the literate populations of the modern world. (Dunn 1999: 27)

Nationalism is a potent force in almost all forms of political life, and like conservatism, it is not easily categorised as a single ideology. Like conservatism, it takes a range of forms, several of which share more than one characteristic, and it may well be better understood as a range of outlooks rather than as a specific body of theory; that may also help account for its enduring character. In addition, nationalism has been associated with many other ideologies, from liberalism through socialism to fundamentalism, and we have already encountered the element of ethno-nationalism in certain forms of fundamentalism.

The fact that nationalism has a very wide range of forms also means that it is not always regarded as a modern development. Azar Gat, for example, sees nationalism as one form of political ethnicity and identifies it as having been a strong force in empires of very ancient times, such as the Assyrian empire which existed in the second millennium BCE; he identifies ethnicity in the sense of national membership as a powerful, if not decisive, political element in the creation and survival of many other ancient empires, including those of ancient India, though he says of India that ethnic diversification occurred at the local level (Gat 2013: 17, 111–25). Gat's wider argument is that forms of nationalism, whether modern or premodern, permeate human history and that they 'spring from deep within the human psyche' (Gat 2013: 17). We need not take issue with that argument in detail here, but we should note that the Greek historian Herodotus (484–425 BCE) may have been the first to use the term *ethnos* to mean 'nation', even if quite what he meant by that is still the subject of argument, as is whether or not the term 'nation' provides a complete translation of the term *ethnos* (Papastephanou 2012).

Nationalism in its modern sense, however, has emerged as other forms of political organisations have declined; these are kingdoms, principalities, and the like (Heywood 2007: 144–45). Nationalism, however, may not have been planned or explicitly intended to replace such forms, as it seems to have had its first modern expression during the French Revolution, where it was among other things a rallying call for the French people to rise up against their aristocratic oppressors.

The term 'nationalism' in its modern sense also has a conceptual relation to another historical development, namely the idea of sovereignty. That idea arose in its modern form when many of the major rulers of Europe signed the Peace of Westphalia in 1648. The treaty marked the end of the Thirty Years' War, which was a truly terrible one, with besieged populations even resorting to cannibalism (Wedgwood 1938: 330, 411–14). This war, which was mainly fought in what is now Germany, involved almost every nation in the then Europe as well as Russia, and also had a substantial religious motivation, with bitter hostility between the Holy Roman Empire and the increasingly widespread new denomination of Protestantism. The Peace of Westphalia, which given the physical conditions of travel and communications at the time took many months to finalise, also played a part in creating the modern concept of sovereignty over territory, whereby rulers would recognise one another's authority within designated boundaries. As we shall see, this element of recognition is central to nationalism and nationalist movements in our time.

Historically, nationalism has had an enormous impact on the human world, from one of its earliest expressions in the French Revolution, which started in 1789, through movements for the unification of formerly separate territories, to powerful and successful demands for the end of colonial subjecthood and the more recent claims to separation from existing countries on the grounds of unrecognised or oppressed nationhood. Perhaps the earliest modern claim to nationhood was made in the French Revolution; the sufferings of the people under Louis XVI and his predecessors had reached a point where the public rose up in the name of the nation; the uprising was extremely violent, probably expressing the bitterness of the leaders and some of their followers, but for us the conceptual point is that the people put an end to their status as subjects of the crown and declared themselves citizens of the nation. Such a development is relatively familiar to us today, as are symbols like national flags, national anthems, stereotypes of national identity, and customs and practices which are considered or claimed to be typical of particular nations. France's national day is 14 July, Bastille Day, the day on which the French public stormed the notorious Bastille prison. India, for its part, has what are in effect two national days, namely 15 August, marking the day the country achieved Independence from Britain in 1947, and 26 January, the day in 1950 on which the Republic of India came into being.

The propagation of such symbols and related language, terminology, and rhetoric was greatly aided and facilitated in the nineteenth century as literacy and the mass media—at that time, newspapers and magazines—spread, but nationalism as an ideology was also located in a particular social class during that period. This was the mercantile upper-middle class which had emerged in the previous century and was overwhelmingly committed to liberalism. That in turn meant the spread of constitutional government, with laws intended to be applied equally to all (Heywood 2007: 145). For that it was necessary to specify the geographical area within which any one constitution would hold, and therefore the idea of national boundaries gained even more currency than it had inherited from the Peace of Westphalia.

Given the many forms nationalism takes and its association with many different ideologies, it can look amorphous or difficult to characterise, but certain themes or concepts seem to be shared by most forms of this ideology; it is therefore an ideology and not just a political sentiment or political doctrine. The main themes in nationalism are:

- The nation
- Community or organic community
- Self-determination
- Identity and identity politics

THE NATION

The idea of a nation is obviously central to nationalism, but it is virtually impossible to say or specify what a nation is or what constitutes a nation. Very often, the claim is made that a nation is made up of a group of people who share a common culture and common traditions; these are often taken to be such things as shared language, shared religion and history, and often a common geographical area.

Yet the problem is that for every one of the criteria we might regard as necessary for nationhood, significant exceptions exist. For example, Kurdish communities are found in south-eastern Turkey, north-western Iran, north-eastern Iraq, and Syria. Kurdish people often see themselves as a nation, a claim which is perfectly intelligible; they also have the Kurdish language in common. Yet it is only in Iraq that Kurds have a designated territory—specifically, an autonomous self-governing province, which also elects representatives to the Iraqi assembly in Baghdad when general elections are held; significantly, this is a politically constituted province, and there is no question of the exclusion of, say, non-Kurdish Iraqis from Iraqi Kurdistan. Tibetans, for their part, can reasonably claim to constitute a nation, despite the fact that Tibet was annexed by China in 1951, but Tibet had earlier been administered by the Qing dynasty (1644–1912) of China, and even when under something resembling self-rule by the Dalai Lama from 1912 to 1951 the region was effectively under British rule. In several of the northern provinces of Sri Lanka, strong claims to nationhood have long been made by Tamil-speaking leaders for the creation of a Tamil nation, and when the terrible 20-year civil war seemed to be ending in 2009, renewed discussion arose of federal or quasi-federal arrangements with the apparent intention of giving some recognition to those claims without creating a separate self-governing state. In this connection, we need to note that there seems to have been no serious claim by any political body that the Tamil-speaking regions of Sri Lanka be united with the Indian state of Tamil Nadu, where Tamil (albeit involving a range of dialects other than Sri Lankan Tamil) is the majority language.

While the Tamil language is one of the main unifying factors in Sri Lankan Tamils' claim to nationhood, in other areas of the world, languages are shared without any corresponding claims to national identity. English is spoken in the United Kingdom, where it is the most widely spoken language, and is also the language of Australia and New Zealand, but no claim is made that the peoples of these three states constitute a single English nation. It would, furthermore, be at best implausible to regard, say, even those who are first-language English speakers in South Asia and the former British territories in East or West Africa as even potential members of an English nation. In addition, a common language makes no difference at all to deep and often violent religious divisions in some parts of the world, such as those which have obtained in the devolved British region of Northern Ireland. Indeed, in Northern Ireland, the majority of Protestants favour continuing membership of the United Kingdom, while most of the minority Catholic community favour union with the Republic of Ireland. (In any case, as the United Kingdom and the Republic of Ireland are both members of the European Union (EU), the border between Northern Ireland and the Irish Republic is in effect an open one.)

If language is not by itself sufficient to define a nation, it may therefore look as though religion provides a definite ground for the concept of a nation. The partition of British India into India and Pakistan in the years leading to the British departure in 1947 was at least in theory founded on that principle, though the resulting upheaval and mass slaughter were truly terrible; the consequences are very obvious even today, but all the three countries concerned—that is, India, Pakistan, and Bangladesh—have very substantial numbers of people of all faiths. Even within a single faith, religious or doctrinal divisions do not always generate claims to nationhood. The United Kingdom, where the official state religion has been the Anglican faith since King Henry VIII rejected the authority of the Pope and made himself head of the Church of England in 1534, has a wide range of Christian denominations, but these have not given rise to rival nationalisms. The same is true of the United States (Heywood 2007: 148–49). Similarly, Poland, Italy, Brazil, the Philippines, and the Republic of Ireland, in each of which the Catholic faith has overwhelmingly the largest number of followers, do not constitute a 'Catholic nation' (Heywood 2007: 149).

COMMUNITY

Partly in response to the many problems with the idea that either language or religion is foundational to nationalism, various theorists have argued that nationalism has to be understood in the light of people's self-understandings, or the ideas that peoples around the world have of themselves. As we have seen, particular peoples may share languages or faiths and yet not consider themselves collectively to be a nation. One response to this has been that languages and faiths have to be seen like other forms of commonality, such as class or gender, and that any of these will be pertinent in particular contexts without forming a foundation for the idea of a nation. The nation, according to this line of argument, is some kind of organic entity more like ties of kinship, and has its origins in primordial or ancient cultural inheritances which long predate modern states. This also implies that membership of a modern nation is closely tied to historical ethnicity; the term 'ethnies' has been used for such earlier groupings (Smith 1986, cited in Heywood 2007: 152).

Today's nations, however, are not simple or direct developments from the ethnies of Smith's conception. They are often extremely or even enormously large either geographically or in the size of their respective populations. Russia uses eleven time zones spanning ten hours; China's population, at the time of writing, is about 1.38 billion, and India's is about 1.34 billion. Even in very small countries, it is inconceivable that people can think of one another as some sort of extended tribe or family; it is far from clear what it might even mean to think that or what sort of connections or obligations we would have towards one another if that situation did obtain. Nevertheless, the idea of a nation endures almost all around the world, and some have proposed that it has put down deep roots in modern societies, even though a return to premodern or primordial societies is unthinkable; according to such theories, the value of this idea of a nation is that it provides social and other forms of cohesion in today's much more individualistic societies. It follows that the idea of a nation is closer to what the German philosopher Ferdinand Tönnies called *Gemeinschaft*, in the sense of community, than it is to *Gesellschaft*, in the sense of the much looser and often contractual associations which we find in much of contemporary life (Heywood 2007: 152).

One result is that the idea of a nation has a powerful role in our imagination, and Benedict Anderson has articulated this in detail, arguing that nations are 'imagined communities'; this also means that we can see ourselves as being members of our nation without needing direct contact with every other member of it, and that we can share various common understandings of ourselves and our fellow members even if we are very far away from them either geographically or historically. Anderson says communities are to be distinguished not by whether they are genuine or false, but by the 'style in which they are imagined'. He adds here that until recently, Javanese society had no word for the abstract term 'society', and that in pre-revolutionary France, aristocrats would not have identified themselves as members of a ruling class or ruling aristocracy but as the duke of a place, or as a relative of another aristocrat, and so on (Anderson 1991: 6–7).

A problem arising, however, is that of how an imagined entity like the nation can command such loyalty or devotion that millions or tens of millions are even willing to lay down their lives for it, even if they have known one another for generations and have grown up together. Michael Ignatieff writes of the time he spent on the Serbian–Croatian front line during the terrible nationalist wars in the Balkans in the early 1990s:

> This is a village war. Everyone knows everyone else: they all went to school together; before the war, some of them worked in the same garage; they dated the same girls. Every night, they call each other up on the CB radio and exchange insults—by name. Then they go back to trying to kill each other. (Ignatieff 1999)

Anderson, for his part, recognises that the idea of a nation, or its history, therefore cannot be reduced to official histories or official documents, and that the kind of attachment he sees as central to national membership seems to be at its strongest in a time of war (Anderson 1991: 144; Balakrishnan 1996: 208–13). That, however, also implies that nationalism itself is a construction, and even a myth; the argument here is that historical continuity and cultural homogeneity or purity are themselves ideological creations which conceal class relations and class interests. More specifically, according to this line of reasoning, powerful classes have invented the ideas of historical and cultural unity; the nation itself becomes a creation, even an invention, which conceals class interests, and the argument is therefore that it was nationalism that invented nations (Hobsbawm 1983, cited in Heywood 2007: 152). We have already noted an example of this in the way the idea of the United States has until very recently involved almost no recognition of the foundational role slavery played in the establishment and consolidation of capitalism in the United States.

SELF-DETERMINATION

This term figures less in today's political discourse than it did during the first two or three decades following the Second World War; at that time, the two major imperial powers of the previous two and a half centuries, Britain and France, were rapidly leaving their imperial territories, or were being thrown out—as happened to France when the Viet Cong defeated French forces at Dien Bien Phu in 1954. Across Africa and Asia in the period after the Second World War, subject peoples claimed and usually won the right to self-determination. Article 1 of the Charter of the United Nations states that one of the four purposes of the UN is 'To develop friendly relations among nations based on respect for the principle of equal rights and self-determination of peoples, and to take other appropriate measures to strengthen universal peace'.

Since 1945, when the UN was founded, large numbers of new countries—called states in international law—have been founded in recognition of the Article 1 principle. The UN has been directly involved in at least one such case, namely the creation of Timor Leste in 2002. The country had formerly been East Timor, a Portuguese colony since the early seventeenth century and then part of Indonesia, which had annexed the territory in 1975. The independence movement was brutally suppressed, and Timor Leste achieved its independence only after the then-UN Secretary-General Kofi Annan persuaded the Indonesian president to accept UN intervention in accordance with Chapter VII of the UN Charter (Annan with Mousavizadeh 2012: 101–18).

The UN principle of the right to self-determination is not the first such to be stated in international affairs. The US president Woodrow Wilson put it forward as part of the victorious powers' proposals for the reconstruction of Europe after the First World War; the underlying thinking is that nations are largely homogeneous linguistic and cultural entities, and that therefore they occupy identifiable single areas or territories (Heywood 2007: 154, 158). In other words, Wilson seemed to think nations and states were coterminous. We shall see below that this conception caused terrible problems and that it may well involve very serious misconceptions about the very nature of human association.

IDENTITY POLITICS

Nationalism, like conservatism and fascism, relies on and develops conceptions of identity by drawing upon, for example, territory, religion, and language, and on less obviously tangible things such as will, memory, and political loyalty. This also has the effect of reminding or telling people who they are and what brings them together as a people. In its stronger or more strident forms, it can also inculcate a sense of destiny or purpose; these less tangible elements may explain how it is that nationalism is often very prominent in politics and why nationalist politicians or writers are often very popular, in some cases for long periods, even if—as we shall see—much of the theory of nationalism is contradictory and even incoherent (Heywood 2007: 155–56).

Nationalism based on identity politics also involves the idea of a national consciousness, and proponents of such forms of nationalism often draw on what they claim are national myths, traditions, folk tales, and legends to define or specify the national consciousness which they advocate. In Germany, the philosophers Johann Herder (1744–1803) and Johann Fichte (1762–1814) were among the most noted proponents of this form of nationalism, and Herder seems to have held that each nation possesses its own national spirit. He seems, however, to have considered this to be a matter of language and culture, and he also seems to have rejected the idea of hierarchy of nations (Foster 2007). That kind of thinking is often called cultural nationalism, and at least in theory is somewhat different from nationalist theories based on ethnic membership, or ethnic nationalism. This is both racially and culturally exclusivist (Heywood 2007: 156–57). In extreme forms, it amounts to fascism, and it has permanently fascistic undertones.

Historically, nationalism which involves a strong element of identity politics has often arisen when peoples have been subjected to colonial or imperial rule. What we now know as Germany was an area of 39 states, including city-states, before the Prussian army's victories over Austria in 1866 and France in 1870–71 enabled the Prussian ruler Wilhelm I to proclaim himself the German emperor and to claim that Germany had been unified; in effect, it was the spread of Napoleonic rule across much of Europe that had given rise to nationalistic uprisings. Similar developments occurred in Italy and in Latin America, where the major nationalist leader Simón Bolívar (1783–1830) led successful uprisings against imperial Spain; several independent countries, such as Bolivia, Colombia, Ecuador, Peru, and Venezuela were founded as a result (Heywood 2007: 144).

Similar things could be said about India; before the achievement of Independence in 1947, the idea of India as a single nation may not even have figured in the thinking of the hundreds of rulers in the geographical area now called South Asia. Even in the First War of Independence in 1857, some of those involved in the uprising, such as the Rani of Jhansi, seem to have been relatively indifferent to the fate of the kingdoms or other areas around them, let alone the wider region of India. Indeed, even the most courageous among those who fought against the colonisers in 1857 seem to have had no awareness of what has been called 'a great cause for which they were prepared to sacrifice their narrow selfish interests' (Abel 2005: 31–32). This state of affairs continued until and even after Independence; it is well enough known that the 561 princely states were extremely suspicious of and even hostile to the Indian National Congress for a range of reasons, and that very few of them had any wish to accede to the incipient Indian Union (Reid 2016: 235–38). In the end, it may have been nothing other than the facts of geography, and the fact that almost none of the princely states had the slightest chance of defending themselves against attack by other countries, that led to their accession to the Union (Reid 2016: 235–38). That of course has changed very greatly in the last few decades; the princely states are now simply part of the states of India where they happen to be, and many of the former rulers are now significant political participants in the Indian republic, joining political parties and standing for election in the usual way.

As nationalism is such an elastic or even amorphous ideology, its political expressions inevitably draw from other ideologies and therefore fall into relatively clear strands, which show strong inheritances from particular ideologies, and we need to be able to identify the main forms. These are:

- Liberal nationalism
- Conservative nationalism and reactionary nationalism
- Expansionist nationalism

LIBERAL NATIONALISM

This may well be one of the oldest forms of nationalism, dating from the French Revolution and the ideas which informed some of it, in particular those put forward by Jean-Jacques Rousseau (1712–78). Polish struggles for independence from Russia led Rousseau to conclude that there is such a thing as the general will, and that this is vested in any culturally unified people. Therefore, monarchical or autocratic government was illegitimate, and governments, according to Rousseau, must express the public will. Sovereignty would therefore reside with the people and not the monarch, and the people ceased to be subjects of a monarch; instead they became citizens of a nation, that is, citizens who possessed inalienable rights and duties. This is a highly political vision, as citizenship is both a national and a political status involving a certain form of political organisation (Heywood 2007: 153–54). This in turn gives rise to the idea of the nation-state, a concept I shall examine in a later section below.

The emergence of the modern conception—as expressed by Rousseau's inheritors—of citizenship as involving nationalism as well as citizenship in liberal forms had the result that liberal principles of mutual non-interference, tolerance, and the right to national liberty or self-determination are also central to relations between states. Citizens who enjoyed rights within their national boundaries were also obliged to ensure that their own governments did not restrict the rights of citizens in other countries to live their lives as they wished. This goes beyond nationalism to a form of internationalism, and many of the founding ideas of global or multilateral bodies, such as the UN or the EU, show the widespread acceptance of such principles. A further result is that member states of such bodies are expected to work towards negotiated agreements; the South Asian Association for Regional Cooperation (SAARC), which was founded in 1985, explicitly excludes discussion of bilateral issues. In relation to other regions of the world, the UN often has a very substantial role in agreements between states and, for example, the British Good Friday Agreement, which was signed in 1998 and effectively ended violence so severe in Northern Ireland that it amounted to civil war, is a UN treaty; it comprises two parts, one signed by most of the Northern Ireland political parties, and the other signed only by the British government and the government of the Republic of Ireland.

CONSERVATIVE AND REACTIONARY NATIONALISM

Conservative thinkers and leaders have often regarded nationalism as a dangerous and destabilising force, especially when their own subjects have a variety of ethnic, religious, linguistic, or other origins. Yet towards the end of the nineteenth century, leaders like the British prime minister Benjamin Disraeli, the first German chancellor Otto von Bismarck, and the Russian tsar Alexander III came to see nationalism as a unifying force which helped them to maintain order and the traditional institutions of their countries and societies (Heywood 2007: 161).

Strong forms of conservative nationalism, often expressed in vehemently exclusivist and even racist terms, are very obvious today; for example, in the United Kingdom, in the form of hostility to continued membership of the EU, the law of which takes precedence over domestic law in the event of an actual or possible clash of laws, and in the form of aggressive and sometimes violent hostility to citizens of other EU states who, under EU law, are entitled to live and work in the United Kingdom. While the Conservative Party has always been deeply divided over membership of the former European Economic Community and now the EU, the most visible nationalist party at present is the UK Independence Party or UKIP, which won 15 per cent of the votes in the 2015 general election but, under the simple-majority electoral system gained only one seat in the House of Commons. In the 2017 general election, however, the UKIP vote-share collapsed to 1.8 per cent and the party won no seats.

Other Western countries where forms of ethno-nationalism are currently very prominent include Germany, where the Alternative für Deutschland party (AfD) has gone from opposing the eurozone bailouts for Greece in 2013 to a much more wide-ranging and extreme nationalist position; this involves expressing particular hostility towards Germany's substantial Turkish-descended minority and towards the West Asian refugees whom the German government has admitted to the country in the last three years or so (BBC 2016b). Even the AfD's first leader Bernd Lucke left the party over its increasing xenophobia, but in 2016 the party took second place in the elections to the provincial assembly in Mecklenburg–Western Pomerania, with 21 per cent as against the Social Democratic Party's 36 per cent. The AfD has repeatedly won seats in other provincial assemblies as well, and openly asserts that multicultural and multinational societies cannot work (BBC 2016b).

Perhaps the most successful conservative-nationalist party in continental Europe is the French Front National (or National Front), which was founded in 1972 as an assemblage of far-Right parties and is now a strong national party; the party won several municipalities in the 2014 municipal elections and topped the regional elections in 2015 with 28 per cent of the vote; it also won the French elections to the European Parliament in 2014, with a quarter of the votes. The party's leader, Marine Le Pen came second in the first round of the next presidential election, which was held on 23 April 2017, with 21.30 per cent of the vote. In the second and decisive round, held on 7 May 2017, Emmanuel Macron, who had won the first round with 24.01 per cent, won by 66.1 per cent to Le Pen's 33.9 per cent. The party's main positions are socially conservative and economically protectionist; economic protectionism runs directly counter to the EU's Single European Act. Much of the National Front's support, however, results from its hostility to mass immigration; the party's expressions of this often come close to open Islamophobia and seem to be based on the idea that large cultural and religious minorities are a threat to French national unity. As the National Front has gained more widespread support, however, the leader has moderated some of the party's more obviously xenophobic positions. She has even presided over the expulsion of the previous leader, her father Jean-Marie Le Pen, whose attitudes were very extreme and who publicly all but denied the Holocaust; indeed his reference to Nazi gas chambers as 'a detail' of the Second World War was what led to his expulsion from the party. Certain other European countries, however, continue with extreme forms of xenophobic nationalism, and one of the most obvious is Hungary, where the prime minister Viktor Orbán started his second term in 2010 on an explicit and extreme nationalist platform which he calls illiberal democracy. Orbán's

Fidesz–Hungarian Civic Union (Fidesz–Magyar Polgári Szövetség), which currently rules in coalition with the Christian Democratic People's Party (Kereszténydemokrata Néppárt or KDPN), has espoused positions so extreme that the EU has warned that Hungary risks suspension from the EU.

It is highly significant that none of the current ethno-nationalist, racist-nationalist, or xenophobic-nationalist parties in contemporary Europe makes any mention of the fact that for the task of reconstruction after the terrible destruction of the Second World War, almost all the larger European countries imported what amounted in all to several million cheap labourers from extremely poor regions of the world; these territories included former imperial territories as well as Yugoslavia and Portugal. Many of the conditions laid down were extremely restrictive; Germany, for example, made it very difficult, if not impossible, for imported workers or *Gastarbeiter* to obtain German citizenship. The obliteration of this fact from European public discourse is in effect not nationalist but racist, and constitutes racism on a continental scale.

Conservative nationalism does, however, have less extreme and less xenophobic forms, and its greatest moderate European exponent was probably Charles de Gaulle, who led the exiled French forces during the Second World War and then was president of France from 1959 (he played a substantial part in creating the French Fifth Republic to end a serious constitutional crisis). De Gaulle's form of conservative nationalism, which he had introduced as head of the provisional government towards the end of the war, involved substantial state support for and direction of the economy. This kind of nationalism seems to appear in established states, and it shares many of its main contentions with conservatism. These include a view of society as organic and also place great value on the traditions and historical inheritances which, according to conservatism, make countries what they are (Heywood 2007: 162). The resulting policies can cause tensions even with international allies; de Gaulle, for example, made France an associate member of the North Atlantic Treaty Organization (NATO) from 1965 onwards rather than a full member; he also insisted, to the anger and dismay of his NATO allies, on an independent defence and foreign policy.

EXPANSIONIST NATIONALISM

This is connected with both imperialism and fascism. We have already seen that fascism rejects all state boundaries as false and artificial creations which divide and weaken the unity of races—which in turn are the defining units of human membership. Therefore, according to fascist theory, the superior races must unite across all frontiers, and must ultimately be assembled into some sort of fascist territory which only they occupy. The process will inevitably involve violent conquest, mass expulsions, and finally mass extermination.

Aggressive or expansionist nationalism, for its part, had its historical peak in the eighteenth and nineteenth centuries, when the major European powers extended their empires across most of the world. This form of expansion was accompanied by often crude but highly popular expressions of racial and cultural superiority, including the conviction that the so-called white races, especially the European ones, had a duty to colonise all others with a view to elevating them morally and culturally. The British imperialist politician T. B. Macaulay, speaking about India, even told parliament that:

> To have found a great people sunk in the lowest depths of slavery and superstition, to have ruled them so as to make them desirous and capable of all the privileges of citizens, would indeed be a title to glory all our own. (Macaulay 1833, cited in Reid 2016: 2)

Other forms of expansionist nationalism have sometimes been expressed in Russia, and involve the idea that Russians are the 'natural' leaders of all Slavic peoples, that is, all who speak Slavic languages, and that Slavs are in some way culturally superior to peoples who inherit other cultures (Heywood 2007: 165). Similar claims are made from time to time all around the world, in varying cultural and political contexts, and the attitudes concerned have given rise to particular forms of terminology. One of the words used for expansionist nationalism is jingoism, which was coined in the 1870s and means aggressive or militarist nationalism; another is chauvinism, which follows the name of Nicolas Chauvin, a French soldier who was a fanatical follower of Napoleon Bonaparte (Heywood 2007: 163–64).

NATIONALISM AND COLONIALISM

Certain forms of nationalism are direct responses to the experience of colonialism and imperialism. In 1920, Britain ruled a quarter of the land surface of the globe and 420 million people, just under a quarter of the world's population at the time; France, including its European territories, ruled about a third of that area, encompassing about 110 million people. These were the largest empires yet known in human history. Together with the Dutch and Portuguese empires, they also subjugated and controlled well over half a billion people, often in conditions of great cruelty and brutality (for example, the aboriginals of Tasmania were exterminated by white invaders) and in a climate of racism and cultural contempt which have generated lasting bitterness and continue very obviously in our own time.

We need not be at all surprised that colonial and imperial rule resulted in the emergence of nationalist movements and that they even played a part in creating the idea of nations where, before colonial conquest, other senses of association and authority had obtained. A further important element in many of the anticolonial national liberation movements was a commitment to economic self-determination. This was partly because the modern imperial powers had industrial economies which both needed enormous supplies of raw materials and produced far more than their own populations could possibly consume. They had plundered raw materials from their colonies and had then sold the resulting finished goods back to what were in effect captive markets, where the populations were prevented from developing their own productive systems. In India, the move by the Indian independence leaders to defy this forced consumption by starting the Swadeshi movement caused the colonials great alarm. Lenin regarded imperialism as the highest stage of capitalism, and also noted that the colonisation of markets applies to rivalries between industrialised countries, which compete for markets in one another's economies (Lenin 1963: 265–75).

The economic element in anticolonial or postcolonial nationalism often drew on ideas the colonials themselves, largely unintentionally, imparted to those colonial leaders who had been to school or had done higher studies in imperial countries. Academics who founded and taught in universities in the British and French empires also played a part in teaching the philosophic and political ideas of the imperial powers' own intellectual traditions, and thereby may well have had the effect of aiding the developing independence movements among colonised peoples. Many leaders of the independence movements also saw the inequalities of their own societies as a moral and political evil, and included a strong socialist element in their nationalist campaigns for independence. The resulting political economy ranged from the broadly social-democratic outlook of Jawaharlal Nehru to the more explicitly Marxist commitments of Hồ. Chí Minh in Vietnam and of Fidel Castro, the Cuban leader. Perhaps the most extreme form of anticolonial Marxism was that adopted by Mao Zedong, who led China from 1949 to 1976.

The specific relation of Mao's politics and the system he created to Marx's analysis of capitalism is a more complex issue and one that I shall not cover here, but we need to note that India's commitment to social democracy with a broadly state-managed economy caused the country's emerging business elites such concern that in 1944, they effectively forced a plan—known as the Bombay Plan—on the Indian National Congress, whereby the state would install the basic infrastructure of a modern economy by the late 1970s and then hand much of this over to the private industrial sector (Prashad 2015: 32–45). We also need to note that Fidel Castro and his fellow revolutionary Ernesto 'Che' Guevara decided not to follow the Soviet model of political economy (Guardiola-Rivera 2013: 96–98).

That is only one of many examples which show that anticolonial nationalism is as complex a phenomenon as any other form of nationalism. That in turn means that proponents of it face political issues just as much as proponents of any other ideology do, and that they can be manipulated. In India, the colonials often used differences among nationalists to deadly and terrible effect. In the early 1920s, the viceroy Lord Reading warned the British government in London of the dangers of communalism in India, but he acted very effectively on the orders he received to split the Indian National Congress, the Muslim League, and the Khilafat movement from one another (Reid 2016: 45–46). The colonials may not have thought it themselves, but what they were doing was playing upon different Indian nationalist groups' ideas of the post-independence India they wanted. Furthermore, the colonials as a whole did little to change the caste system, despite Winston Churchill's frequent and vitriolic attacks on untouchability in Hindu society and despite the fact that many colonials besides Churchill openly held that imperial rule involved a duty to protect India's minorities, including tribals, against Hindu dominance, which they largely associated with the Indian National Congress (Reid 2016: 94–109).

CONCEPTUAL PROBLEMS IN NATIONALISM

Nationalism has a number of conceptual problems, and a particular historical period helps to show these clearly. This period is the decade or so immediately following the First World War, when the newly constituted League of Nations attempted to prevent a repetition of the conditions which they thought had led to the war; their approach required the creation of new states in continental Europe on the assumption that nations are made up of populations with common ethnic or linguistic inheritances and that such populations had to have their own states; these new nation-states would be defined by territorial boundaries.

One major problem was that the war had put an end to the Austro–Hungarian Empire, which had imposed central, if often despotic, authority and bureaucracy on the many nationalities within its reach. Now, with that authority gone, many of the nationalities turned against one another, especially when they were geographical neighbours; the Slovaks were against the Czechs, the Serbs against the Croats, the Ukrainians against the Poles, and so on. In addition, national majorities started oppressing national or linguistic minorities, and some of the minorities turned against one another (Arendt 1958: 268). The source of the problem was that the nations which emerged from the collapse of the defeated countries in the First World War had signed individual peace treaties with the League of Nations, and that these treaties—by recognising nation-states—had themselves created national minorities and made possible the expulsion of such minorities on the grounds that they did not belong to the particular nation-states where they happened to live; in some cases, they had lived there for centuries (Arendt 1958: 269–72).

Yet the French Revolution had created the idea of the rights of man (as they were then called) and combined it with the idea of national sovereignty, so at least in theory, all minorities should have been protected, even if they did not live in their supposedly own nation-state but in another nation-state. Indeed the post-war treaties included Minority Treaties—but these agreements themselves placed no obligation at all on the new nation-states to protect minorities. Instead, the treaties required the League of Nations to safeguard the rights of those in such a situation; that meant legal protections for minorities, but those legal protections would have been provided by an international body, namely the League of Nations. Unsurprisingly, the minorities themselves did not trust the League to protect them, because the League itself was made up of national leaders; in 1922, the League's Third Ordinary Assembly even adopted resolutions stating the duties of minorities, and it turned out that the minority treaties had been devised with a view to the assimilation of minorities into the new nation-states (Arendt 1958: 272 and 272 n. 9).

That, unsurprisingly, infuriated the newly created minorities, but it was part of a new and insoluble problem, namely the recognition of the new nation-states' sovereignty over their territories. The existing great powers could not impose any limits on the new nations' sovereignties without exposing their own hypocrisy in maintaining their own sovereignty at the same time; those great powers' representatives knew, as Arendt says, 'only too well that minorities within nation-states must sooner or later be either assimilated or liquidated' (Arendt 1958: 273).

The state as a constituted legal body had been transformed from an instrument of the law into an instrument of the nation, and the consequences were deadly. The most obvious manifestation of this was the expulsion of national minorities by nation-states; the human suffering involved might possibly have been mitigated if all the minorities had even had some kind of nation-state to go to, but tens of millions of them had no such nation-state, and at one point the combined number of the national minorities was greater than the combined populations of all the nation-states (Arendt 1958: 274).

The worst result of all was the creation of a new category of people, namely those who had no nation-state and were therefore liable to be rendered stateless at any time. This was only possible because of the creation of the nation-state, and between the wars almost every country in continental Europe passed legislation giving itself the power to expel very large numbers of its own inhabitants at almost any time. As no other country was under any obligation to take any responsibility for such people, their condition was even worse than those of criminals, who were at least recognised as human agents by the legal system in which they had committed their crime or crimes (Arendt 1958: 286–87). It hardly needs saying that the system created by the League of Nations after the First World War was part of what made it possible for fascist governments across Europe to see their Jewish populations as belonging to a Jewish nation with no defined territory and to send millions of Jews to concentration camps and extermination camps.

Yet the victims of these kinds of developments were, at least theoretically, possessors of the supposedly inalienable rights of man, because they were human beings first and foremost and because the rights involved are supposedly independent of citizenship, nationality, or anything else. Being made stateless, however, meant that not one public body on the planet had either obligations or powers to protect those rights; those rights became totally meaningless. Thus Arendt on the stateless:

> Their plight is not such that they are equal before the law, but that no law exists for them; not that they are oppressed but that nobody wants even to oppress them. (Arendt 1958: 296–97)

If we are stateless, we may continue to exist, but we do so as nothing identifiable. We are not even outlaws in a more ancient sense. What we have undergone instead is the loss of a polity, the loss of our membership of a political body. That is what has expelled us from humanity, and it is the very idea of a nation as a defining political entity that has made this expulsion possible. As a foundation for political association, the idea of the nation may well be completely incoherent, and certainly its history is one of disaster and tragedy for hundreds of millions all around the world. It is nevertheless the case that few lessons have been learnt as a result; despite the utter failure of the attempt to create nation-states in Europe after the First World War, the concept of nation-states was used after the even greater destruction caused by the Second World War, when large-scale repatriations were tried in a hopeless attempt to end the truly modern problem of statelessness (Arendt 1958: 276–77).

CONTEMPORARY NATIONALISM: THE IMPLAUSIBLE EXAMPLE OF BREXIT

In a referendum held on 23 June 2016, the British electorate voted by 51.9 per cent to 48.1 to leave the European Union; the turnout was 72.2 per cent of an electorate numbering just over 46.5 million. The referendum (in which this writer voted) was, like almost all referenda held in the United Kingdom, advisory and not of itself binding; on 24 January 2017, the UK Supreme Court ruled that Parliament and not the government had the sole power to invoke Article 50 of the Treaty of Lisbon. On 29 March 2017, the British Parliament voted to invoke or trigger Article 50.

The referendum itself concluded an extremely ugly campaign, and the result brought about the resignation of the prime minister, David Cameron, who had called the referendum and had campaigned for the country to remain in the EU. If the campaign was ugly, the aftermath was even uglier, with police recording sharp rises in racist and xenophobic attacks; the BBC journalist Sima Kotecha, interviewing people in her home town of Basingstoke in Hampshire, was racially abused by an interviewee, and people of Polish origin were often attacked; one was murdered by a gang who set upon him. Some white British people were attacked, sometimes very seriously, by strangers who thought they were Polish, and in January 2017 a visiting Swedish minister publicly expressed shock at the xenophobia Swedes living in Britain had been experiencing.

In addition, other aspects of the political atmosphere after the referendum are at best puzzling. The leading pro-Brexit party, the United Kingdom Independence Party (UKIP), all but collapsed despite getting the result it wanted. The leader, Nigel Farage, resigned on 4 July 2016, saying he wanted 'to get his life back', and the party descended into bitter public infighting; the next leader Diane James herself resigned after 18 days, and her successor Paul Nuttall faced continuing public dissent from some of the membership. He resigned the leadership on 9 June 2017, the day after the general election. Among other leading Brexit campaigners, the former central-government justice minister Michael Gove seemed to have left politics after saying his greatest campaign ally Boris Johnson was not fit to be prime minister, and Johnson himself accepted the post of foreign minister in the new prime minister Theresa May's cabinet. This looked more like the conduct of people who had lost instead of winning, and there was public talk of their not having wanted to win at all, because none of them seemed to have any plan for what they would do or wanted to see done by the UK government in the event of their winning the referendum.

As for the analysis of the referendum, the great bulk of it has been, and continues to be, about what the referendum result means or expresses. That issue is made much harder by the regional and other variations in the vote itself. Among the devolved regions, which unlike England have their own elected assemblies, Scottish voters opted by 62 per cent to 38 to stay in the EU, and Northern Irish voters took the same position, by 55.8 per cent to 44.2 per cent. In Wales, the vote to leave was 52.5 per cent to leave, with 47.5 per cent to remain (BBC 2016a; Electoral Commission 2016). The English vote was 53.4 per cent to leave, a margin of nearly 7 per cent over the 46.6 per cent who voted to stay.

The complexity of the evidence undermines claims that the result expressed the will of the British people, or that it showed the remoteness of an urban or metropolitan elite from the much larger numbers living in former industrial heartlands or in rural areas. There are elites in Scotland just as there are in Northern Ireland or anywhere else in the United Kingdom, and they do not seem to have seen the referendum as any kind of issue to do with national identity, even though the campaign was notably devoid of any serious analysis of what EU membership means or of any articulated alternative (Boyle 2017).

Secondly, the English vote in particular is very revealing; there is no English regional assembly, and English identity (whatever that might mean, following the impact of the Norman Conquest in 1066 and the enormous transformations that wrought upon the then English society and the then English language) has been subsumed under a British identity by the 1707 Treaty of Union between England and Scotland, by the Acts of Union with Ireland in 1800, and by the fact of the British empire. As Boyle puts it, the fact of EU membership has brought to the surface what may well be an English and not a Scottish or Irish issue over having to be something of an equal in partnership with others (Boyle 2017; Kenny and Pearce 2017). The irony, or absurdity or worse of the situation as it stands is that the partnership in question is the world's outstanding example of cooperation between sovereign states, a truly mighty achievement in the light of the terrible violence and destruction of the Second World War, which started in the heart of Europe.

If what the Brexit referendum means is therefore anything but clear, the direction events will take is completely unpredictable. As the implications of even a hypothetical Brexit emerge (for example, what will happen to the estimated 1.2 million Britons currently living in the other 27 EU states if they become non-EU aliens?), some poll evidence suggests at the time of writing that a second referendum would produce a 'remain' result. Secondly, all the major parties except the Scottish National Party and possibly the Liberal Democrats are divided over EU membership, and all that seems to obtain at present is chaos and confusion. Whatever else, this is not the resurgence of serious nationalism but more like something out of *Monty Python's Flying Circus*—sadly, without the hilarious entertainment and with far worse consequences for tens of millions of people.

STATEHOOD WITHOUT NATIONALISM

In view of pervasiveness of the idea of a nation, it may seem as if no claim to political independence or self-determination can be made without some sort of foundational claim to national identity, even if that kind of foundation crumbles when examined, or results in the creation of brutally exclusive systems based on ideas of racial, ethnic, religious, or linguistic homogeneity or uniformity.

That, however, is not the case, and both in theory and in practice significant attempts have been made and continue to be made to assert claims to statehood without any claim to the usual nationalist foundations. Among the theoretical or analytical attempts, for example, is an argument for Kurdish statehood without any assertion of national or religious exclusivity (Besifki 1996).

In practice, a striking and illuminating example is provided by Scotland, which at the time of writing seems virtually certain to achieve not only independence from the United Kingdom but also full membership of the EU and the UN. Constitutionally, Scotland as it stands today is a devolved region of the United Kingdom under the Scotland Act 1998, which created the Scottish Parliament and specified the extensive range of powers which would thenceforth lie with the Scottish Parliament. The Act also specifies those powers which are not devolved to Scotland and are retained by the UK parliament at Westminster; those reserved powers include, for example, foreign affairs and defence (United Kingdom 2013). It hardly needs saying that Scotland is very recognisably a First-World country without being—or without yet being—a state in its own right.

The historical background to this is unusual in the history of nationalist ideas and movements. In 1603, the Scottish king, James VI, succeeded quite legitimately to the throne of England and Ireland, but in 1706 and 1707, the English and Scottish parliaments respectively legislated to abolish themselves and create a single parliament at Westminster. This parliament, under the 1688 constitutional settlement, is still the sovereign body of the United Kingdom, and therefore the 1707 Treaty of Union meant that Scotland had given up statehood but had retained so much of the institutional and cultural ethos associated with statehood that it had become a 'decapitated state' without an associated or assimilated nationality; this amounts to a 'quasi-national legacy' (Nairn 1981: 128–31).

One major result was that Scotland's emerging bourgeois or mercantile classes played little or no part in the formation of Scottish institutions and processes of state. In this they were noticeably different from similar classes in other northern European countries, particularly England, where the bourgeois class broke into the ruling landed and aristocratic castes so successfully that the latter made very sure they coopted the new class into their ranks, and thereby also crushed an earlier English revolutionary tradition (Nairn 1981: 28–41 and 132–33). In Scotland, however, the expansion in philosophic and scientific ideas which accompanied the eighteenth-century economic and mercantile transformations in England gave rise to what has been called a Scottish intelligentsia. The figures involved were among the greatest intellects of their time, and in some cases of all time; they include the philosophers David Hume and Adam Smith, the poet Robert Burns, the engineer-inventor James Watt, the architect Robert Adam, and many others (Nairn 1981: 134–40).

Scotland did of course have its own new bourgeois class, but this class in effect inherited a position so favourable that it was neither threatened by industrial modernity nor excluded from it; the new bourgeoisie also benefited greatly from the expansion of British imperial power and wealth through the eighteenth and nineteenth centuries. The position of this class, however, was not unchallenged; as the inequalities between the coastal southern areas—the Lowlands—and the rural areas, mainly in the north and the Highlands grew, a serious insurrection in 1745 almost succeeded. Scotland, as Nairn says, was unusually well equipped for recognisable nationalist struggles, but these never took place (Nairn 1981: 142–48).

The recent and rapid rise of what amounts to an independence movement without the usual nationalist burdens and trappings therefore needs another form of explanation. The main factors seem to lie in very modern or contemporary economic and political factors. One is the discovery and exploitation of oilfields under the bed of the North Sea from the early 1970s onwards, and another has to do with the political or constitutional position of Scotland in relation to the UK parliament at Westminster. By the mid-1970s, the Scottish National Party, the SNP, was starting to win significant elections to Westminster seats, including some in Labour strongholds. One reason was increasing resentment over the fact that revenues from North Sea oil were not under the control of Scottish local authorities or indeed any Scottish elected bodies but instead went straight to the UK treasury, and were mainly used to reduce the budget deficit rather than being invested in physical infrastructure or in health and education. Secondly, as the 1980s progressed, the Conservative central government in London imposed a new and highly unpopular form of local taxation, a per capita tax called the Community Charge, on Scotland a year before it did so in England. The tax, which the public, the media, and even Conservative politicians immediately renamed the Poll Tax after a hated tax in the fourteenth century, provoked widespread civil disobedience and non-payment when it was introduced in England, and was soon abandoned, but a large proportion of the Scottish electorate never forgot the way they had been treated over it.

A third factor almost certainly had to do with internal turmoil and even sclerosis within the British Labour Party, which according to Nairn had grown as 'addicted' to the existing British state as the Conservatives (Nairn 1981: 190). The Scottish electorate, which had elected 56 Labour MPs out of 72 seats in the 1997 general election, sent 54 Scottish National Party MPs to Westminster in 2015, out of 59 Scottish seats. In the Scottish parliament at Holyrood in Edinburgh, the SNP holds 63 out of 128 seats at the time of writing; this parliament is elected by the Additional Member System.

Scotland is nevertheless complex in its linguistic, cultural, and religious composition. Gaelic has not been the first language of a majority of Scots for 500 years, and today fewer than 60,000 Scots speak it; the country's other main languages are Lallans, a word coined by the poet Robert Burns for a form of the language which is closely related to English and is spoken in the southernmost counties, and English (Appiah 2016). Similarly, the largest denomination in the country is the Church of Scotland or the Kirk, which is Protestant, but in Glasgow, Scotland's largest city, Catholics outnumber Protestants. Scotland has for a long time also had a Jewish minority, and a Muslim one (Appiah 2016). At least one minister in the current Scottish government is a Muslim.

Yet the key point here is that the Scottish National Party makes no claim to any of the backward-looking, atavistic, and ultimately incoherent elements of nationalism, such as ethnic, linguistic, racial, or religious exclusivity (Scottish National Party n.d.). Neither do what seem to be more radical movements for Scottish independence, such as Common Weal or the Radical Independence Collective (Common Weal n.d.; Radical Independence Collective n.d.). What all of them do make a claim to is statehood. The contrast with nationalism in any of its forms could not be more obvious.

CHAPTER 11: NATIONALISM

Extension Exercise

1. Read this article
   Stark, Holger. 2016. 'Donald Trump and the New American Nationalism'. *Speigel Online*, 17 May. http://www.spiegel.de/international/world/essay-donald-trump-and-the-new-american-nationalism-a-1092548.html

and use the material in it to show in about 300 words whether Donald Trump is a fascist or some form of American nationalist.

2. Read this article
Stark, Holger. 2017. 'How America Lost its Identity'. *Spiegel Online*, 26 January. http://www.spiegel.de/international/world/letter-from-washington-how-america-lost-its-identity-a-1131294.html
and use the material in it to write 200 words on which version of America Trump intends to restore to its former position.

Further Reading

Abel, Maddela. 2005. *Glimpses of Indian National Movement*. Hyderabad: ICFAI University Press.

12
CHAPTER

Republicanism and Citizenship

Republicanism as a form of political thought has very little to do with the attitudes and policies advocated by the US Republican Party. Republican political thought has a very ancient history, which starts with the Greek philosopher Aristotle (384–322 BCE), and has been adapted for the contemporary world by several modern and contemporary thinkers. In practice, republican thought underlies—usually without recognition or acknowledgment—most contemporary democracies, even though most of those democracies appear to embody liberal principles rather than republican ones. Just as importantly, republicanism could provide a way of preventing the occurrence of many of the main problems and incoherences of liberalism. Indeed several noted contemporary political theorists have explicitly advocated republicanism for that purpose, and in the process have criticised liberalism severely.

The main forms of republicanism have been called classical and modern. Classical republicanism refers to forms of thought and possibly also of practice in parts of ancient Greece. Modern republicanism is usually taken to have its origins in Niccolò Machiavelli's reflections, written mainly in the Italian city-state of Florence in the fifteenth century. We must remember that ancient Greek thought had a number of versions of republicanism, and therefore that there are problems over the argument that Machiavelli's republicanism is a direct continuation of classical republican thought and of the thinking which underlay the organisation of Rome in its republican period (Jurdjevic 2007: 1231–33). Those kinds of arguments are most commonly associated with the work of Quentin Skinner and J. G. A. Pocock (Skinner 1981; Pocock 1985). Machiavelli's concerns here are largely drawn from his great work, *Discourses upon the First Ten (Books) of Titus Livy*, which was published in 1517.

In certain passages, however, Machiavelli shows sharp insight into the contribution citizens can make to the quality of life in a republic, even though he saw the republic as being ruled by an oligarchy of 40 or 50 people. He says that it was the very tension, the frequent 'tumult' between the nobles and the plebeians, which resulted in the creation of good law and of a civic life largely free of serious violence, so that citizens could live freely and yet securely (Machiavelli 1517: 9–11). Machiavelli then has to reconcile these domestic or internal achievements with the need for external security, but we need not examine those concerns of his in detail. The main point for us is that the organisation of the state and even of who governed it and how they did so were matters for the whole polity to settle, even despite frequent internal discord. The state conceived thus is not ruled by the most powerful, by a religious institution, by aristocrats who claim divine right, or the automatic inheritance of political position and power. This recognition of a form of secular political authority which pervades the whole polity is perhaps the central republican principle in Machiavelli's thinking.

This form of political authority, nevertheless, led Machiavelli to be concerned about how citizens might learn or might be taught *virtù* or good conduct in public affairs; he holds that fear is a strong element in ensuring that the republic does not descend into strife and violence, and he cites the end of Tarquin rule in Rome as his example. According to Machiavelli, after the end of the Tarquin dynasty, the nobles conducted themselves well for a time, but they then started to 'vent upon the plebs that poison which they had kept within their breasts'; Machiavelli adds here that we never act well except through necessity (Machiavelli 1517: 10). This may well be one of the main factors that sets Machiavelli apart from modern or more modern senses of republicanism as well as the theory of classical republicanism.

Certain forms of classical republicanism, which draw strongly upon and amount to a significant further development of classical republicanism, have seen a strong revival since the early 1980s. In the next decade or so, a number of eminent philosophers and political thinkers published works which responded to problems in societies apparently mired in the problems of liberalism by identifying resources in classical republican thought, which seemed likely to offer dissolutions of problems liberalism gave rise to and could not address. Among the works which draw upon classical republicanism and adapt it for our times by discarding its historically contingent features are *After Virtue* (1981) by Alasdair MacIntyre, and *What's the Matter with Liberalism?* (1992) by Ronald Beiner. I shall draw on both of these at various points below.

The main republican criticisms of liberalism start with the key liberal principle that we must not impose any theory of the good life or any political or moral ideology, because such attempts have caused enormous amounts of slaughter and other suffering. So people must be free to decide their own beliefs and ways of life, and the state must be neutral about conceptions of the good. Secondly, society is made up of individuals, whose decisions must be freely made. We must therefore tolerate the resulting diversity of occupations, ways of life, and religious and cultural preferences. That means we have a right to choose our political representatives, our political, moral, and aesthetic attitudes, our occupations, our sexual partners, and so on. We also have a right to freedom from interference when we vote, a right to vote in secret, and a right to fair trials in which we are innocent until proven guilty. In liberal theory, all of these are founded on the principle of individual choice protected by rights. Liberalism as a whole requires that we avoid stating any substantive theory of human nature, or any such philosophical anthropology.

In practice, however, liberalism looks very different. We are only too familiar with radically insoluble conflicts between morals and positions which are not only diametrically opposed but have no common ground whatever. For example, the rights of a foetus are counterposed to the rights of the mother; the right to a traditional life is set against the right to choose another way of life, or against the right of a contractor to pursue their occupation even if it means building over traditional habitats. Another example of such a clash is between those who hold that war is destructive and violent, and those who hold that oppressed and colonised peoples have a right to wage war so as to achieve independence or national self-determination. A third example of an irresoluble clash is that justice requires that we all have an equal opportunity to develop our talents, so taxation for public healthcare and education is necessary for the state to give us all that opportunity, but we should be free to incur only the obligations we want to incur, so taxation should be abolished and we should be free to choose schools and doctors, and so on (MacIntyre 2007: 1–50). A very familiar complaint in India is that affirmative action quotas disadvantage those who have achieved the target grades for admission to publicly funded universities and colleges anyway; here, the right to have structural disadvantage recognised is set against the right to the reward for achievement.

We should not be surprised that the supposed arguments degenerate so quickly into bitterly entrenched positions and mutual hatred, if not worse; they were never arguments in the first place, but only assertions of purported rights. Liberalism has no conceptual resources with which to resolve conflicts of rights, and none with which to decide what is to count as a right and therefore as something worth absolute protection. The language of rights has nevertheless come to permeate almost all of our contemporary public discourse, and has become almost the standard language in making a case for, and for judging the legitimacy of, a state or a social and economic system, or any specific law or policy (Bellamy 2000: 162).

In addition, the principle of choice which liberalism claims we have as of right is illusory. In practice, we see only more and more sameness in tastes, perceptions, and clichés in a shopping-mall culture where vast numbers of shops all sell the same junk (Beiner 1992: 23). Much of the junk may also be built to fail after a given time, so that we have to go back and buy the newest version, irrespective of the often unrecyclable rubbish that such a practice generates. The so-called consumer choices involved here are not intelligible as choices at all, and a way of life in which this kind of consumption is the defining feature cannot possibly qualify for the respect liberalism requires us to give all ways of life; why should we respect a way of life that is 'servile, conformist, and unreflective'—or worse (Beiner 1992: 60)? What would it even mean to do so? Are we to respect or be neutral about, say, a way of life whose central principle is genocide or the propagation of hate?

If that makes the idea of moral neutrality unintelligible, liberal requirements for neutrality on the part of the state also collapse. What would it mean for the state to be neutral about scientific discoveries, say, in the treatment of deadly diseases, or about precautions against natural disasters, or about economic growth? Liberalism nevertheless has to assume that the state must be neutral about such things (Beiner 1992: 24).

These dead ends and incoherences have a deeper source in liberalism, namely, its conception of the human being as a radical chooser and nothing else. For liberalism, to choose is to be human; choosing is the essence of personhood. This does not just lead to the problems I have identified above; it amounts to a substantial theory of human nature, a philosophical anthropology of precisely the kind liberalism requires us to refrain from adopting (Beiner 1992: 26; Sivaramakrishnan 2012a: 203–4). Liberalism offered us, and was part of the historical process whereby we achieved, liberation from feudality, inherited privilege, and arbitrary power, but it has only delivered us into another sort of captivity, the captivity of sterile and irresoluble oppositions between competing rights. It has also made possible a combination of private perfection and public squalor or emptiness, because it cannot accommodate the idea of shared predicaments which are other than chance developments. At this point liberalism can only fall silent.

Part of the problem is that by accepting choice as the essence of personhood, liberalism rules out any substantive inquiry into the content and the context of the choices we make. For example, much of the uniformity Beiner and others excoriate is driven by commercial pressures in the markets which constitute an essential element in the liberal conception of human autonomy. Advertising—the sale of lifestyle rather than substance—undoubtedly has much to do with this, and the larger corporations have colossal advertising budgets; they also mount fierce and often coordinated campaigns against, for example, attempts by states to restrict alcohol and tobacco advertising. Even within particular markets, commercial pressures often have a less obvious but no less insidious effect. For example, a free and diverse media is crucial to liberal societies, but competition among commercial media bodies means constant pressure to cut costs, especially by cutting staff. That makes the commercial media more and not less dependent on official and corporate press releases, so the content and tone of a lot of news starts to look and sound more and more uniform; furthermore, liberal doctrine has it that the state must be a neutral enforcer of laws, not an active participant in the media. Staff cuts under market pressures also sharply reduce the time news reporters have to get to know a beat, to make contacts, and to do serious investigative work; even in the supposedly serious press, public relations material, press releases, and wire copy can amount to nearly 70 per cent of news coverage (Davies 2009: 52–53).

One result is that we, the public, whose decisions are crucial to the survival even of liberal democracy, end up less and less well informed about the major issues facing us, and largely unaware of major issues the media choose not to mention at all. The point is not just that liberalism cannot challenge the choices we make, but that it rules out inquiry into whether or not our choices are well-informed, or made under coercion, or deceit, or any other pressures.

Such problems have led to responses which adapt classical republicanism for the contemporary world. The ideas involved have their source in the work of Aristotle, for whom the defining feature of humanity is that we are speakers of language. We are therefore reasoning beings; that in turn makes us political beings, or in Aristotle's phrase *zoa politika*; it is only by speaking reasoningly that we can determine how to organise our lives and our public institutions, and decide what is just and fair in our arrangements and procedures (Aristotle 1905: 28–29). According to Aristotle, the task is to live well, and this is why we need to address our disagreements and differences so that we can bring them under something we all share, namely the concern to live well; for Aristotle, that is the characteristically human purpose or *telos*.

There is no attempt here to pretend that we have no differences or disagreements. Indeed, republican thought starts with the plain fact that differences and disagreements occur all the time in human life, but instead of responding to them by excluding, enslaving, or exterminating those with whom we disagree, or by retreating behind non-negotiable rights which purportedly require no justification, republicanism requires that we reason about our disagreements in order to recognise what those disagreements are about. That means recognising and learning about the factors behind them, so that we can see how these relate to the good, that is, to the concern to live well. Abortion is almost a canonical example here; the sterile positions taken for and against it in a rights discourse exclude the wider questions of the circumstances in which conception occurred. These would include not only matters of forced sex, such as rape, but other less obvious forms of coercion, such as the quality and breadth of sex education for people of all ages, including children and young people, access to contraceptive advice and services, patriarchal cultures in which women are expected to conceive until they have a male child, and so on.

Those are both private and public issues, and the space in which we can address them is not that created by liberalism; it is instead, the republic, that is, the public space for reasoning about the issues we face. The word 'republic' is derived from the Latin phrase *res publica*, which literally means 'a public thing', but is better rendered as 'a public affair', or a matter of public importance. As we have already noted, the idea of human beings as beings who reason in the public space has its origins in the work of Aristotle, and the central element in that reasoning is that we need to learn about the issues so that we address them in well-informed ways and make good practical judgments about them. We need to develop a faculty of practical wisdom, which Aristotle calls *phronesis* (Aristotle 1955: 25–54).

Being a citizen, then, involves engaging with the public issues we face, that is, learning about them, and learning from and participating in the public discourse or discourses on them. Citizenship is therefore an activity and not just a status. In this Aristotelian sense, moreover, the idea of citizenship relieves us of the connotations of saintly conduct, in the sense of being a good citizen, that the idea seems to have acquired in modern times. Secondly, the boundaries of the public space, the range of ideas and issues about which we deliberate, cannot be fixed; we have already seen how greatly our sense of the political has been expanded. The way we treat the natural environment has similarly become part of our political space, and so has the matter of structural disadvantage and discrimination in all democratic societies.

In addition, we are no more automatically capable of good judgment than we are automatically capable of any other complex activity. We need to learn about the issues we face, and learn by the practice of making and reflecting on our decisions, but in the political or public space there are no techniques which will serve us in all situations, and no certificates or qualifications which will equip us for wise conduct. We may often need technical advice, but in the end it is we the citizens who have to make the decisions, and who have to take the responsibility for our decisions. For Aristotle, politics is the supreme human activity, the architectonic activity; it is what integrates and makes sense of our other roles in society and thereby enables us to identify what it is to be fully human (Aristotle 1905: 25–54, 100–44; Aristotle 1955: 26–27; Beiner 1992: 51, 119; Barber 1984: 154).

We might—and we should—wonder what this has to do with the politics we see around us all the time; politics looks like an area of life which is filled with evasions, lies, brutality, mass slaughter, and corruption, all carried out by what seem to be the worst of people with the worst of motivations. Yet the evidence is overwhelmingly that what the corrupt and the unscrupulous fear above all is exposure or detection. The idea of a public space is far from dead. Improving it in keeping with the Aristotelian conception, even if we did so only in part, would of course require enormous transformations in our institutions and our attitudes, though those might change as our practices change. At the very least, we would need far greater transparency in our public processes, including those related to security and defence. We would also need far more explicit and widespread education on our systems of state, including legal and judicial processes, at every level. We might, in addition, need to give elected assemblies far greater powers of scrutiny over government and citizens far greater access to elected representatives than they have at present.

ILLIBERAL DEMOCRACY

The term 'illiberal democracy' seems to have been coined by Fareed Zakaria in 1997, in an article he wrote for the journal *Foreign Affairs*. He identifies a problem which I have remarked upon above, namely that it is not enough for liberal political systems to stop with the institutionalisation of certain values and certain types of political organisation; among these are of course free and fair elections, and also the separation of powers between elected assemblies, the executive branch of government—in parliamentary systems, the cabinet and the civil service—and the judiciary (Zakaria 1997: 22–23). For Zakaria and many others, it is also essential that the freedom of speech, assembly, religion, and property be protected; Zakaria calls this latter set of protections constitutional liberalism, and cites Philippe Schmitter as saying that such constitutional liberalism has never been 'unambiguously linked' with the practice of democracy' (cited in Zakaria 1997: 22–23).

Zakaria, writing at a time when any number of dictatorships around the world were being replaced by democracies, concludes that most, if not all, of the emerging democracies are procedurally democratic but in fact have 'strong executives, weak legislatures and judiciaries, and few civil and economic liberties' (Zakaria 1997: 22). For Zakaria, it is not acceptable to claim that such forms of executive power are sometimes described as necessary for the elimination of rigid social stratification or powerful established interests such as institutionalised religions or landed or corporate wealth (which in many developing countries is tightly concentrated in family hands).

To us, living in a world now permeated by permanent and apparently limitless electronic surveillance by virtually every state in the world, and moreover a world in which open expressions of racial and religious hatred are once again part and parcel—or so it seems—of life in Western democracies, Zakaria's distinction between constitutional liberalism and democracy may well look much less convincing than it might have looked in the late 1990s. We also need to remember that much of the repressive legislation involved has been passed almost unquestioned by impeccably elected legislatures; those laws include the US Homeland Security Act and the Patriot Act, both of which were later criticised for unconstitutional provisions. British legislation of a similar nature includes purported anti-terrorism legislation, such as the Regulation of Investigatory Powers Act 2000, which gave a large number of public bodies at different levels almost unlimited powers of electronic surveillance; the British Parliament passed a further law, the Investigatory Powers Act, in 2016. More recently, the British government has started to require that publicly funded schools decide and record the ethnic backgrounds of their pupils—a procedure which used to be carried out by state officials in the now-abolished apartheid South Africa. In the United Kingdom, the data collection has been outsourced to a private firm, and if parents do not disclose a child's ethnic background, the schools have been told to 'guess' that background (Pells 2016).

Zakaria, therefore, would have even more evidence of the spread of illiberal democracy today than he did when he wrote his article. That spread has of course been noted; Yascha Mounk points out the ways in which several apparently stable and functioning democracies, including many of the richest countries in the world, have seen the rapid political rise of populist and often demagogic politicians (Mounk 2016). Mounk cites the

US Republican presidential candidate Donald Trump, the French National Front leader Marine Le Pen, and the far-Right Dutch politician Geert Wilders as examples. He also mentions the British referendum vote of 23 June 2016 to leave the European Union, and is blunt about the political opportunism of those who use, for example, terrorist attacks or attempted coups to advance their own brands of often xenophobic or ethno-nationalist politics. Mounk specifically names Marine Le Pen's reaction to the mass killing in Nice by a man driving a stolen truck during the Bastille Day celebrations on the city's promenade on 14 July 2016, and he goes into detail over the Turkish president Recep Tayyip Erdoğan's swift centralisation of power after the failed coup that month; Erdoğan dismissed thousands, apparently not for anything they had done but for what they might have thought, and effectively put an end to a long-standing Turkish dispensation under which a secular or secularist elite had legislated to protect religious and ethnic minorities and a reasonable if variable amount of journalistic and academic criticism (Mounk 2016). Similar processes have been very obviously at work in Hungary and Poland, where elected governments have swiftly undermined the country's constitutional court, stacked government institutions like the electoral commission with party loyalists, and turned the most important media outlets into uncritical propaganda machines (Mounk 2016).

This is, of course, much more than just a matter of a political climate. Mounk rightly identifies the enormous democratic deficit in the EU, where three of the four major institutions—the Council of Ministers, the European Commission, and the European Court of Justice—barely figure in the consciousness of over 520 million EU citizens, despite the fact that those bodies' decisions have an enormous impact throughout the EU. He also, equally rightly, points out that the only elected EU institution, the European Parliament, is elected on tiny turnouts and has few, if any, formal powers (Mounk 2016).

That may be a slightly unfair comment on the European Parliament; under the Treaty of Maastricht, the European Commission—the only EU body which drafts legislation—has to send all draft EU law to the European Parliament, which can reject or amend any such draft before the draft goes to the law-making body, the Council of Ministers; this is called the co-decision procedure. Secondly, the European Parliament can sack all the European Commissioners (on the one occasion it would almost certainly have done so, over a substantial corruption scandal, the Commissioners resigned *en bloc*). Thirdly, the debate on the EU's democratic deficit has been underway for a considerable time, with reforms proposed from time to time, and fierce public criticism of the EU's subordination to highly secretive and very powerful corporate bodies has also been made; for example, the European Parliament very rarely uses the co-decision procedure and instead allows almost all draft legislation through under the much less stringent consultation procedure (Føllesdal and Hix 2006; Moravcsik 2002; Monbiot 2001).

Mounk nevertheless concludes that the problems faced by liberal democracy as it turns into illiberal democracy constitute only one half of the problem. The other half is what he calls the tendency of the elites in liberal democracies to see themselves as, in effect, having to protect liberal democracy against the worst populist movements and the worst populist motivations; he calls this undemocratic liberalism, and says it is part of the cause of ordinary people's bitter sense of remoteness and alienation from their own—apparently thoroughly democratic—systems. As we saw in the chapter on liberalism, this elitist tendency and a profound fear and distrust of the public are inherent in liberal theory and in supposedly liberal democracies.

Mounk says that historically, liberalism and democracy only came together coincidentally, that is, during the first three decades after the Second World War, when enormous inequalities were significantly reduced and hundreds of millions, especially in industrial countries, experienced previously unimaginable improvements in their standard of living (Mounk 2016). Mounk does not, however, mention the role of the state or of mass trade-union membership in bringing this about; neither does he mention the impact of vastly expanded public provision in education and healthcare at every level in such countries.

Mounk's explanation for what he considers only a historical coincidence relies on the material conditions and relations of production in industrial countries after the Second World War, and may amount to a Marxist or quasi-Marxist explanation. Zakaria, for his part, makes little or no mention of such material conditions as forming a decisive context for the coincidence of liberalism and democracy, but—like Mounk—sees the collapse or imminent collapse of liberal democracy as alarming and very dangerous for the whole world; given the alternatives on offer (or which a lot of leaders may be about to impose on us), that is an entirely understandable fear. Mounk, writing 20 years later and very much in our own time, sees an urgent need for us to restate and protect the ends of liberalism. Substantive ends, however, are precisely the kinds of things liberalism cannot allow itself to propound; we have seen that problem above, in the chapter on liberalism and earlier in this chapter.

A further set of problems for our predicament as outlined by Zakaria and Mounk is their neglect of how hundreds of millions around the world have come to think they are faced by such threats, including permanent debt, unemployment or underemployment, and even the obliteration or overrunning of their own cultures, that they think only some kind of powerful leader who promises to assert cultural, religious, or ethnic homogeneity can save them. The single greatest source of our knowledge (if that is the right word) of the world is the largely corporate-owned mass media, but the part played by the mass media in creating our current sense of our situation does not figure in either Zakaria's or Mounk's analysis. Powerful and sharp analyses of the media's part in our sense of our problems abound, and many have been written by very experienced journalists (Herman and Chomsky 1988; Edwards and Cromwell 2006, 2012; Rather 2011; McChesney and Nichols 2005; Nichols and McChesney 2013). All is, however, not lost, and despite challenges, threats, and other problems, other forms of the mass media, broadly under the umbrella term complementary media, have emerged, mainly on the Internet (Sivaramakrishnan 2014: 146–54).

In addition, examples of public involvement often show that when ordinary people, almost irrespective of their background, have the chance to address public issues seriously, they can and frequently do engage openly and seriously with the issues before them to reach very sound decisions. In 2000, the Canadian province of British Columbia used a form of nearly random selection to create a 160-member Citizens' Assembly, which considered several electoral systems and then decided on a particular one to replace the existing simple-majority or first-past-the-post system (Warren and Pearse 2008: 8–9). The existing system had twice in succession produced anomalous results in the elections for the province's assembly. In 1996, the Liberal Party won the popular vote, with 41.8 per cent against the New Democratic Party's 30.5, but lost the election because it won fewer seats, and in 2000 the Liberals won 77 out of 79 assembly seats on a 57.6 per cent share of the vote. In that election, the New Democrats won 21.6 per cent of the vote and two seats, and the Green Party won no seats on a 12.4 per cent share. The result was a one-party assembly, in a climate of declining public confidence in the formal political process (Warren and Pearse 2008: 9).

In response, the incoming provincial government created the Citizens' Assembly, which received funding and administrative support from the provincial government. The members had initial training at weekends, then held over 50 public hearings all round the province, and concluded with six more meetings. The assembly discussed several different electoral systems before recommending by a vote of 123 to 31 that the province change to a proportional system based on the single transferable vote. The members chose criteria for an electoral system from a list of nine, and decided that the main ones were effective local representation, a fair proportional way of translating votes into seats, and maximum voter choice. Crucially, all the evidence was that they made a reasoned and intelligible choice based on deepening knowledge of the subject, and that they did so without collapsing into aggregates of opinion or vote banks (Pearse 2008: 70–84; Blais, Carty, and Fournier 2008: 127–44).

In India, the state of Maharashtra is one of several where the central government's National Rural Health Mission (NRHM) has drawn upon local non-governmental organisations to help include citizens as monitors of the Health Mission; the Mission itself was started in April 2005, as a response to a healthcare system (if the word 'system' is at all applicable here) widely acknowledged to be a national disgrace (Vyasulu 2008; Sivaramakrishnan 2012a: 117–23; J. Singh 2014). The NRHM specifically mandates community monitoring, and states that community monitoring cannot be implemented by state health-department officials alone, that it is largely the officials concerned who must be monitored, and that this involves a change in the balance of power between ordinary people and the officials. The plan explicitly intends ordinary people to have an authoritative voice in evaluating the Mission and in influencing decisions (National Health Mission 2013).

The Pune-based non-governmental organisation (NGO) SATHI notes that community-based monitoring (CBM) generates popular pressure on officials to maintain the quality of services, and independently generates information about the functioning of health services that the standard management systems almost always miss. These include whether or not doctors actually turn up, whether nursing staff make the outreach visits they are supposed to make, the way staff behave towards patients, prescription practices, corruption, denial of care, ordering patients to go to private providers, and illegal charges demanded by staff from patients (Kakde 2010: 43–50; Community Based Monitoring and Planning 2012).

It is hardly surprising that at the outset, perceptions of what citizen monitoring involved varied greatly, with even NGOs seeing the task as data generation and form filling, while the villagers insisted on having more open-ended questions so that they could state their perceptions of the way the NRHM was being implemented; the creation of a newsletter across the districts, together with media coverage of the public hearings or *jan sunwais* (literally, people's hearings) involved may have helped here (Kakde 2010: 37–42, 73–77).

The very fact of public hearings at a range of levels, from primary health care (PHC) to district level, was nevertheless crucial; it revealed some embarrassing failures in the way the NRHM worked, and exposed other gaps in the system—but significant improvements resulted, and seem to have resulted without the creation of the grossly excessive, burdensome, and destructive monitoring systems which are inevitable in managerialist regimes. It may be equally significant that the NRHM requires the lowest elected tier of government in India's constitution, the village *panchayats*, to be involved in the monitoring process.

As time went by, the citizens concerned started to participate in planning the services, and officials' dismay, even shock, at the very idea of such involvement started to fade; crucially, the quality of citizen involvement improved as the citizens came to know more about the official systems and powers, and about the funding systems involved (Kakde 2012: 43–50). Even many of the doctors in the NRHM had no idea about such matters (Khunte and Walimbe 2012: 30–31). Similar benefits from citizen involvement have been noted in, for example, the Iindaba Ziyafika citizen journalism project conducted jointly by the South African newspaper *Grocott's Mail* and the Rhodes University School of Journalism and Media at Grahamstown in Natal (Lang 2010: 119–20). That project, however, was time-limited, as funding was provided only for a set period.

One implication is that citizenship as informed engagement is inherently egalitarian, as we are all reasoning beings; a further implication is that inequalities and the processes which generate and maintain them would need to be publicly justified. The public to whom those inequalities would have to be justified would inevitably include victims of the relevant processes and structures. This egalitarian character amounts to a development in republican thought since Aristotle, who is often criticised for accepting the exclusion of women and slaves from citizenship, and for holding that only those who can afford the time—that is, those who have the wealth and leisure—to reflect on public matters are entitled to be citizens (Mulgan 2000: 82–85). Aristotle seems to recognise that this would exclude large numbers of men who have to make their living through labour or trade and commerce but would otherwise be fit for citizenship (Mulgan 2000: 87–89). Aristotle does also say that domestic equality is the closest private approximation to public justice, but today we would not accept that as sufficient, and today's republican theorists rightly regard gender equality as an inherent element in citizenship; indeed, citizenship would be unintelligible without it, and without the element of universal entitlement to citizen membership that characterises all democracies today.

That also means that we do not need to concern ourselves excessively with whether or not Aristotle is a recognisable social democrat, or a liberal by today's standards, or a conservative supporter of the established order; that issue has been debated by Aristotle scholars such as Richard Mulgan and Martha Nussbaum, but it is not directly pertinent to our concerns here (Mulgan 2000; Nussbaum 2000). What we need to do instead is to see where Aristotle's recognition that we are reasoning beings and therefore *zoa politika* takes us; it certainly takes us far beyond Aristotle's historically contingent limitation of the entitlement to citizenship.

The point here is that severe inequalities, including structural and systemic inequalities, would almost certainly undermine any wide sense of citizenship in the sense in which I have outlined it here. They would render unintelligible and perhaps impossible any sense of shared predicaments, and in very unequal societies that is often very obvious, with elites increasingly buying themselves out of most of the effects of grossly dysfunctional public processes and public institutions, even if they probably cannot buy themselves indefinitely out of the diseases and dangers caused by water or air pollution, and cannot indefinitely buy themselves locations away from sites of radioactive contamination.

As for distributional or material equality, this cannot be separated from wider questions of the mode of production, but there is no justification for removing that kind of issue from serious and open examination by citizens (Marx 1875; Beiner 1992: 104–5, 156, 161). Any serious discourse on such a topic would, furthermore, need to abandon the current promises or assumptions of ever-increasing wealth and ever-expanding consumption. What it could well do, on the other hand, is initiate serious examination of what we produce and how we produce it, and of what we consume and how we consume it. What would be matters of private preference under liberalism, with the state seen as a permanently alien and potentially hostile institution, become matters of public concern and decision under republicanism; that in turn means the boundary between the public and the private is itself a matter to be decided by reasoned public consideration.

One important implication here is that certain noted approaches taken by liberal theorists stop short of this point. For example, the detailed and valuable outlook sometimes called the capabilities approach is a vast improvement on the idea that, for example, national gross domestic product (GDP) is an automatic index of quality of life; GDP by itself can say nothing about the dignity of the lives people lead, or about the sense of meaning—or lack of it—people feel their lives embody or possess. As outlined by Martha Nussbaum, the capabilities approach encompasses crucial necessities for a decent or dignified life, such as literacy, access to health care, to education, to even reasonable financial independence and control over earnings or income, and much else besides (Nussbaum 2011: ix–xii and 1–45). Nussbaum rightly reminds us that the necessities which figure in the capabilities approach are not exhaustive; the approach leaves many matters as optional and requiring settlement by what Nussbaum calls the political process (Nussbaum 2011: 32). It is also significant that capabilities are not a matter of innate abilities or qualities; we develop capacities and capabilities in and through our lives and in the contexts in which we live, and in making this point, Nussbaum draws on thinkers as varied as Aristotle, Mill, and Tagore (Nussbaum 2011: 23).

Yet Nussbaum, as a self-avowed liberal, explicitly states that she will not offer 'any comprehensive account of value' (Nussbaum 2011: 23). I shall not address the question here of whether or not the idea of central capabilities is itself a very substantial value, because Nussbaum herself sees the development of capacities as centrally involving choice and freedom (Nussbaum 2011: 39). Rather is it the case that Nussbaum's idea of central capabilities cannot itself be decided by definition or stipulation. The central capabilities themselves will have to be decided by reasoning public discourse; we have already noted, in Chapter 3, that liberal theory cannot sustain its own distinction between procedural rights and substantive rights, and Nussbaum seems in effect to have accepted that point, but it also follows that what is to count as a decent life cannot be defined from above but will have to be addressed in and through public discourse.

Furthermore, the idea of informed political observation and participation plays what seems to be at best an uncertain role in the account of capabilities which Nussbaum provides. Nussbaum notes that—at least in the Western tradition—a long line of thought has it that one of the major tasks of government is to ensure that people have the central entitlements, by which she presumably means the main capacities (Nussbaum 2011: 168). She also notes that we 'badly need' to address the whole issue of political structure, including the separation of powers, the role of interest groups, voting procedures (and presumably also electoral systems), and she is right to say that unless such matters are addressed in political discourse, such discourse is 'mere hand-waving'. Addressing these kinds of issues will almost certainly mean reconstituting our existing states, including institutions and laws, on an immense scale, and doing so with the necessary involvement of citizens in ways which completely negate the liberal idea of the state as some kind of external or alien authority which merely holds the ring while people make their own market and lifestyle choices within it.

In addition, practical reason as characterised by Nussbaum seems not to include the element of reliable and freely accessible knowledge of and about our systems and procedures of state and our economic structures and processes. It is not enough to assume that practical reason—if enabled—will *eo ipso* create such knowledge, or access to it, or to avenues for informed and authoritative participation. Practical reason will itself have to be put towards the creation of spaces and systems in which we can freely gain reliable knowledge about our public processes and institutions.

PROBLEMS FOR REPUBLICANISM AND CITIZENSHIP

In practice, we would expect powerful political and economic forces and interests to resist the creation of any kind of public space which would enable the practice of republican citizenship. Indeed, that is precisely what often happens; in Iceland, the complete failure to replace the 1944 constitution (itself only a minor variation on the 1874 one) combined with the effects of the 2007–09 financial crash, in which the corruptly privatised Icelandic banks were heavily implicated, generated very great public anger. In 2009, the first post-crash Icelandic government—which was the first majority government not to include either of the two main parties—agreed that the public should draft the new constitution, and appointed a seven-member constitutional committee to select a random sample of 950 citizens to a national assembly as the first stage of the task.

Two of the main issues to be addressed in the new constitution were reform of the electoral system and ownership of natural resources. A constituent assembly of 25 was elected nationally from 522 candidates from all walks of life to do the detailed work—but this was too much for the now-opposition parties, who seem to have got the election result annulled on the most implausible of technicalities, despite there having been no claim that the election had been affected thereby (Gylfason 2013).

The constituent assembly nevertheless went ahead, and within four months, had drafted a constitution incorporating all the points raised by the national assembly; they had consulted domestic and international authorities, and despite opposition attempts to filibuster the consequent bill, a national referendum approved the new constitution by 67 per cent in favour, on a 49 per cent turnout (Gylfason 2013). Even then the bill failed after a series of breathtakingly convoluted and utterly hostile manoeuvrings by the main opposition parties. It may well be that elected politicians fear interested and committed citizens above all else.

Secondly, it is not clear if the idea of citizenship by itself can generate enough of a sense of civic membership to sustain common commitments or the commitment to informed engagement with issues which can be very difficult. A sense of civic membership inevitably varies across cultures, classes, and regions, and may well be as vulnerable to substantial inequalities or rigid social stratification as attempts to establish citizenship as a practice. Republics constituted by citizens, however, remain among the oldest and longest-enduring concepts in political thought, and their potential appeal may well be shown by their sustained exclusion from all other ideologies.

CHAPTER 12: REPUBLICANISM AND CITIZENSHIP

Extension Exercise

1. Read this:
   Fung, Archon. 2009. 'British Columbia Citizens' Assembly on Electoral Reform'. *Participedia* blog. Last modified 17 December 2016.
   http://participedia.net/en/cases/british-columbia-citizens-assembly-electoral-reform
   In short-note form, write down the key points of the article. Include at least one of the author's criticisms.
2. Read this:
   Keruwala, Naim. 2013. 'Participatory Budgeting in India—The Pune Experiment'. *Development Central* blog, 2 July.
   https://developmentcentral.wordpress.com/2013/07/02/participatory-budgeting-in-india-the-pune-experiment
   In short-note form, write down the main points in the article. Include details of the comparison between New York and Pune. Also identify one significant difference between the approach taken in Pune and that taken in British Columbia.

Further Reading

Bellamy, Richard. 2008. *Citizenship: A Very Short Introduction*. Oxford: Oxford University Press.

Artistole. Any edition. *Politics*.
Short, accessible, and one of the great works.

[illegible]

[illegible]

[illegible]

[illegible]

[illegible]

BIBLIOGRAPHY

Abel, Maddela. 2005. *Glimpses of Indian National Movement*. Hyderabad: ICFAI University Press.

Abraham, John, and Julie Sheppard. 1997. 'Democracy, Technocracy, and the Secret State of Medicines Control: Expert and Nonexpert Perspectives'. *Science, Technology, & Human Values* 22 (2): 139–67.

Aginam, Obijiofor. 2012. 'Rape and HIV as Weapons of War'. Accessed 2 October 2015, http://unu.edu/publications/articles/rape-and-hiv-as-weapons-of-war.html

Anandhi S., and M. Vijayabaskar. 2013. 'Where Buying a Motorcycle Can Spark a Riot'. *Hindu*, 7 January.

Anderson, Benedict. 1991. *Imagined Communities: Reflections on the Origin and Spread of Nationalism*. London: Verso.

Anderson, Terry, and P. J. Hill. 1979. 'An American Experiment in Anarcho-Capitalism: The Not So Wild, Wild West'. *Journal of Libertarian Studies* 3 (1): 9–29.

Annan, Kofi, and Nader Mousavizadeh. 2012. *Interventions: A Life in War and Peace*. New Delhi: Penguin/Allen Lane.

Appiah, Kwame Anthony. 2016. 'Mistaken Identities: Country'. The Second Reith Lecture. Accessed 16 January 2017, http://downloads.bbc.co.uk/radio4/transcripts/2016_reith2_Appiah_Mistaken_Identities_Country.pdf

Arendt, Hannah. 1951. *The Burden of Our Time*. London: Secker & Warburg.

Arendt, H. 1958. *The Origins of Totalitarianism*. Cleveland: World Publishing Company.

Arendt, H. 1963. *On Revolution*. Harmondsworth: Penguin.

Arendt, H. 1977. *Eichmann in Jerusalem: A Report on the Banality of Evil*. Harmondsworth: Penguin.

Aristotle. 1905. *Politics*. Translated by Benjamin Jowett. Oxford: Clarendon.

Aristotle. 1955. *Ethics*. Translated by J. A. K. Thomson. Harmondsworth: Penguin.

Avineri, Shlomo. 1968. *The Social and Political Thought of Karl Marx*. London: Cambridge University Press.

BBC. 2005. 'India Wins Landmark Patent Battle'. *BBC News*, 9 March. Accessed 2 January 2017, http://news.bbc.co.uk/1/hi/sci/tech/4333627.stm

BBC. 2016a. 'EU Referendum: Results'. 24 June. Accessed on 24 January 2017, http://www.bbc.com/news/politics/eu_referendum/results

BBC. 2016b. 'What Does Alternative for Germany (AfD) Want?' 5 September. Accessed 16 December 2016, http://www.bbc.co.uk/news/world-europe-37274201

Bakunin, Mikhail. 1867. 'Federalism, Socialism, Anti-Theologism'. Mikhail Bakunin Reference Archive. Accessed 10 September 2015, https://www.marxists.org/reference/archive/bakunin/works/various/reasons-of-state.htm

Balakrishnan, Gopal. 1996. 'The National Imagination'. In *Mapping the Nation*, edited by G. Balakrishnan, 198–213. London: Verso.

Baldwin, Katherine. 2012. 'Factbox—The Worst and Best G20 Countries for Women'. Accessed on 5 October 2015, http://www.trust.org/item/20120613010100-sk134/?source=spotlight

Balmer, Randall. 2014. 'The Real Origins of the Religious Right'. *Politico*, 27 May. Accessed 12 March 2016, http://www.politico.com/magazine/story/2014/05/religious-right-real-origins-107133

Bambrough, Renford. 1956. 'Plato's Political Analogies'. In *Philosophy, Politics and Society: First Series*, edited by Peter Laslett. Oxford: Blackwell.

Baptist, Edward. 2014. *The Half Has Never Been Told: Slavery and the Making of American Capitalism*. New York: Basic Books.

Barber, Benjamin. 1984. *Strong Democracy: Participatory Politics for a New Age*. Berkeley: University of California Press.

Barry, Peter. 2002. *Beginning Theory: An Introduction to Literary and Cultural Theory*. Manchester: Manchester University Press.

Barsamian, David. 2003. 'Monocultures of the Mind', Interview with Vandana Shiva, *India Together*, 1 April. Originally published in Z Magazine (December 2002). Accessed 2 January 2017, http://indiatogether.org/vandana-interviews

Bates, Laura. 2014. *Everyday Sexism*. London: Simon & Schuster.

Beiner, Ronald. 1992. *What's the Matter with Liberalism?* Berkeley: University of California Press.

Bell, Daniel. 1974. *The End of Ideology: On the Exhaustion of Political Ideas in the Fifties*. London: Heinemann.

Bell, Duncan. 2014. 'What is Liberalism?' *Political Theory* 42 (6): 682–715.

de Bellaigue, Christopher. 2015. 'Stop Calling for a Muslim Enlightenment'. Guardian, 19 February. Accessed 17 September 2015, http://www.theguardian.com/world/2015/feb/19/stop-calling-for-a-muslim-enlightenment

Bellamy, Richard. 2000. *Rethinking Liberalism*. London: Pinter.

Belsey, Catherine. *Poststructuralism: A Very Short Introduction*. Oxford: Oxford University Press.

Bergstrøm, Ida Irene. 2015. 'Toril Moi: Feminist Theory Needs a Revolution'. Accessed 2 January 2017, http://kjonnsforskning.no/en/2015/09/toril-moi-feminist-theory-needs-revolution

Berlin, Sir Isaiah. 1969. 'Two Concepts of Liberty'. In *Four Essays on Liberty*. Oxford: Oxford University Press. Accessed 4 July 2015, https://www.wiso.uni-hamburg.de/fileadmin/wiso_vwl/johannes/Ankuendigungen/Berlin_twoconceptsofliberty.pdf

Besifki, Nawzat. 1996. *The Kurdish National Liberation Movement since 1975: Success or Failure*. Unpublished PhD thesis, University of Southampton.

Bhabha, Homi. 2004. 'Sly Civility'. In *The Location of Culture*, 132–44. London: Routledge.

Bhatnagar, Gaurav Vivek. 2016. 'Rights Groups Demand Implementation of Anti-Caste Discrimination Law in the UK'. *The Wire*, 14 September 2016. Accessed 9 January 2017, https://thewire.in/65823/65823/

Bibby, Andrew. 2013. 'Workers Occupy Plant as Spanish Co-operative Goes Under'. *Guardian*, 15 November. Accessed 1 October 2015, http://www.theguardian.com/social-enterprise-network/2013/nov/15/spanish-co-op-workers-occupy-plant

Birch, Kean, and Vlad Mykhnenko, eds. 2010. Introduction to *The Rise and Fall of Neoliberalism: The Collapse of an Economic Order?* 1–20. Bangalore: Books for Change.

Blais, André, R. Kenneth Carty, and Patrick Fournier. 2008. 'Do Citizens' Assemblies Make Reasoned Choices?' In *Designing Deliberative Democracy*, edited by Mark E. Warren and Hilary Pearse, 127–44. Cambridge: Cambridge University Press.

Boardman, John. 2013. 'Soil Erosion in Britain: Updating the Record'. *Agriculture* 3 (3): 418–42.

Bose, Mihir. 2004. *Raj, Secrets, Revolution: A Life of Subhas Chandra Bose*. Horsford: Grice Chapman Publishing.

Boyle, Nicholas. 2017. 'The Problem with the English: England Doesn't Want to be Just Another Member of a Team'. *The New European*, 17 January. Accessed 29 January 2017, http://www.theneweuropean.co.uk/topstories/the_problem_with_the_english_england_doesn_t_want_to_be_just_another_member_of_a_team_1_4851882.

Brighouse, Harry. 2006. *On Education*. Abingdon: Routledge.

Burke, Edmund. 1790/2014. *Reflections on the Revolution in France*. Accessed 22 May 2017, https://ebooks.adelaide.edu.au/b/burke/edmund/reflections-on-the-revolution-in-france/

Burnham, James. 1945. *The Managerial Revolution*. Harmondsworth: Penguin.

Callaway, Ewen. 2013. 'Mystery Humans Spiced Up Ancients' Sex Lives'. *Nature*, 19 November. doi:10.1038/nature.2013.14196

Callinicos, Alex. 1989. *Against Postmodernism: A Marxist Critique*. Cambridge: Polity.

Casolari, Marzia. 2000. 'Hindutva's Foreign Tie-Up in the 1930s: Archival Evidence'. *Economic and Political Weekly* 35 (4): 218–28.

Cavell, Stanley. 1976. 'A Matter of Meaning It'. In S. Cavell, *Must We Mean What We Say? A Book of Essays*, 213–37. Cambridge: Cambridge University Press.

Centeno, Miguel Angel. 1993. 'The New Leviathan: The Dynamics and Limits of Technocracy'. *Theory and Society* 22 (3): 307–35.

Center for Reproductive Rights. 2003. 'The Bush Global Gag Rule: Endangering Women's Health, Free Speech and Democracy'. Dated 1 July. Accessed on 17 September 2015, http://www.reproductiverights.org/document/the-bush-global-gag-rule-endangering-womens-health-free-speech-and-democracy

Chaudhuri, Maitrayee. 2012. 'Feminism in India: the Tale and its Telling'. *Revue Tiers Monde* 209, 19–36. Accessed on 29 January 2017, http://www.cairn.info/revue-tiers-monde-2012-1-page-19.htm doi: 10.3917/rtm.209.0019

Cheliotis, Leonidas. 2006. 'Penal Managerialism from Within: Implications for Theory and Research'. *International Journal of Law and Psychiatry* 29 (5): 397–404.

Chester, Mikhail, and Arpad Horvath. 2010. 'Life-Cycle Environmental Assessment of California High Speed Rail'. *Access* 37 (Fall): 25–30. Accessed 27 September 2010, http://www.uctc.net/access/37/access37_assessing_hsr.pdf

Chilvers, Jason. 2008. 'Deliberating Competence: Theoretical and Practitioner Perspectives on Effective Participatory Appraisal Practice'. *Science, Technology, & Human Values* 33 (3): 421–51.

Chronicle of Higher Education. 1993. 7 July: 7 (§A18), p 7.

Chomsky, Noam. 2003. *For Reasons of State*. New York: The New Press.

Chomsky, N. 2008. 'Humanitarian Imperialism: The New Doctrine of Imperial Right'. *Monthly Review* 60 (4). Accessed 26 September 2015, http://monthlyreview.org/2008/09/01/humanitarian-imperialism-the-new-doctrine-of-imperial-right/

Cobain, Ian. 2013. 'Revealed: The Bonfire of Papers at the End of Empire'. *Guardian*, 29 November, Accessed 17 September 2015, http://www.theguardian.com/uk-news/2013/nov/29/revealed-bonfire-papers-empire

Collier, Andrew. 2004. *Marx*. Oxford: Oneworld.

Common Weal. n.d. Accessed 17 January 2017, http://allofusfirst.org

Community Based Monitoring and Planning. 2012. 'CBMP Policy Brief'. Accessed 20 September 2015, http://www.cbmpmaharashtra.org/cbmdata/books/CBM%20Policy_Brief_English_Dec.12.jpg

Concerned Citizens Tribunal—Gujarat 2002. *Crime Against Humanity* (2 vols). Mumbai: Citizens for Justice and Peace.

Conflict Armament Research. 2014. *Islamic State Ammunition in Iraq and Syria: Analysis of Small-Calibre Ammunition Recovered from Islamic State Forces in Iraq and Syria. Dispatch from the Field* series, October. Accessed 15 September 2014, http://www.conflictarm.com/wp-content/uploads/2014/10/Dispatch_IS_Iraq_Syria_Ammunition.pdf

Cooper, David. 1974. *The Death of the Family*. Harmondsworth: Penguin.

Crowder, George. 2004. 'Are Post Modernists Fascists?' *Australian Review of Public Affairs*, 25 October. Accessed 14 September 2015, http://www.australianreview.net/digest/2004/10/crowder.html

Culler, Jonathan. 1997. *Literary Theory: A Very Short Introduction*. Oxford: Oxford University Press.

Cunningham, Lillian. 2015. 'Accenture: One of World's Biggest Companies to Scrap Annual Performance Reviews'. *Independent*, 28 July. Accessed 15 August 2015, http://www.independent.co.uk/news/business/news/accenture-one-of-worlds-biggest-companies-to-scrap-annual-performance-reviews-10421296.html

Dahiya, Sunil, Lauri Myllyvirta and Nandikesh Sivalingam. 2017. *Airpocalypse: Assessment of Air Pollution in Indian Cities*. New Delhi: Greenpeace Environmental Trust. Accessed 24 January 2017, https://secured-static.greenpeace.org/india/Global/india/Airpoclypse--Not-just-Delhi--Air-in-most-Indian-cities-hazardous--Greenpeace-report.pdf

Daily Telegraph. 2008. 'Police Chief Pledges to Drive out Target Culture'. 31 May. Accessed 15 August 2015, http://www.telegraph.co.uk/news/uknews/2056114/Police-chief-pledgesto-drive-out-target-culture.html

Das, Pushpita. 2012. 'The History of Armed Forces Special Powers Act'. In *Armed Forces Special Powers Act: The Debate*, edited by Vivek Chadha, 10–21. New Delhi: Lancer and Institute for Defence Studies and Analyses.

Davies, Nick. 2009. *Flat Earth News: An Award-winning Reporter Exposes Falsehood, Distortion and Propaganda in the Global Media*. London: Vintage.

Deakin, Elizabeth. 2010. 'Environmental Impact of High Speed Rail in California'. Working paper, Center for Environmental Public Policy, University of California, Berkeley. Paper presented at a symposium on 'Environmental and Other Co-benefits of Developing a High Speed Rail System in California: A Prospective Vision 2010–2050', 2–3 December. Accessed 27 September 2015, https://gspp.berkeley.edu/assets/uploads/page/HSR10_Deakin.pdf

Derrida, Jacques. 1976. *Of Grammatology*. Translated by Gayatri Chakravorty Spivak. Baltimore: Johns Hopkins University Press.

Derrida, J. 1978. 'Structure, Sign, and Play in the Discourse of the Human Sciences'. In Jacques Derrida, *Writing and Difference*, Translated by Alan Bass, 278–93. London: Routledge & Kegan Paul.

Dews, Peter. 1987. *Logics of Disintegration: Post-structuralist Thought and the Claims of Critical Theory*. London: Verso.

DiLeo, Petrino. 2009. 'The Return of Keynes?' *International Socialist Review* 63. Accessed 30 September 2015, http://isreview.org/issue/63/return-keynes

Drugwatch. 2014. 'Vioxx Recall Information'. Last modified 14 May 2014. Accessed 26 September 2015, htttp://www.drugwatch.com/vioxx/recall

Dunn, John. 1999. 'Nationalism'. In *Theorizing Nationalism*, edited by Ronald Beiner, 27–50. Albany: State University of New York Press.

Edwards, David, and David Cromwell. 2006. *Guardians of Power: the Myth of the Liberal Media*. London: Pluto Press.

Edwards, David, and David Cromwell. 2012. *Why Are We the Good Guys? Reclaiming Your Mind from the Delusions of Propaganda*. Alresford: Zero Books.

Eisenhower, Dwight. 1961. 'Military-Industrial Complex Speech'. In *Public Papers of the Presidents of the United States: Dwight D. Eisenhower, 1960*: 1034–40. Accessed 13 January 2017, http://coursesa.matrix.msu.edu/~hst306/documents/indust.html

Electoral Commission. 2016. 'EU Referendum Results'. Accessed 24 January 2017, http://www.electoralcommission.org.uk/find-information-by-subject/elections-and-referendums/past-elections-and-referendums/eu-referendum/electorate-and-count-information

Enteman, Willard. 1993. *Managerialism: The Emergence of a New Ideology*. Madison: University of Wisconsin Press.

Erdman, Howard. 1978. 'Conservatism in India'. *Journal of Contemporary History* 13 (4): 791–802.

EUR-Lex. N.d. *M. H. Marshall v Southampton and South-West Hampshire Area Health Authority (Teaching)*. Accessed 6 September 2015, http://eur-lex.europa.eu/legal-content/EN/TXT/?uri=CELEX:61984CJ0152

EUr-Lex. N.d. *A. Foster and others v British Gas plc*. Accessed 6 September 2015, http://eur-lex.europa.eu/legal-content/EN/TXT/?uri=CELEX:61989CJ0188

EUR-Lex. N.d. Andrea Francovich and Danila Bonifaci and others v Italian Republic. Accessed 6 September 2015, http://eur-lex.europa.eu/legal-content/EN/TXT/?uri=CELEX:61990CJ0006

Fay, Brian. 1996. *Contemporary Philosophy of Social Science: A Multicultural Approach.* Oxford: Blackwell.

Fetscher, Iring. 1973. 'Karl Marx on Human Nature'. Social Research 40 (3): 443–67.

Fine, Ben. 2010. 'Zombieconomics: The Living Death of the Dismal Science', In *The Rise and Fall of Neoliberalism: The Collapse of an Economic Order?* edited by Kean Birch and Vlad Mykhnenko, 53–70. Bangalore: Books for Change.

Fleming, Anne Taylor. 2012. 'The Female Body as Battlefield'. *Reader Supported News*, 11 February. Accessed 27 September 2015, http://readersupportednews.org/opinion2/273-40/9917-the-female-body-as-battlefield

Føllesdal, Andreas, and Simon Hix. 2006. 'Why There is a Democratic Deficit in the EU: A Response to Majone and Moravcsik'. *Journal of Common Market Studies* 44 (3), 533–62.

Forster, Michael. 2007. 'Johann Gottfried von Herder'. *Stanford Encyclopedia of Philosophy*, Accessed on 11 June 2017, https://plato.stanford.edu/entries/herder/

Foucault, Michel. 1970. *The Order of Things: An Archaeology of the Human Sciences.* Translated by Alan Sheridan-Smith. London: Tavistock.

Foucault, M. 1972. *The Archaeology of Knowledge.* Translated by Alan Sheridan-Smith. London: Tavistock.

Foucault, M. 1987. 'What is Enlightenment?', in *Interpretive Social Science*, edited by Paul Rabinow and William M. Sullivan, 2nd ed., 157–74. Berkeley: University of California Press.

Fountain, Ben. 2016. 'American Crossroads: Reagan, Trump and the Devil Down South'. Guardian, 5 March. Accessed 2 June 2017, https://www.theguardian.com/us-news/2016/mar/05/trump-reagan-nixon-republican-party-racism

Friedman, Milton. 1968. 'The Role of Monetary Policy'. *The American Economic Review* 58 (1): 1–17.

Friends of the Earth. 2011. 'Briefing: High Speed Rail. Friends of the Earth's Views'. Accessed 27 September 2015, http://www.foe.co.uk/sites/default/files/downloads/high_speed_rail.pdf

Funnell, Warwick, Robert Jupe, and Jane Andrew. 2009. *In Government We Trust: Market Failure and the Delusions of Privatisation*. London: Pluto Press.

Gannon, Zoe, and Neal Lawson. 2013. *Co-Production: The Modernisation of Public Services by Staff and Users*. London: Compass. Accessed 26 September 2015, http://www.compassonline.org.uk/wp-content/uploads/2013/05/CO-PRODUCTION.pdf

Gat, Azar, and Alexander Yakobson. 2013. *Nations: The Long History and Deep Roots of Political Ethnicity and Nationalism.* Cambridge: Cambridge University Press.

Glimcher, Paul W., Michael C. Dorris and Hannah M. Bayer. 2005. 'Physiological Utility Theory and the Neuroeconomics of Choice'. *Games and Economic Behavior* 52 (2): 213–56. doi: 10.1016/j.geb.2004.06.011

Goldman, Emma. 1911. 'The Tragedy of Women's Emancipation'. In *Anarchism and Other Essay.* New York & London: Mother Earth Publishing Association. Accessed 5 October 2015, http://theanarchistlibrary.org/library/emma-goldman-anarchism-and-other-essays#toc12

Gowdy, John, and Susan Mesner. 1998. 'The Evolution of Georgescu-Roegen's Bioeconomics'. *Review of Social Economy* 56 (2): 136–56. Accessed 5 October 2015, http://homepages.rpi.edu/~gowdyj/mypapers/RSE1998.pdf

Graeber, David. 2012. *Debt: The First 5000 Years.* New Delhi: Penguin India.

Green, Leslie. 1995. 'Internal Minorities and their Rights'. *The Rights of Minority Cultures*, edited by Will Kymlicka, 257–72. Oxford: Oxford University Press.

Greenstone, Michael, Janhavi Nilekani, Rohini Pande, Nicholas Ryan, Anant Sudarshan and Anish Sugathan. 2015. 'Lower Pollution, Longer Lives: Life Expectancy Gains if India Reduced Particulate Matter Pollution'. *Economic and Political Weekly* 50 (8): 40–46.

Greenpeace. n.d. 'Koch Industries: Secretly Funding the Climate Denial Machine'. Accessed 5 October 2015, http://www.greenpeace.org/usa/global-warming/climate-deniers/koch-industries

Grice, Andrew. 2013. 'Vodafone's £84bn Tax Avoidance Bonanza: Nothing for Taxpayers in Verizon Deal while Bankers share £500m in Fees'. *Independent*, 2 September. Accessed 30 September 2015, http://www.independent.co.uk/news/business/news/vodafones-84bn-tax-avoidance-bonanza-nothing-for-taxpayers-in-verizon-deal-while-bankers-share-500m-8794169.html

Guardiola-Rivera, Oscar. 2013. *Story of a Death Foretold: The Coup against Salvador Allende, 11 September 1973*. London: Bloomsbury.

Gubb, James. 2009. 'Have Targets Done More Harm than Good in the English NHS? Yes'. *BMJ* 338 (7692). doi: 10.1136/bmj.a3130

Guérin, Daniel. 2010. *Anarchism*. Translated by Mary Klopper. New Delhi: Aakar Books.

Guha Thakurta, Paranjoy, Subir Ghosh and Jyotirmoy Chaudhuri. 2014. *Gas Wars: Crony Capitalism and the Ambanis*. Gurgaon: Paranjoy Guha Thakurta.

Gunnell, John G. 1982. 'The Technocratic Image and the Theory of Technocracy'. *Technology and Culture* 23 (3): 392–416.

Guttmacher Institute. 2012. 'Guttmacher Statistic on Catholic Women's Contraceptive Use'. Press release, February 15. Accessed 14 September 2015, http://www.guttmacher.org/media/inthenews/2012/02/15

Gylfason, Thorvaldur. 2013. 'Democracy on Ice: A Post-Mortem of the Icelandic Constitution'. Accessed 21 September 2015, www.opendemocracy.net/can-europe-make-it/thorvaldurgylfason/democracy-on-ice-post-mortemof-icelandic-constitution

Hamilton, Alexander. 1804. Letter to Thomas Sedgwick, 19 July. Accessed on 24 September 2015, http://founders.archives.gov/documents/Hamilton/01-26-02-0001-0264

Hanley, Alex. 2017. 'Germany Breaks A Solar Record — Gets 85% Of Electricity From Renewables'. *Cleantecnica*, 8 May. Accessed 29 May 2017, https://cleantechnica.com/2017/05/08/germany-breaks-solar-record-gets-85-electricity-renewables/

Harte, Julia, and R. Jeffrey Smith. 2014. 'Investigators find Islamic State Used Ammo Made in 21 Countries, including America'. Center for Public Integrity, 22 October. Updated 16 November 2015. Accessed 11 March 2017, http://www.publicintegrity.org/2014/10/05/15827/investigators-find-islamic-state-used-ammo-made-21-countries-including-america

Harvey, David. 2013. The Crisis and the Consolidation of Class Power: Is This *Really* the End of Neoliberalism? *Counterpunch*, 13 March 2015. Accessed 1 January 2017, http://www.counter-punch.org/harvey03132009.html

Hayek, Friedrich. 1976. Law, Legislation and Liberty. Vol 2. London: Routledge & Kegan Paul.

Hegel, Georg Wilhelm Friedrich. 1967. *The Philosophy of Right*. Translated by T. M. Knox. Oxford: Clarendon.

Hegel, G. W. F. 1979. *Hegel's Phenomenology of Spirit*. Translated by A.V. Miller Oxford: Oxford University Press.

Herman, Edward S. and Noam Chomsky. 1988. *Manufacturing Consent: The Political Economy of the Mass Media*. New York: Pantheon.

Heywood, Andrew. 2007. *Political Ideologies: An Introduction*, 4th ed. Houndmills: Palgrave Macmillan.

Hill, Joshua. 2015. 'Wind Power Generates 140% Of Denmark's Power Demand'. *CleanTechnica*, 13 July. Accessed 4 October 2015, http://cleantechnica.com/2015/07/3/wind-power-generates-140-denmarks-power-demand/

The Hindu. 2011. 'Tunisian Voters Lead the Way'. Editorial, 1 November. Accessed 26 September 2015, http://www.thehindu.com/todays-paper/tp-opinion/tunisian-voters-lead-the-way/article2586963.ece

Human Rights Watch. 2010. 'Back to the Future: India's 2008 Counterterrrorism Laws'. Published 27 July. Accessed 4 October 2015, https://www.hrw.org/report/2010/07/27/back-future/indias-2008-counterterrorism-laws

Hume, David. 1969. *A Treatise of Human Nature*. edited by Ernest C. Mossner. Harmondsworth: Penguin.

Ignatieff, Michael. 1999. 'Nationalism and the Narcissism of Minor Differences'. In *Theorizing Citizenship*, edited by Ronald Beiner, 91–102. Albany: State University of New York Press.

Institute of Race Relations. 2017. Ethnicity and Religion Statistics. Accessed on 8 January 2017, http://www.irr.org.uk/research/statistics/ethnicity-and-religion/

Intergovernmental Panel on Climate Change. 2013. 'Summary for Policymakers'. In *Climate Change 2013: The Physical Science Basis. Contribution of Working Group I to the Fifth Assessment Report of the Intergovernmental Panel on Climate Change*, edited by Thomas F. Stocker, Dahe Qin, Gian-Kasper Plattner, Melinda M. B. Tignor, Simon K. Allen, Judith Boschung, Alexander Nauels, Yu Xia, Vincent Bex and Pauline M. Midgley, 1–30. Cambridge and New York: Cambridge University Press.

Jacoby, Russell. 1981. *Dialectic of Defeat: Contours of Western Marxism*. Cambridge: Cambridge University Press.

Jameson, Fredric. 1991. *Postmodernism, or, the Cultural Logic of Late Capitalism*. Durham, North Carolina: Duke University Press.

Jha, Praveen, and Pooja Parvati. 2008. *India's Tryst with Elementary Education in the Time of Reforms: Policy Constraints and Institutional Gaps*. Bangalore: Books *for* Change & New Delhi: ActionAid.

Jurdjevic, Mark. 2007. 'Machiavelli's Hybrid Republicanism'. *English Historical Review* 122(499): 1228–57.

Kakde, Dhananjay. 2010. *Compiled Report of Community Based Monitoring of Health Services under NRHM in Maharashtra 2007–2010*. Pune: SATHI (Support for Advocacy and Training to Health Initiatives).

Kant, Immanuel. 1933. *Kant's Critique of Pure Reason*. Translated by Norman Kemp Smith. London: Macmillan.

Kant, I. 1948. *The Moral Law*. Translated by H. J. Paton. London: Hutchinson.

Karat, Brinda. 2015. 'The Economics of Cow Slaughter'. *Hindu*, 16 November 2015. Updated 6 September 2016. Accessed 22 April 2017, http://www.thehindu.com/opinion/op-ed/the-economics-of-cow-slaughter/article7880807.ece.

Karmi, Ghada. 2007. *Married to Another Man: Israel's Dilemma in Palestine*. London: Pluto Press.

Kennedy, Robert F., Jr, and Greg Palast. 2008. 'Drinking the ACORN Kool-Aid: How Cries of Voter Fraud Cover Up GOP Elections Theft'. *Huffington Post*, 27 November. Updated 25 May 2011. Accessed 16 September 2015, http://www.huffingtonpost.com/robert-f-kennedy-jr-and-greg-palast/drinking-the-acorn-koolai_b_138390.html

Kennedy, R. 2011. 'Imperfect Cosmopolitanisms'. *Curriculum Inquiry* 41 (1): 62–66. doi: 10.1111/j.1467-873X.2010.00519.x

Kenny, Michael, and Nick Pearce. 2017. 'The Empire Strikes Back'. *New Statesman*, 23 January.

Khoday, Kishan, and Leisa Perch. 2012. 'Green Equity: Environmental Justice for More Inclusive Growth'. *Policy Research Brief* 19, International Policy Centre for Inclusive Growth. Accessed 27 September 2015, http://www.ipc-undp.org/pub/IPCPolicyResearchBrief19.pdf

Khunte, Prashant, and Amruta Walimbe. 2012. *People are Reclaiming the Public Health System: Qualitative Report on Community Based Monitoring and Planning of Health Services in Maharashtra Supported by NRHM*, Translated by Vidya Kulkarni, Rashmi Padhye, and Arun Gadre. Pune: SATHI (Support for Advocacy and Training to Health Initiatives).

Khurana, Rakesh. 2007. *From Higher Aims to Hired Hands: The Social Transformation of American Business Schools and the Unfulfilled Promise of Management as a Profession*. Princeton: Princeton University Press.

Kothari, Abhijit, and Rita Kothari. 2011. 'Interrogating Management Studies: Legacies and Preoccupations'. *Economic and Political Weekly* 46 (1): 35–40.

Kropotkin, Peter. 1902. *Mutual Aid: A Factor of Evolution*. Accessed 24 May 2017, https://www.marxists.org/reference/archive/kropotkin-peter/1902/mutual-aid/

Kymlicka, Will. 1995. *Multicultural Citizenship: A Liberal Theory of Minority Rights*. Oxford: Oxford University Press. doi: 10.1093/0198290918.001.0001

Lang, Steven. 2010. 'Citizen Journalism Project Offers Case Study in Collaboration'. In *Brave News Worlds: Navigating the New Media Landscape*, edited by Bill Mitchell, 119–21. Vienna: International Press Institute.

Laing, R. D., and Aaron Esterson. 1970. *Sanity, Madness and the Family*. Harmondsworth: Penguin.

Lenin, Vladimir Ilyich. 1963. *Imperialism, the Highest Stage of Capitalism: A Popular Outline*. Accessed 17 December 2016, https://www.marxists.org/archive/lenin/works/1916/imp-hsc

Leys, Colin. 2001. *Market-Driven Politics: Neoliberal Democracy and the Public Interest*. London: Verso.

Leys, Colin, and Stewart Player. 2011. *The Plot against the NHS*. London: Crane.

Lindley, Mark. 2015. 'The Ecological Economists of the 20th Century'. Paper presented at a research seminar at the Madras Institute of Development Studies, 1 October.

Locke, John. 1960. *Two Treatises of Government*. Edited by Peter Laslett. London: Cambridge University Press.

Locke, Robert R. 2009. 'Managerialism and the Demise of the Big Three'. *Real-World Economics Review* 51: 28–47.

Losurdo, Domenico. 2011. *Liberalism: A Counter-History*. Translated by Gregory Elliot. London: Verso.

Lovelock, James. 1989. 'Geophysiology, the Science of Gaia'. *Reviews of Geophysics* 17: 215–22. Accessed 27 July 2015, http://www.jameslovelock.org/page37.html

MacIntyre, Alasdair. 1962. 'A Mistake about Causality in Social Science'. In *Philosophy, Politics and Society: Second Series*, edited by Peter Laslett, W. G. Runciman and Quentin Skinner, 49–61. Oxford: Blackwell.

MacIntyre, A. 1990. *Three Rival Versions of Moral Inquiry: Encyclopaedia, Genealogy, and Tradition*. London: Duckworth.

MacIntyre, A. 1981. *After Virtue: A Study in Moral Theory*. London: Duckworth.

MacIntyre, A. 2007. *After Virtue: A Study in Moral Theory*, 3rd ed. London: Duckworth.

McChesney, Robert, and John Nichols. 2005. 'The Rise of Professional Journalism: Reconsidering the Roots of our Profession in an Age of Media Crisis'. *In These Times*, December 7. Accessed 23 October 2011, http://www.inthesetimes.com/article/2427/the_rise_of_professional_journalism

McLaughlin, Jenna. 2015. 'The US Military's Sexual-Assault Problem is So Bad the UN is Getting Involved'. *Mother Jones*, 14 May. Accessed 27 September 2015, http://www.motherjones.com/politics/2015/05/un-human-rights-council-us-military-do-better-victims-sexual-violence

Machiavelli, Niccolo. 1517. *Discourses upon the First Ten (Books) of Titus Livy*. The Constitution Society. Accessed 19 January 2017, http://www.constitution.org/mac/disclivy.pdf

Marcuse, Herbert.1964. *One-Dimensional Man: Studies in the Ideology of Advanced Industrial Society*. Accessed 13 January 2017, https://www.marxists.org/ebooks/marcuse/one-dimensional-man.htm

Marginson, Simon. 1998. 'Value Creation in the Production of Services: A Note on Marx'. *Cambridge Journal of Economics* 22 (5): 573–85. doi: 10.1093/cje/22.5.573

Marx, Karl. 1843. Letter to Arnold Ruge, September. Accessed 21 January 2017, https://www.marxists.org/archive/marx/works/1843/letters/43_09.htm

Marx, K. 1844. *Economic and Philosophic Manuscripts of 1844*. Accessed 27 September 2015, https://www.marxists.org/archive/marx/works/download/pdf/Economic-Philosophic-Manuscripts-1844.pdf

Marx, K, and Friedrich Engels. 1848. *Manifesto of the Communist Party*. Accessed 28 August 2015, https://www.marxists.org/archive/marx/works/1848/communist-manifesto/ch01.htm

Marx, K. 1875. *Critique of the Gotha Programme*. Accessed 21 September 2015, https://www.marxists.org/archive/marx/works/1875/gotha/index.htm

Marx, K. 1887. *Capital*, vol. 1. Accessed 26 September 2015, https://www.marxists.org/archive/marx/works/1867-c1

Marx, K. 1999. 'The Law of the Tendency of the Rate of Profit to Fall', Part III of K. Marx, *Capital*, vol. 3: *The Process of Capitalist Production as a Whole*, edited by Friedrich Engels, Part III, ch. 13, 148–59. Accessed 3 October 2015, https://www.marxists.org/archive/marx/works/download/pdf/Capital-Volume-III.pdf

Marx, K. 1999. 'Economy in the Employment of Constant Capital'. Chapter 5 of K. Marx, *Capital: A Critique of Political Economy, Volume III: The Process of Capitalist Production as a Whole*, edited by Friedrich Engels, 49–73. Accessed 21 January 2017, https://www.marxists.org/archive/marx/works/download/pdf/Capital-Volume-III.pdf

Marx, K. 2000. *Karl Marx: Selected Writings*. Edited by David McLellan. Oxford: Oxford University Press.

Masci, David, and Michael Lipka. 2014. 'Fighting over Darwin, State by State'. Pew Research Center. Last updated 3 February. Accessed 17 September 2015, http://www.pewforum.org/2009/02/04/fighting-over-darwin-state-by-state

Meer, Nasar, and Tariq Modood. 2011. 'How Does Interculturalism Contrast with Multiculturalism?' *Journal of Intercultural Studies* 33 (2): 175–196. doi: 10.1080/07256868.2011.618266

Merquior, Jose Guilherme. 1985. *Foucault*. London: Fontana.

Moi, Toril. 2009. 'I Am Not a Woman Writer'. *Eurozine*, 12 June. Accessed on 2 January 2017, http://www.eurozine.com/articles/2009-06-12-moi-en.html

Molyneux, John. 2008. 'More than Opium: Marxism and Religion'. *International Socialism* 119. Accessed 23 January 2017, http://isj.org.uk/more-than-opium-marxism-and-religion

Monbiot, George. J. R. 2001a. 'Stealing Europe'. *Guardian*, 20 June. Accessed 5 September 2015, http://www.theguardian.com/politics/2001/jun/20/eu.politicalcolumnists

Monbiot, G. J. R. 2001b. *The Captive State: The Corporate Takeover of Britain*. London: Pan Macmillan.

Monbiot, G. J. R. 2007. *Heat: How We Can Stop Our Planet Burning*. London: Penguin.

Moravcsik, Andrew. 2002. 'In Defence of the "Democratic Deficit": Reassessing Legitimacy in the European Union'. *Journal of Common Market Studies* 40 (4): 603–24.

Morley, Louise, and Naz Rassool. 2000. 'School Effectiveness: New Managerialism, Quality and the Japanization of Education'. *Journal of Education Policy* 15 (2): 169–83.

Morton, Matthew, Jeni Klugman, Lucia Hanmer and Dorothe Singer. 2014. *Gender at Work: A Companion to the World Development Report on Jobs*. Washington, DC: World Bank Group. Accessed 6 March 2017, http://documents.worldbank.org/curated/en/884131468332686103/Gender-at-work-a-companion-to-the-world-development-report-on-jobs

Mounk, Yascha. 2016. 'The Week Democracy Died'. *Slate*, 14 August. Accessed 29 October 2016, http://www.slate.com/articles/news_and_politics/cover_story/2016/08/the_week_democracy_died_how_brexit_nice_turkey_and_trump_are_all_connected.html

Mulgan, Richard. 2000. 'Was Aristotle an "Aristotelian Social Democrat"?' *Ethics* 111 (1): 79–101.

Muralidharan, Sukumar. 2007. 'The Tyranny of Identity: Party Politics in India and its Changing Forms of Authoritarianism'. In *Short on Democracy: Issues Facing Indian Political Parties*, edited by Arvind Sivaramakrishnan, 28–55. Gurgaon: ImprintOne.

Murdock, George Peter. 1965. *Social Structure*. New York: The Free Press.

Næss, Arne. 1990. *Ecology, Community and Lifestyle: Outline of an Ecosophy*. Translated and revised by David Rothenburg. Cambridge: Cambridge University Press.

Nahory, C. 2004. 'The Hidden Veto'. *Global Policy Forum*. Accessed on 10 September 2015, https://www.globalpolicy.org/home.html

Nairn, Tom. 1981. *The Break-up of Britain: Crisis and Neo-nationalism*. London: Verso.

National Health Mission, Ministry of Health and Family Welfare, Government of India. 2013. 'Community Action: Suggested Broad Process of Initial Facilitation and Capacity Development.' Accessed 22 September 2015, http://nrhm.gov.in/communitisation/community-action/suggested-broad-process-of-initial-facilitation-and-capacity-development.html

Neslen, Arthur. 2015. 'Wind Power Generates 140% of Denmark's Electricity Demand'. *Guardian*, 10 July. Accessed 4 October 2015, http://www.theguardian.com/environment/2015/jul/10/denmark-wind-windfarm-power-exceed-electricity-demand

Nichols, John, and Robert W. McChesney. 2013. *Dollarocracy: How the Money and Media Election Complex is Destroying America*. New York: Nation Books.

Noorani, Abdul. 2000. *The RSS and the BJP: A Division of Labour*. New Delhi: LeftWord Books.

Norris, Christopher. 1993. *The Truth about Postmodernism*. Oxford: Blackwell.

Nussbaum, Martha. 2000. 'Aristotle, Politics, and Human Capabilities: A Response to Antony, Arneson, Charlesworth, and Mulgan'. *Ethics* 111 (1): 102–40.

Nussbaum, M. 2011. *Creating Capabilities: The Human Development Approach*. Ranikhet: Permanent Black.

Oakeshott, Michael. 1962. 'Rationalism in Politics'. In *Rationalism in Politics and Other Essays*, 1–36. London: Methuen.

Oakeshott, M. 2006. *Lectures in the History of Political Thought*. Edited by Terry Nardin and Luke O'Sullivan. Exeter: Imprint Academic.

Ollman, Bertell. n.d. 'Marx's Vision of Communism'. Accessed 21 January 2017, https://www.nyu.edu/projects/ollman/docs/vision_of_communism.php

Orsini, Francesca. 2002. *The Hindi Public Sphere 1920–1940: Language and Literature in the Age of Nationalism*. New Delhi: Oxford University Press.

Papastephanou, Marianna. 2012. 'Deconstructing the *Ethnos*–Nation Distinction'. *Journal of Politics and Law* 5 (4): 147–58.

Pappé, Ilan. 2006. *The Ethnic Cleansing of Palestine*. Oxford: OneWorld.

Parekh, Bhikhu. 1999. 'What is Multiculturalism?' *Seminar* 484. Accessed 17 January 2017, http://www.india-seminar.com/1999/484/484%20parekh.htm

Passmore, Kevin. 2002. *Fascism: A Very Short Introduction*. Oxford: Oxford University Press.

Pearse, Hilary. 2008. 'Institutional Design and Citizen Deliberation'. In *Designing Deliberative Democracy*', edited by Mark E. Warren and H. Pearse, 70–84. Cambridge: Cambridge University Press.

Penny, Laurie. 2011. *Meat Market: Female Flesh under Capitalism*. Alresford; Zero Books.

Pells, Rachael. 2016. 'Schools Told to "Guess" Pupil Ethnicity". *Independent*, 24 October.

Pissarro, Joachim. 2009. 'Greenberg, Kant and Modernism?' *Notes in the History of Art* 29 (1): 42–48.

Plant, Raymond. 1982. 'Jürgen Habermas and the Idea of Legitimation Crisis'. *European Journal of Political Research* 10 (4): 341–52. doi: 10.1111/j.1475-6765.1982.tb00029.x

Plant, R. 2010. *The Neo-liberal State*. Oxford: Oxford University Press.

Plant, Raymond, Harry Lesser and Peter Taylor-Gooby. 1980. *Political Philosophy and Social Welfare: Essays on the Normative Basis of Welfare Provision*. London: Routledge and Kegan Paul.

Plato. 1956. *The Republic*. Translated by H. D. P. Lee. Harmondsworth: Penguin.

Pocock, J. G. A. 1985. 'The Machiavellian Moment Revisited: A Study in History and Ideology'. *The Journal of Modern History* 53(1): 49–72.

Prakash, Aseem, and Yugank Goyal. 2013. 'A Development Index with Missing Links'. *The Hindu*, 22 October. Accessed 15 August 2015, http://www.thehindu.com/todays-paper/tp-opinion/a-development-index-with-missing-links/article5259266.ece.

Prashad, Vijay. 2015. *No Free Left: The Futures of Indian Communism*. New Delhi: LeftWord Books.

Press Trust of India. 2016. 'PIL seeks scrapping of BJP's Lotus symbol'. *Indian Express*, 7 July. Accessed 22 April 2017, http://indianexpress.com/article/india/india-news-india/bjp-lotus-symbol-pil-ec-election-commission-scrapping/

Price, John Vladimir. 1966. 'Hume's Concept of Liberty and The History of England'. *Studies in Romanticism* 5 (3): 139–57.

Radical Independence Collective. n.d. Accessed 17 January 2017, https://radical.scot/

Rampton, Martha. 2008. 'The Three Waves of Feminism'. *Pacific Magazine, 41*(2), 363–37. Accessed on 12 July 2015, http://www.pacificu.edu/about-us/news-events/three-waves-feminism

Rao, Nitya. 2009. 'Structural Constraints in Sarva Shiksha Abhiyan Schools'. *Economic and Political Weekly* 44 (16): 17–20. Accessed 4 March 2017, http://www.jstor.org/stable/40279149

Rather, Dan. 2011. 'And, We Have Gotten Used to It'. *Reader Supported News*, 28 November. Accessed 2 August 2012, http://readersupportednews.org/opinion2/276-74/8633-and-we-have-gotten-used-to-it

Raworth, Kate. 2017. *Doughnut Economics: Seven Ways to Think Like a 21st-Century Economist*. London: Penguin Random House.

Read, Rupert. 2013. 'How Ecologism is the True Heir of Both Socialism and Conservatism'. *LSE British Politics and Policy Blog*, 22 July. Accessed 30 January 2017, http://blogs.lse.ac.uk/politicsandpolicy/how-ecologism-is-the-true-heir-of-both-socialism-and-conservatism

Reid, Walter. 2016. *Keeping the Jewel in the Crown: The British Betrayal of India*. Edinburgh: Birlinn Books.

Richardg. 2014. 'Brazil's Biggest Slaughterhouses are Cleaning Up their Meat Supply. Others Must Follow Suit'. *Greenpeace Blog*. Accessed on 27 September 2015, http://www.greenpeace.org.uk/blog/forests/brazil%E2%80%99s-biggest-slaughterhouses-are-breaking-link-between-forest-destruction-and-meat-production-now-others-must-f

Riddington Young, John, unnamed second author and Peter Tomlin. 2008. *The Hospital Revolution: Doctors Reveal the Crisis Engulfing Britain's Health Service*. London: John Blake.

Rohde, Robert A., and Richard A. Muller. 2015. 'Air Pollution in China: Mapping of Concentrations and Sources'. *PLOS One* 10 (8). doi: 10.1371/journal.pone.0135749

Rosenman, Ellen. 'On Enclosure Acts and the Commons'. *BRANCH: Britain, Representation and Nineteenth-Century History*, edited by Dino Franco Felluga. Extension of *Romanticism and Victorianism on the Net*. Accessed on 24 September 2015, http://www.branchcollective.org/?ps_articles=ellen-rosenman-on-enclosure-acts-and-the-commons

RUPE. 2003. 'Ford Foundation—A Case Study of the Aims of Foreign Funding'. Appendix 1 of *Aspects of India's Economy 35: Economics and Politics of the World Social Forum*. Accessed 29 September 2015, http://rupe-india.org/35/app1.html

Sanders, Andrew. 2004. *The Short Oxford History of English Literature*. Oxford: Oxford University Press.

Sankararaman, Sriram, Swapan Mallick, Michael Dannemann, Kay Prüfer, Janet Kelso, Svante Pääbo, Nick Patterson and David Reich. 2014. 'The Genomic Landscape of Neanderthal Ancestry in Present-Day Humans'. *Nature* 507: 354–57. doi:10.1038/nature12961

Sardar, Ziauddin. 2008. 'Islam and Science: Beyond the Troubled Relationship'. In Ziauddin Sardar, *Breaking the Monolith Essays, Articles and Columns on Islam, India, Terror and Other Things that Annoy Me*, 57–83. Gurgaon: imprintOne.

Scottish National Party. n.d. Accessed 17 January 2017, www.snp.org

Sen, Amartya. 2009. 'Capitalism Beyond the Crisis'. *The New York Review*, 26 March.

Simkins, Tim. 2000. 'Education Reform and Managerialism: Comparing the Experience of Schools and Colleges'. *Journal of Education Policy* 15 (3): 317–32.

Sims, Alexandra. 2016. 'Sweden on Target to Run Entirely on Renewable Energy by 2040'. Independent, 26 October. Accessed 29 May 2017, http://www.independent.co.uk/news/world/europe/sweden-renewable-energy-target-2040-country-on-track-a7381686.html

Singer, Peter. 1980. *Marx*. Oxford: Oxford University Press.

Singh, Hira. 2014. *Recasting Caste: From the Sacred to the Profane*. New Delhi: SAGE Publications.

Singh, Jyotsna. 2014. 'Operation Cover-up'. *Down To Earth*, 31 December. Accessed 20 September 2015, http://www.downtoearth.org.in/coverage/operation-coverup-47822

Sivaramakrishnan, Arvind. 1995. 'Foucault and the Enlightenment: An Epistemological Note'. *Studies in Humanities and Social Sciences* 2 (2)—*Discourse and Truth*: 31–40. Shimla: Indian Institute for Advanced Studies.

Sivaramakrishnan, A. 1998. 'Living with Alienation: A Response to Stephen Mulhall'. *Angelaki* 3(1): 103–4. doi: 10.1080/09697259808571968

Sivaramakrishnan, A. 2008. 'Archbishop's Opening is More than a Gambit'. *Hindu*, 21 February. Accessed 9 October 2016, http://www.thehindu.com/todays-paper/tp-opinion/Archbishoprsquos-Opening-is-more-than-a-gambit/article15170404.ece

Sivaramakrishnan, A. 2011. 'An Epitaph for Neoliberalism'. *Hindu*, 11 January. Accessed 1 January 2017, http://www.thehindu.com/books/An-epitaph-for-neoliberalism/article15515602.ece

Sivaramakrishnan, A. 2012a. *Public Policy and Citizenship: Battling Managerialism in India*. New Delhi: SAGE Publications.

Sivaramakrishnan, A. 2012b. 'Never Mind the Elections, Just Rig the Rolls'. *Hindu*, 14 April. Updated 21 April. Accessed 11 March 2017, http://www.thehindu.com/opinion/op-ed/never-mind-the-elections-just-rig-the-rolls/article3311962.ece

Sivaramakrishnan, A. 2012c. 'Paid Laws, American Style'. *Hindu*, 28 May. Accessed 11 July 2016, http://www.thehindu.com/todays-paper/tp-opinion/paid-laws-american-style/article3463524.ece

Sivaramakrishnan, A. 2014. *Public Interest Journalism: A Guide for Students*. Hyderabad: Orient BlackSwan.

Skinner, Quentin. 1981. *Machiavelli: A Very Short Introduction*. Oxford: Oxford University Press.

Smith, Adam. 2007. *An Inquiry into the Nature and Causes of the Wealth of Nations*. Edited by S. M. Soares. ΜεταLibri Digital Library. Accessed 20 August 2015, http://www.ibiblio.org/ml/libri/s/SmithA_WealthNations_p.pdf

Sreeraj, T. K. 2015. 'Breaking Stereotypes a Highway at a Time, these Women Drive Trucks and Buses in India'. *ScoopWhoop*, 21 May. Accessed 7 March 2017, http://www.scoopwhoop.com/news/tamil-nadu-woman-truck-driver

Stone, Clarence. 1983. 'Whither the Welfare State? Professionalization, Bureaucracy and the Market Alternative'. *Ethics* 93 (3): 588–95.

Thatcher, Margaret. 1987. Interview with Douglas Keay for Woman's Own, 23 September. Accessed 22 May 2017, http://www.margaretthatcher.org/speeches/displaydocument.asp?docid=106689

Taylor, Frederick. 2011. *Exorcising Hitler: The Occupation and Denazification of Germany*. London: Bloomsbury.

Thompson, C. Bradley. 2011. 'Neoconservatism Unmasked'. *Cato Unbound*, Accessed on 18 January 2017, https://www.cato-unbound.org/2011/03/07/c-bradley-thompson/neoconservatism-unmasked

Transparency International. 2011. *Daily Lives and Corruption: Public Opinion in South Asia*. Accessed 24 September 2015, http://issuu.com/transparencyinternational/docs/2011_southasiabaromter_en?e=2496456/2494566

Transparency International. 2013. 'Global Corruption Barometer, GCB 2013, Nigeria'. Accessed 24 September 2015, https://www.transparency.org/gcb2013/country/?country=nigeria

Tremlett, Giles. 2013. 'Mondragon: Spain's Giant Co-operative where Times are Hard but Few Go Bust'. *Guardian*, 7 March. Accessed 4 October 2015, http://www.theguardian.com/world/2013/mar/07/mondragon-spains-giant-cooperative

United Kingdom. 2010. *Caste Discrimination and Harassment in Great Britain*, Accessed 9 January 2017, https://www.gov.uk/government/uploads/system/uploads/attachment_data/file/85521/caste-discrimination-summary.pdf

United Kingdom. 2013. 'Devolution Settlement: Scotland'. 20 February. Accessed 31 December 2016, https://www.gov.uk/guidance/devolution-settlement-scotland

Union of Concerned Scientists. n.d. 'Global Warming Skeptic Organizations'. Accessed 5 October 2015, http://www.ucsusa.org/global_warming/solutions/fight-misinformation/global-warming-skeptic.html

Vincent, Andrew. 2001. 'Green Political Theory'. In *Political Concepts*, edited by Richard Bellamy and Andrew Mason, 182–95. Manchester: Manchester University Press.

Vitousek, Peter M., Carla M. D'Antonio, Lloyd L. Loope, Marcel Rejmanek and Randy Westbrooks. 1997. 'Introduced Species: A Significant Component of Human-Caused Global Change'. *New Zealand Journal of Ecology* 21 (1): 1–16.

Vyasulu, Vinod. 2008. 'The Case against Health Insurance'. *Economic and Political Weekly* 43 (39): 15–17.

Ward, Colin. 2004. *Anarchism: A Very Short Introduction*. Oxford: Oxford University Press.

Warren, Mark, and Hilary Pearse. 2008. 'Introduction: Democratic Renewal and Deliberative Democracy'. In *Designing Deliberative Democracy: The British Columbia Citizens' Assembly*, edited by M. E. Warren and H. Pearse, 1–19. Cambridge: Cambridge University Press.

Wedgwood, Dame Cicely. 1938. *The Thirty Years War*. London: Jonathan Cape.

Weiser, Wendy R., and Lawrence Norden. 2011. *Voting Law Changes in 2012*. New York: Brennan Center for Justice, New York University School of Law.

Winch, Peter 1958. *The Idea of a Social Science and Its Relation to Philosophy*. London: RKP.

Wolff, Richard D. 2012. *Democracy at Work: A Cure for Capitalism*. Chicago: Haymarket Books.

Wolin, Sheldon S. 1954. 'Hume and Conservatism'. *The American Political Science Review* 48 (4): 999–1016.

Wood, Graeme. 2015. 'What Isis Really Wants'. *The Atlantic*, March. Accessed 13 March 2016, http://www.theatlantic.com/magazine/archive/2015/03/what-isis-really-wants/384980

World Bank. 2011. *Gender Equality and Development*. World Development Report 2012. Washington DC: The World Bank.

Zakaria, Fareed. 1997. 'The Rise of Illiberal Democracy'. *Foreign Affairs* 76 (6): 22–43.

INDEX